They Never Came Home

THE STARDUST STORY

D1585951

NEIL FETHERSTONHAUGH
and
TONY MCCULLAGH

First published in 2001
Merlin Publishing
16 Upper Pembroke Street
Dublin 2, Ireland
www.merlinwolfhound.com

First edition: ISBN 1-903582-09-1
Second edition: ISBN 1-903582-63-6

Fetherstonhaugh, Neil
They never came home: the Stardust story
1. Stardust - Fire, 1981 2. Fires - Ireland -
Dublin 3. Fires - Casualties - Ireland - Dublin
I. Title II. McCullagh, Tony
363.3'7'0941835

Typeset by Gough Typesetting Services, Dublin

Printed in the E.U.

This book is dedicated to the forty-eight young people who lost their lives in the Stardust tragedy:

Michael Barrett
Richard Bennett
Carol Bissett
Jimmy Buckley
Paula Byrne
Caroline Carey
John Colgan
Jacqueline Croker
Liam Dunne
Michael Farrell
David Flood
Thelma Frazer
Michael French
Josephine Glen
Michael Griffiths
Robert Hillick
Brian Hobbs
Eugene Hogan
Murtagh Kavanagh
Martina Keegan
Mary Keegan
Robert Kelly
Mary Kennedy
Mary Kenny

Margaret Kiernan
Sandra Lawless
Francis Lawlor
Maureen Lawlor
Paula Lewis
Eamon Loughman
George McDermott
Marcella McDermott
William McDermott
Julie McDonnell
Teresa McDonnell
Gerard McGrath
Caroline McHugh
Donna Mahon
Helena Mangan
James Millar
Susan Morgan
David Morton
Kathleen Muldoon
George O'Connor
Brendan O'Meara
John Stout
Margaret Thornton
Paul Wade

Acknowledgments

The authors would like to thank: the Stardust victims and relatives who co-operated with this book, in particular Christine, Lorraine and Antoinette Keegan of the Stardust Victims' Committee, who have supported the project from its inception; Darren Kinsella, whose feedback to the work-in-progress was essential, as was his research assistance; our boss, Robin Webb, managing director of the *Dublin People Group*, for his patience, support and understanding; all the staff of the *Dublin People Group* and *Bluepages*, particularly Karl Doyle of the production department; Christy Moore, for his generous support; Selga Medenieks, Managing Director of *Merlin Publishing*, possibly the most efficient editor we're ever likely to encounter; Chenile Keogh, Sales and Marketing Manager of *Merlin*, for keeping us on our toes; Paul Howard for his worldly advice on writing books; Gerard Fanning for his legal advice; and Linda Kenny, our publicist, for all the hard work that lies ahead.

Neil Fetherstonhaugh would like to thank: the Stardust families who invited me into their homes and shared their painful memories with me; my mam, Dot Fetherstonhaugh; Liz, for her patience; J&A, F&M, K&F; Deirdre Ní Raghallaigh and Declan McCulloch of Dublin Corporation's press office; Paul Shannon and Michael Fitzsimons for their expert advice and valuable recollections; and my co-author, Tony McCullagh, who also assisted with the editing of my chapters.

Tony McCullagh would like to thank: Kathryn Flynn for her constant support and encouragement; Mick Duggan for his advice and time; John Cleere for his knowledge of all things technical; Lir Canoe Club for leaving me alone; the McCullagh family – Tony Sr, Phyllis, Sharyn, Jennifer, Jamie and Chloe; my grandfather, Peter

Seagrave; all my friends for their support; and my co-author, Neil Fetherstonhaugh, who was a dynamic ally throughout.

Darren Kinsella, the book's researcher and photographer, would like to thank: his wife, Claire; Mark Maxwell, *Maxwell's Picture Agency*; Liam Mulcahy, *Independent Newspapers*; Susan Kennedy, *Lensman*; Joan Hyland, *Irish Press*; and all the Stardust families who provided him with precious photographs of their loved ones.

Foreword

by Christy Moore

This book will help to keep the issue of the Stardust tragedy and scandal alive – not that the bereaved or injured will need reminding, for their pain and sense of loss will be lifelong.

However, others among us need to realise the consequences of shoddy, anti-social and sinful behaviour; to be reminded of what happens when quick profit and greed come before public safety and common decency.

At the time of the tragedy, certain politicians promised answers to the important questions raised by the Stardust disaster. Many of these questions remain unanswered. For many years, successive Irish governments also neglected the needs – emotional and physical – of the fire's victims and their families.

Neil Fetherstonhaugh and Tony McCullagh's book will serve to remind us all that, in the end, indifference will destroy not only the guilty but also the innocent.

Christy Moore
June, 2001

The Last Valentine

by Martina Keegan, RIP

Oh Father up in Heaven, oh Lord up above,
Please guide and protect the guy that I love.
Keep him from danger, save him from fear,
Show me the way his actions to steer.

You know, Lord, I love him with all my heart,
So keep us together, never to part.
But if this guy should ever leave me,
When he gets to heaven please tell him from me,
I love him forever.

But if I am first to rise above,
Please give him a message, a sign of love.
Written in marker (pen, sorry), sealed with a kiss,
His name is David, the guy that I miss
(When you're not around).

February 13, 1981

Contents

Prologue

In the early hours of Saturday morning, February 14, 1981, John Keegan got up from his seat in Cadbury's factory on the Oscar Traynor Road in the north Dublin suburb of Coolock and made his way to the men's room. He overheard two of his colleagues standing in the corridor discussing a late-night radio news report. One of the chargehands had heard that a fire had broken out at the Stardust disco in nearby Artane.

John stopped in his tracks, with the words "a fire in the Stardust" catching his immediate attention. He asked his colleague to repeat what he had heard on the radio. The man told John that, according to the news bulletin, emergency services had rushed to the scene of a fire at the popular disco and cabaret venue earlier that night. People had been hurt. Without another word, John turned around and went quickly back to his workstation. He grabbed his jacket and walked out into the night.

On his way home, John felt a rising tide of fear. Earlier that evening he had reluctantly given permission to four of his eight children to go to the St Valentine's Eve disco in the Stardust. A stern father who commanded respect from his children without ever resorting to physical force, John had nevertheless acted uncharacteristically when his children asked his permission to go to the nightclub. He was steadfastly opposed to the idea and had mentioned to his wife, Christine, before he went to work his nightshift in Cadbury, that he had almost stopped them leaving the house that night. John reminded Christine that he was superstitious about the number thirteen: he had suffered a leg injury when he landed badly on his thirteenth jump with the Territorial Army in England. However, John had relented and allowed Mary, 19 years of age, Antoinette, 18, John Jr, 17, and Martina, 16, to go out that night, Friday, February 13, 1981.

As he reached the quiet, terraced house on Greencastle Crescent, just a short distance from his workplace, John's sense of foreboding swelled into panic. The porch light was still on. The house rule was that the light was to be turned off by the last of the children to come home after a night on the town. A darkened porch would have been a simple, reassuring signal to John that everyone was safely home. He knew the disco would have been over by 2 a.m. – now the light indicated that someone had not yet arrived home.

After searching the empty bedrooms, he woke Christine and told her there had been a fire in the Stardust; the kids were not in their beds. As soon as she fully realised what he was saying, Christine sprang out of bed and got dressed. She had been in a deep sleep since 2 a.m. when her 13-year-old daughter, Lorraine, had told her to go to bed after she starting dozing during a late night movie. Christine always stayed up waiting for her children to come home from a night out so she could quiz them playfully about what they had got up to, who they had danced with, and what fellas they had kissed. Aged 45, Christine was nonetheless as much one of the girls as her daughters.

Not long after the girls left the house that night in a flurry of excited teenage laughing and catcalling, John Jr had arrived home on his own. He slumped in the chair in the sittingroom, complaining that the bouncers on the door of the Stardust had refused him entry. Typically of doormen, there was no specific reason – they had just disliked the look of him. There was a loose policy among the door staff of the nightclub to randomly select queuing punters and turn them away, especially young men in a group. John had been with a gang of his friends and he had been refused entry, despite the fact that he was dressed smartly that night in a shirt and tie. Arriving home, he didn't appear too disappointed to his mother and told her he wasn't that bothered. A simple decision by an anonymous doorman that fateful evening probably saved his life.

Later that night, after John and his two younger brothers had gone upstairs, Lorraine had convinced her mother that the others would be home much later than usual because the Stardust had a bar extension for Valentine's night. Besides, they would probably go to a chipper on the way home.

Now, as she dressed frantically, Christine noticed thick clouds of black smoke drifting past her bedroom window. Opening the window, she heard the sirens and sweeping noise of commotion coming from the direction of the Stardust, just over one mile away. On the silent drive to Artane with her husband to look for their daughters, Christine didn't imagine that anything serious might have actually happened to them. As they drove the final few minutes down the Kilmore Road and turned into the car park of the complex, it never occurred to her that anybody might have been harmed.

It was then, when the first ambulance sped past the car in the opposite direction, quickly followed by another, then another, all with sirens roaring, that Christine and John realised the seriousness of the fire. Christine blessed herself as they turned the corner and witnessed the horrific scene before them. Police cars, ambulances, fire engines and taxis blocked their path at the entrance to the Stardust complex. Gardaí, ambulance men and firemen had gathered together in little knots, and were pushing and shoving the dazed onlookers back. Parking twenty yards away, Christine and John got out of the car and were immediately overwhelmed with a blast of heat from the burning building. They could hear screaming. Christine's heart almost stopped.

Stunned teenagers were being carried into ambulances while those less seriously injured were being guided gently towards a fleet of waiting taxis. Blackened figures shuffled across the car park, some in a state of silent shock, others screaming. Blankets covered people-shaped heaps on the ground and a fireman was sobbing with his head buried in his hands as he slumped at the side of the road. The shell of the building that had been the Stardust was in darkness, lit up only in parts by the flickering flames. The blackened windows on both sides of the main entrance door bore mute testimony to the attempts firemen had made to gain access to those trapped within the inferno. Draped across the windows were the scorched awnings on which the word "Stardust" were emblazoned.

Christine saw one figure, which she could not make out as male or female, being led to an ambulance with only one small patch of white clothing standing out against badly burnt skin. A young Garda tried to push Christine back but she grabbed him by the arm and asked if he had seen the three Keegan sisters. He told her that the best thing she could do at that point would be to go to the hospitals and start looking there.

John and Christine drove first to the Mater Hospital. Two ambulances and a fire engine were parked at the entrance to the Accident and Emergency unit. Inside, complete pandemonium reigned, as casualties were brought in through the door and rushed to intensive care rooms and operating theatres. A nurse blocked Christine's way as she tried to rush through the reception area and into the treatment room, and asked the panicked mother who she was looking for. Christine stammered that she was trying to find the Keegan girls and attempted to get past the nurse, even when she was told that nobody of that name had been admitted to the hospital. Then Christine spotted a girl in a pink dress similar to the one worn by 19-year-old Mary. But when she got to the bed Christine realised the unburnt patch of pink did not belong to her daughter. Now Christine noticed the dead lined up in the corridors in the hospital. A team of doctors rushed past her with a young girl on a trolley, her face burnt beyond recognition.

The Keegans drove to the next hospital, where they saw similar scenes of horror replayed in the casualty department. Hysterical families begged medical staff for information on loved ones as victim after victim was wheeled through the doors. All this time John kept repeating that his children must have got out of the Stardust in one piece. "They must be here," he insisted to Christine as they reached yet another distressing scene of chaos and carnage. But every fruitless round of panicked questioning of doctors and nurses would yield the same answer: "Nobody of that name was admitted here – try the next hospital."

By 7 a.m. John and Christine had driven to every major hospital in the city but had not found any of their daughters. They arrived back home to find young Lorraine sobbing in the kitchen, but trying to get the younger kids their breakfast. Against fading hope, the grief-stricken family quizzed John Jr about Mary, Martina and Antoinette's last movements, but he had not seen his sisters since they left the house. He would never see two of them again.

By this time the early morning children's television programmes on RTÉ were being interrupted by emergency broadcast news of the fire at the Stardust. A roll call of the dead and injured was starting to appear on the screen – but there were still no Keegan names there.

John and Christine got back into the family car to recommence their search, as Dublin woke up to the single worst fire disaster to hit Ireland in the history of the State.

Over eight hundred young people went to the Stardust disco on the most romantic night of the year, February 13–14, 1981. Forty-eight of them never came home.

One

An Accident Waiting to Happen

"I personally take great care to make sure all exits are clear."

– Eamon Butterly, owner of the Stardust, in a letter to
Dublin Corporation, January 27, 1981.

For many reasons, 1981 was to be a bleak year in modern Irish history. It was a year of worsening Anglo-Irish relations against the backdrop of H-Block hunger strikes at the Maze Prison. On May 5 IRA prisoner Bobby Sands, who had been elected MP for the Fermanagh-South Tyrone constituency the previous month, was pronounced dead after sixty-six days on hunger strike. Nine others would die before October as British Prime Minister Margaret Thatcher refused to concede to republican demands for political prisoner status. That summer would see scenes of riot and unrest outside the British Embassy in Dublin.

The Charles Haughey-led Fianna Fáil Government was about to plunge Ireland into years of economic uncertainty with borrowing and spending reaching record – or reckless – levels. Haughey's populist approach to public spending, clearly designed to win over the electorate, would see him humiliated at the polls that summer as Fine Gael took office in coalition with the Labour Party.

Ironically, Haughey's plans for a spring election that year would be thrown into disarray by the Stardust tragedy, which occurred in the heart of his own Dublin North Central constituency. Fianna Fáil had planned to mobilise its troops with a triumphant Ard Fheis on Valentine's Day. The leader's main address was to be the springboard for a snap election which Haughey believed he could win. Since taking over as Taoiseach from Jack Lynch in 1979, Haughey was keen to put his leadership of Fianna Fáil to the test for the first time.

As the nation awakened to the news of a fire in Artane, Haughey postponed the Ard Fheis until April and abandoned plans for an early election.

By the time the general election was held in May, Fianna Fáil's popularity had plummeted. Political fallout from the hunger strikes, which saw two republican prisoners take Dáil seats at the expense of Fianna Fáil, and Haughey's mismanagement of the economy resulted in the party's poorest showing in twenty years. The Stardust tragedy would continue to haunt Haughey in different ways for the next two decades.

Other notable events of 1981 included the kidnapping of Dunnes Stores' joint managing director, Ben Dunne. He was abducted by the IRA and released six days later. A threatened oil strike materialised a week after the Stardust fire. Top films in Irish cinemas that year included "The Elephant Man", "The Jazz Singer" and "Airplane". House prices in Dublin were below what most people today are paying for a deposit on a property. A four-bedroom home at Hazelwood Court in Artane, for example, set its purchasers back just £31,850.

But of all the newsworthy events of 1981, a fire in a north Dublin nightclub would dominate the headlines. Owned by the Butterly family, the Stardust was formerly a jam factory. It was later used for food processing and as a plastics factory. Since its opening in 1978, the Stardust had become the premier entertainment venue on the north side of Dublin. Located just four miles from the city centre on the Kilmore Road, the Artane venue regularly played host to some of the biggest names in music around at the time. Showband legend Joe Dolan had performed at the Stardust's gala opening night. There were also concerts by Gary Glitter, the Drifters, Dana, the Nolan Sisters and Dickie Rock. At the height of the Ska music era, U.K. bands such as The Beat and The Specials performed to full houses at the complex. Popular Irish folk singer, Paddy Reilly, was billed to play there on February 14, 1981. By then, however, the venue would be burnt to the ground.

The Stardust was located in one of the country's most socially and economically disadvantaged blackspots. With national unemployment that year over the 130,000 mark, its effects were acutely felt in areas such as Coolock where early school-leaving figures were high and college entry levels disproportionately low compared to other parts of the city. The local unemployment rate was forty per cent, well above the national average. The concentration of massive local authority estates in the area, which had been built haphazardly throughout the 1960s and 1970s, would contribute to social problems that remain to the present day. For many local people, the Stardust disco provided a weekly escape from badly paid jobs or life on the dole. The adolescent longing for glamour or the possibility of a new and exciting relationship made the club a magnet for young people.

Only for the sheer persistence of the Butterly family, the Stardust would have remained an industrial unit. In the early 1970s Patrick Butterly began his long battle with the city's planning authorities to have the factory converted into a major entertainment complex comprising a pub, function rooms and cabaret venue.

In November 1972 Patrick Butterly submitted an application to Dublin Corporation seeking planning permission to use a portion of his factory at 3b Kilmore Road as a licensed premises and restaurant. Outline planning permission was refused by the Corporation in January 1973. However, Butterly appealed the decision and in April 1975 was granted outline planning permission by the Minister for Local Government.

In February 1976 Butterly applied successfully for permission under the Planning Acts and Building Bye-Laws to convert his factory into a licensed amenity building. Dublin Corporation deemed these plans to be inadequate, however, and refused planning permission. The refusal was subsequently upheld on appeal to the Minister for Local Government. The plans were also found to be inadequate for consideration under the Building Bye-Laws.

Patrick Butterly refused to accept defeat and submitted a revised plan. After protracted correspondence between Butterly and Dublin Corporation's planning department, permission was eventually granted by the end of the year. Before work began on the entertainment complex in June 1977, Butterly had to submit further revisions to his original plan.

An application for a liquor licence for the Kilmore Road complex was made in June 1973 under the name of R&W Scott (Ireland) Limited, with registered offices at Fairdale Works, Kilmore Road,

Artane, through its nominee, Patrick Butterly. Maps and plans of
the premises were produced in the Dublin District Court in support
of the application. Butterly already held a licence as nominee of
Silver Swan Limited in respect of a premises at 4 George's Quay in
Dublin. This licence was being surrendered for extinguishment in
support of the new application for Artane. The application was
adjourned from court term to court term due to Buttlerly's difficulties
securing planning permission.

The application for a liquor licence was allowed to lapse in
1976 when the company changed its name to Scott's Foods Ltd and
statutory notices under the new name were served. In the meantime,
Butterly's plan to transfer his existing pub licence to Artane had run
into trouble. On July 1, 1975, the Superintendent at Pearse Street
Garda Station objected in court to the renewal of Butterly's publican's
licence. This was on the grounds that no licensing business had been
carried out at the George's Quay premises during the year 1973–
1974. District Justice Donnelly upheld the objection and refused to
renew the licence.

More setbacks were to follow. Later that month the Eastern
Health Board gave notice of its intention to object to the application
being made for the complex in Artane on the grounds that the
proposed premises:

- did not disclose the proposed methods of ventilation, drainage and
  lighting accommodation;

- did not disclose any sanitary accommodation and cloakroom for
  staff;

- did not disclose the number of water closets being provided; and

- did not disclose the general structural methods and finishes to be
  used.

In April 1976 Butterly succeeded in winning back his publican's
licence for the George's Quay premises. That June, as nominee of
Scott's Foods Ltd, he made an application to the Dublin Circuit Court
for a licence for the Kilmore Road complex, despite the fact that
work was yet to start on the troubled project. The Declaration Order
was granted by the judge and the existing licence held by Patrick

Butterly for his George's Quay pub was handed in to the court.

In January 1978 Butterly served notice on the Superintendent at Coolock Garda Station that he was about to apply for a liquor licence in respect of the Artane complex. Dublin Corporation and the Eastern Health Board informed the Superintendent that they had no objection to the application. The following month Superintendent O'Dea forwarded a report on the matter to the Chief State Solicitor, stating that the premises was not completed but was expected to be in order before the licence application came before the court. He was to inspect the premises again prior to the hearing.

At the Dublin Circuit Court on February 17, 1978, Judge Clarke made an order granting a publican's licence to Scott's Foods Ltd, through nominee Patrick Butterly, in respect of 3b Kilmore Road, Artane. The existing licence for the George's Quay pub was retained by the court. On March 28, 1978, the new licence was issued. Butterly was finally in business.

According to records, Butterly began to trade from Kilmore Road in March 1978. The complex comprised the Silver Swan public house; a restaurant/function room called the Lantern Rooms; and the Stardust, which was used for dances, concerts and cabaret shows. Although Patrick Butterly held all licences in relation to activities at the complex – including a restaurant licence, a public dancing licence and a music and singing licence – the premises was managed by his son, Eamon, who was to become a central figure in the Stardust disaster. Another Butterly-controlled company, Silver Swan Limited, had leased the businesses carried on at the Lantern Rooms, the Silver Swan bar and the Stardust. This arrangement would later be found to be in breach of the licensing laws which were apparently flouted with impunity by the Butterlys until the Stardust disaster brought their operations under scrutiny. It would later emerge that Silver Swan Ltd should have obtained a transfer of the publican's licence from Scott's Foods Ltd. In effect, Silver Swan Ltd was selling alcohol without a licence.

The Butterlys' considerable business empire was mainly controlled by Patrick Butterly and two of his sons, Eamon and Colm, although other family members were listed as shareholders of their various companies. Patrick, Eamon and Colm were listed as directors of Scott's Foods and Silver Swan Ltd at the time of the tragedy.

They were also directors and shareholders of numerous other family-controlled businesses. The registered office for most of these companies was listed as Ferndale Works, Kilmore Road, Artane.

A self-made man from the north County Dublin village of Rush, Patrick Butterly was feared and respected in equal measure by his employees. Locals who worked for his fruit and vegetable growing business in Rush recall him being notoriously mean with money, earning him the nickname 'The Jew Man' in certain quarters. He was also known as 'The Turf' Butterly, as he had sold turf in the area during the war years.

Patrick Butterly's privately published memoirs, *From Radishes to Riches*, paint a clear picture of a man obsessed with money and profit. Prior to his death at the age of eighty in January 2000, Butterly had decided that some record of his life should be passed on to his family, particularly his grandchildren. He wanted them to know where the family had come from and "how he had got his money". By his own admission, Patrick Butterly was "a divil" for money and "wouldn't spend it easy". The book documents the rise and rise of the Butterly business empire, from his market gardening companies to his industrial business park and the Stardust complex. Butterly made great play of the fact that his journey to financial success started out with one pony and cart.

In contrast to the mostly working-class punters attending discos at the Stardust, the Butterlys were successful and wealthy. Their hunger for profit would lead to some reckless decisions affecting safety that most likely contributed to the scale of the holocaust in the early hours of February 14, 1981. Later, there would be conflicting evidence between management of the Stardust and many of the survivors of the blaze as to whether a number of the exits were chained or locked during the fire. Eamon Butterly would be accused of operating a scandalous policy of keeping the exits locked until at least midnight during events at the Stardust. This was to stop customers letting their friends into the premises for free through the emergency exits. For Butterly, it was a security issue and, apparently, security took precedence over safety at the Stardust. Although Eamon Butterly would later claim – falsely – that each and every exit was open at the time of the fire, his policy of keeping doors locked in the first place would come in for trenchant criticism at the tribunal of inquiry into the disaster.

Some of Eamon Butterly's questionable practices had already come to the attention of Dublin Corporation. The premises had been visited on a number of occasions by Martin Donohoe, the Corporation's inspector of places of public resort. He inspected the venue on three occasions in 1979, twenty-four occasions in 1980 and three times in 1981, just weeks before the Stardust fire.

Donohoe noted a number of matters of concern following these inspections. On April 24, 1979, he found that one side of an exit door on the western side of the Lantern Rooms was not opening properly. On August 8 of that year, he discovered loose tables obstructing an exit in the Stardust. A piece connecting the floating arm to the panic bolt was missing from another exit. Returning to the Stardust one month later, Donohoe requested a further adjustment to this exit. In August 1980 he noted that six bulbs were out of order in the Stardust's emergency lighting system. On that occasion, the movable stage extension had been placed close to an exit, causing an obstruction. Loose seats obstructed the passageway on the eastern side of the venue. These matters were all brought to the attention of Eamon Butterly by Mr Donohoe. A few weeks later, a panic bolt on another exit was found to be sticking, which would prevent it from opening easily. More bulbs were defective in the emergency lighting system. A plastic skip containing empty bottles was causing an obstruction at an exit.

On September 4, 1980, an exit door in the Silver Swan bar was found chained and locked. When this was brought to the attention of Eamon Butterly, he said he didn't realise that he had to have the door unlocked at all times. He undertook to have the door unlocked in the future. On November 24, 1980, Exit door 5 was found chained and locked. The panic bolt was broken and the upright piece was hanging loose. When Donohoe informed the person in charge of security of this, he was told that the panic bolt had been broken during the evening. It had been locked for security reasons. The inspector insisted that the lock and chain be removed immediately. This was done and a security man was put on the door that night.

On visiting the premises on January 15, 1981 – just one month before the fire – Martin Donohoe had cause for serious concern. A passage leading to Exit 3 in the Stardust was obstructed by a large box, which was later removed at his request by security staff. More worryingly, the venue appeared to be excessively overcrowded. He estimated the attendance at about two thousand, although Patrick Butterly's licence only allowed a maximum of 1,400 people. Due to the large number of patrons on the premises, Donohoe had difficulty moving from one exit to another through the passageways. When Donohoe complained about this, Butterly informed him that he had removed some of the seating in front of the stage area to allow a free flow of people.

On Dublin Corporation's last inspection of the premises – approximately three weeks before the fire – Donohoe discovered more problems. An extra-long electrical flex, approximately 12 to 15 ft, was feeding two florescent lights. This did not comply with the bye-laws for places of public resort. A similar problem was noted in the Lantern Rooms.

Martin Donohoe's concerns were raised by Dublin Corporation in a letter to Patrick Butterly dated January 19, 1981. It read: "The Inspector for Places of Public Resort (Electrical) visited the above premises on 15th January 1981, at 9.00 p.m., and noted the following: (1) Exit passageway at side of stage obstructed with cases, boxes, etc. (2) Overcrowding – the number of persons present in the Cabaret Room was greatly in excess of the permitted number (of 1,400) for which exiting is provided. This constitutes a very serious infringement of this bye-law. Your attention is drawn to the requirements of Bye-law 38 of the Bye-laws relating to Places of Public Resort which require that special care shall be taken to ensure that the means of escape provided for all persons on the premises are at all times maintained unobstructed and immediately available. Unless I receive your immediate assurances that the Exit ways will in future be maintained unobstructed at all times the public are on the premises and immediately available it will be necessary to institute proceedings against you for contravention of the above bye-law and also to raise the matter during the hearing of your application for renewal of your annual licence."

This letter was answered by Eamon Butterly on January 27, 1981: "The back Exit in question was cleared immediately [after] it was brought to my attention and I assure you that it will not happen again. I personally take great care to make sure all exits are clear.

Re overcrowding, I had discovered that tickets were forged for the show on that particular night and I have forged tickets if you wish to see them. This would account for the number of people who were on the premises. I have also decided not to stage concerts of this type again. Again, I assure you that all Exits will be kept clear when the public are on the premises."

This letter would later be described by a tribunal of inquiry report as "a deliberate attempt" by Eamon Butterly to mislead Dublin Corporation into thinking that all the exits would be kept in an unlocked and unobstructed condition while members of the public were on the premises. In fact, the inquiry found that a policy of locking and chaining the exits until midnight, at the earliest, had been operated by Eamon Butterly, despite the reminders he had been given by Martin Donohoe in the past. It was a policy pursued by Butterly up until and including the night of the fire.

Dublin Corporation should have been well aware of Patrick Butterly's cavalier attitude towards the planning process and his poor record on fire safety. Many years before the Stardust opened, Patrick Butterly had brazenly breached the planning laws. His Silver Swan pub on George's Quay adjoined an old sacking building called JP Keogh's, which Butterly eventually bought and converted illegally into a nightclub. Butterly opened the Two Ages disco with no planning permission. "We just went ahead and did it," he admitted in his memoirs.

Butterly was forced to apply for retention of the disco but was refused permission on fire safety grounds. The fire safety officer ordered him to put in another fire escape. However, as the only other possible location for an extra fire escape led onto the yard of another licensed premises, Butterly was unable to comply with the request. He simply knocked an extra hole in the wall, but this wasn't enough to satisfy the authorities.

Butterly approached a Government Minister, Kevin Boland. Butterly knew the Minister well and had even canvassed for him during election campaigns. He was confident that Boland's intervention could swing planning permission for his disco. But Boland was unable to help and told Butterly that he couldn't go against the fire safety officers.

Ironically, it was Patrick Butterly's failure to secure permission for the Two Ages disco that led to his decision to convert the old Scott's factory into the Stardust complex. Butterly boasted that the Stardust was the biggest licensed premises of its day and one of the best known nightclubs in Dublin at the time. Despite the club's huge turnover, Butterly complained that there was no big money being made, a fact he attributed to dishonest staff putting their fingers in the till or mishandling stock. Such was his obsession with money that Butterly trusted very few and was paranoid about being ripped off.

For a club of its size, the Stardust generated little crime or anti-social activity. In fact, local gardaí were of the opinion that it was reasonably well run up until the night of the disaster. Garda records only show minor instances of vandalism and damage to cars in the vicinity of the complex since its opening in March 1978. A small number of complaints were also received by Coolock Garda Station from people living in the area. These mainly related to youths acting in a disorderly manner late at night. The complaints became more frequent from September 1980, which gardaí attributed to the increase in the number of disco dances held at the Stardust. All of them related to disorder and noise being caused by youths leaving the club between 2 a.m. and 3 a.m.

The Stardust was also at the centre of bogus bomb scares on three occasions in 1980. In addition, just over a month before the tragedy, Dublin Fire Brigade attended a fire which had broken out in a hedge between the Stardust and Eamon Butterly's house next door, "Newlands". On another occasion, on January 9, 1981, a call was received by the emergency services stating that there was a fire at the Stardust. A fire engine from Killbarrack station attended the scene but no fire was found and the call was designated a malicious false alarm.

On the night of Friday, February 13, a St Valentine's Eve disco dance was held at the Stardust. A Special Exemption Order had been granted for the occasion allowing late-night opening. The hours of dancing were from 10 p.m. 'till 2 a.m. with a bar extension in force until 1 a.m. According to Garda figures, a total of 841 patrons attended the dance that night. In the Lantern Rooms that same night, a private function was held for members of the Marine Port and General Workers' Union.

The granting of extended hours was not unusual. Special Exemption Orders were granted to Butterly for 128 occasions between March 16, 1979 and February 14, 1981. These were availed of 25 times during 1979 and 99 times during 1980. On January 28, 1981 – just two weeks before tragedy struck – Butterly applied for Special Exemption Orders for eight occasions. These included the hours of 11 p.m. to 2 a.m. on the fateful night of February 13–14 and four occasions after St Valentine's Day.

The special occasion mentioned for each application was a house dinner dance. Admission to the disco that night cost three pounds and the price included a meal of sausages and chips. The event was run by Silver Swan Ltd and George O'Reilly Enterprises, a company engaged in the management of artists and musicians and the booking of entertainers and disc jockeys. Danny Hughes was booked as the main DJ to promote the eagerly anticipated final of the K-Tel sponsored disco dancing competition, which had been advertised in newspapers that day.

For the young people queuing outside the Stardust, it was shaping up to be a great night. Sadly, within the space of a few hours, 48 of them would have their lives snuffed out in the country's worst ever fire disaster. Many others would suffer horrific, disfiguring injuries. More still would bear the emotional scars of loss and grief for the remainder of their lives.

Two

Friday, February 13, 1981
(9.20 p.m.–1.41 a.m.)

*"There was a very real buzz about the Stardust. It was
a great place to go and have a good time."*

– Albert Buckley, survivor.

A light drizzle was settling over Dublin as the weekend drew
near. Thousands of workers were making their way home in
the rain from shopping centres and factories across the north side of
the city. For many, the journey home was filled with anticipation as
thoughts turned to the night ahead. Thankfully, the long winter weeks
were broken up with a Friday or Saturday night out at the Stardust
disco.

For 21-year-old Albert Buckley it was a special night for a
number of reasons. His older brother, Jimmy (23), was bringing his
wife, Christine, out to celebrate the first birthday of their daughter,
Julie-Ann. The young couple had been married for just six months
before the arrival of their beautiful baby girl. This St Valentine's
Day, they were determined to have a good night out after a busy
year dominated by the new addition to their family.

The three decided to mark the occasion by watching Albert and
Jimmy's younger brother, Errol, participate in the final of the disco-
dancing competition in the Stardust nightclub that Friday. It was a
big night for Errol, who prided himself on his dance moves. He had
successfully fended off the competition in previous heats and had
his sights set on winning the title. As Albert arrived home from his
job as an apprentice plumber, Errol was going through his dance
routine in the small sitting room of the house they shared on Clanree
Road in Donnycarney.

The two brothers had moved in together after their mother left Dublin to settle in Birr, County Offaly. Apart from the usual sibling rows about whose turn it was to do the washing and cleaning, Albert and Errol were enjoying their new-found freedom. Albert had eagerly followed his younger brother's progress throughout the competition rounds and was looking forward to watching him show off his moves in the final. He remembers the 18-year-old as "a whiz" on the dance floor. "He had all the dance moves of the time down," says Albert. "He was absolutely brilliant. Whenever Errol got going on the dance floor, there was no stopping him."

After showering, Albert decided to put on the only suit in his wardrobe. He wasn't very comfortable in the restrictive clothes but thought he would make a special effort to dress up on this important night. He grinned as he put on the suit, thinking back to the time when he first wore it. He had bought it for Jimmy and Christine's wedding, eighteen months previously. After the ceremony, Albert had almost met an untimely end when he fell down the Hill of Howth with an unfortunate girl in his arms. Albert had been attempting to show his chivalrous side by lifting the girl through some undergrowth on their way to another pub. He had convinced the girl to take a shortcut through some fields but, feeling a little worse for wear after the wedding celebrations, he tripped and the two tumbled down the hill. Albert got a nasty gash on his buttocks for his efforts which required six stitches by a bemused doctor. He later discovered that the brand new suit was also sporting a tear of similar length. Fortunately, a tailor was found who was equally adept with a sewing needle.

On the night of the Stardust fire, Albert was wearing the wedding suit with a pair of brown boots. The boots stuck in Albert's mind because he had loaned them to his brother, Jimmy, to wear to a job interview. Jimmy got the position of store manager with Scott's Foods Ltd, which was run by the Butterly family. At work he proved himself to be a capable and popular employee. He later represented the company at a talent competition held in the Stardust for local workers. Various businesses competed during the novelty night and Jimmy picked up a prize for his impression of Elvis.

Having spruced himself up, Albert made his way over to his girlfriend's house, but he was in for a disappointment. Although it was St Valentine's night, he would not have the pleasure of the young lady's company. Her mother kept a tight rein on her and was not prepared to let her out in Albert's company on the most romantic night of the year. However, he was in no mood to argue the point as he sat with his girlfriend under the watchful gaze of her mother. He was more interested in getting down to the Stardust where he knew the night was kicking off. He stuck around the girlfriend's house for what seemed like an acceptable amount of time and then made his excuses. As a result, he didn't arrive at the Stardust until after 11 p.m., by which time the night was well and truly underway.

Albert had no problem getting past the security men on the door; they recognised him as a regular. He and his brothers had become familiar faces to the management and staff at the nightclub. They enjoyed nights out at the Stardust, where they were assured of having a good time. Albert remembers a very real buzz about the place and that the talk during the working week would be about the upcoming disco on Friday or Saturday.

The Stardust had a solid reputation as a place where people generally had a fun night out. Before the Butterlys converted the former jam factory into the Stardust four years earlier, local people had to travel to Dublin city or further afield for entertainment. After opening in 1978, the Stardust quickly became the premier nightspot in this working class part of north Dublin. It offered a convenient, walking distance alternative to the city centre venues and was frequently hyped as Dublin's most exciting disco.

Word of the Stardust spread over the years and the car park at the venue was regularly filled with expensive cars from more affluent nearby suburbs, such as Malahide and Portmarnock. Since Danny Hughes had taken the mike as resident DJ, the Stardust had become *the* place to be on a Friday evening. A series of special event nights were held to attract more business but the disco dancing competition on February 13, 1981, generated particular excitement. Hundreds were expected to attend the final heat in which Albert Buckley's brother was taking part.

Albert nodded to one of the doormen he knew as he walked past queuing patrons waiting impatiently outside. As the Stardust grew in popularity, the door staff could afford to be more selective about who they let into the premises. Groups of young men, in particular, often fell victim to an increasingly strict door policy. It was a well-known ploy of customers to split up in the queue so the bouncers wouldn't suspect that a particular group of friends were all attending together. However, this plan didn't always work and some would wait outside the venue for an opportunity to slip past the doormen. There was always the chance that another bouncer would relieve a colleague on the door and be unaware of a previous refusal.

Albert had no such problems as he paid his £3 at the cloakroom on his way in. He declined the token for the plate of sausages and chips included in the price of admission. He was too excited at the prospect of meeting up with his brothers to contemplate eating. He turned the corner from the foyer and stepped into the main ballroom. A disco hit from the popular group Shalimar was blaring and the floor was crammed with teenagers dancing to the music. Hundreds more were gathering to watch as the disco-dancing competition got underway.

Albert made his way through the throng of dancing youngsters and found his brother and sister-in-law sitting on the banked seating near the back of the hall. He waved over to them and decided to get a drink before he sat down. Gradually, he made his way to one of the 'Star Bars' and ordered a pint. As he pushed through the crowd, he noticed the competitors taking their places on the dance floor as the competition got started. The disco was in full swing and from where he was standing he could just catch glimpses of his younger brother, Errol, impressing the onlookers with his sharp moves. Albert returned to where Jimmy and Christine were sitting and left his jacket on a seat next to them because he was sweating from the heat in the packed ballroom. After sitting with his brother and chatting away, he downed his pint and tried to convince the couple to get up for a dance. Christine agreed to go but Jimmy wanted to stay. He kissed Christine on the cheek and said he would join them in a little while. He told Albert to go and enjoy himself and promised he would be down soon. "You go on down, I'll just finish my gargle and I'll see ya in a minute," he shouted after Albert. They would be the last words Albert would ever hear his brother speak.

* * * *

As Albert joined Christine on the dance floor, Antoinette, Martina and Mary Keegan were in fits of giggles across the other side of the hall. The girls had played a practical joke on one of Antoinette's friends, but it was about to backfire.

The unfortunate victim of the joke was known for her vanity and the mischievous sisters hatched a devious plan they knew she would fall for. Mary Keegan and her friend, Mary Kenny, had bought an impressive Valentine's Day card and spent an entire evening composing dramatic phrases of love. They covered the card with poems and tributes, signing it with the imaginary initials of a boy who was supposedly smitten with their friend. Then, for good effect, they sprinkled cuttings of hair from a Cindy doll and sealed them in the card as a mark of this non-existent boy's love for their friend. Finally, they dropped the card in the post box with the girl's address printed on the front and swore each other to secrecy.

Now the girls could barely contain themselves as their excited friend searched the faces in the crowded nightclub for a sign of her lover-to-be. Soon she started to suspect that the squeals of laughter coming from the table where the pranksters were sitting might have something to do with the fact that her mystery man had not appeared.

The three Keegan sisters were sitting together with Mary Kenny in the first tier of seats, close to the dance floor, when they decided to cash in their food vouchers. They went back to their seats with their sausages and chips, and offered a plate to the girl who was still looking around for her admirer. As the girls fell into another fit of hysterics, it finally dawned on their gullible pal that she had been set up. She turned down the food in disgust and stormed off in a huff. Months would pass before Antoinette would speak to this girl again because she left the Keegans on bad terms that night. But Antoinette's two sisters would never get the chance to apologise for their harmless prank.

Earlier in the evening Antoinette had rushed home from her job as a receptionist in Kilmore Joinery and Bonding. She had all her clothes laid out in her room, ready for the night ahead. Antoinette remembers wearing a pair of straight trousers and a white satin blouse, which belonged to Martina. She also put on a grey jacket with silver lining. She could not have known that in a few hours these clothes would contribute directly to saving her life.

For the three Keegan sisters, this was a big night out. Antoinette had just finished seeing a young man from the area after a disastrous blind date. As Mary and Martina were both dating local lads, Antoinette made arrangements to meet up with former school pals from Coláiste Dhulaigh in Coolock. The girls regularly went to the Stardust and had attended a disco there on the previous Friday. They would sometimes hang out in the Black Sheep pub when they could spare a few quid; all the talk over drinks that week was of the upcoming St Valentine's night at the Stardust.

The three girls got ready in their bedrooms in the bustling house on Greencastle Crescent, which they shared with their parents, three brothers and two younger sisters. In between arguing with each other over various articles of clothing, Antoinette remembers Mary asking her mother to stitch her bra strap to her pink suit so it wouldn't show under the material. At 19 years of age, Mary was the eldest of the four Keegan girls. Her mother, Christine, remembers her as a giving child who had serious ambitions to become a nun. She was a home bird who enjoyed cooking and baking cakes in the family's small kitchen. She regularly wrote notes to the other members of her family, telling them how much she loved them. Her diary was packed with expressions of happiness for her life. She was never that interested in putting on make-up to impress the local lads and was content to spend the money she made working at the RTV electrical shop on her friends and family. She wouldn't go out to spend money on clothes to keep up with the changing fashions of her sisters. Instead, she would make up her wardrobe from the leftovers and cast-offs of her siblings.

A quiet, unassuming girl, fate had looked over Mary's shoulder when she wrote in her diary: "My life will change in 1981." She told her mother that this would be the year when she would finally find her path, most likely in a religious order as a nun. Christine never took her daughter's religious leanings too seriously, however, believing she would miss home too much to take off to the convent. While Mary acknowledged that she would miss her family very much, she told Christine very quietly, but with determination: "You wait and see." Christine would jokingly reply: "Okay then, I'll buy you your first habit."

Mary's dad, John Keegan, had built an extension at the back of the small garden behind the house where the girls could bring their friends. Mary and her best friend, Mary Kenny, would spend hours huddled there, yapping away and playing music tapes. To make their hangout more comfortable, they convinced their father to buy them a suite of furniture. Sadly, the settee he ordered would not arrive at the Keegans' door until the following week – the very day the two close friends were buried beside each other.

Mary was never the first one to suggest going out for a night on the tiles but she was easily persuaded to join her more excitable sisters. She was content to let Antoinette or Martina make the plans. On this Friday night she was more than happy to join her sisters at the final of the disco dancing competition. She had a loose arrangement to meet a young man at the Stardust, whom Antoinette had previously dumped because she didn't like his red hair.

Martina, sixteen years old, was panicking because she was late meeting up with her new boyfriend, David Morton, who lived on Montrose Drive near the Stardust. Martina and David had made a great couple from the moment they met and most of their friends already teased them about getting married. Christine remembers Martina looking particularly glamorous that night. "With her hair done up and wearing her lurex trousers she looked just like a model," she says. "She was like a movie star."

As they were exchanging their goodbyes with their mother at the front door, Martina rushed out of the house and down the road without her bright pink lurex belt. Antoinette offered to go back for it but, before she got to the house, the youngest Keegan girl, 13-year-old Lorraine, ran after her sisters with the belt in her hand. Even at that young age, Lorraine wished she could go along with the group and had even made a weak attempt to convince her father to allow it. However, she knew there was no chance, considering that her father had been reluctant to let even his eldest daughters go out that night.

As the girls walked quickly down the Kilmore Road in the direction of the Stardust, Mary turned off to go and meet one of her friends. The three sisters arranged to hook up again in the Stardust later that night. Antoinette and Martina called on another friend, Helen Henvey, and they eventually joined the queue of youngsters outside the Stardust a little after 9.30 p.m. They were standing three and four deep, stretching from the main door of the Stardust along the width of the front of the building and around to the side.

The girls stood in the queue, getting increasingly excited about the night ahead of them. Although they were not particularly interested in the outcome of the disco-dancing competition, they were soon caught up in the jovial atmosphere and were having a good laugh. "There was very little hassle in the queue outside the Stardust any time we went there," recalls Antoinette. "I even remember that this character from Duffy's Circus would sometimes turn up outside and walk up and down along the queue, playing his trumpet as the crowd cheered him on."

However, behind much of the bravado displayed by those in the queue, there was a ripple of anxiety. The bouncers at the door had earned a reputation for random refusal as the popularity of the Stardust attracted ever-increasing numbers. Antoinette remembers a few people in front of her saying that they were sure they would be refused because they had been turned away the previous Friday night. In fact, the girls were unaware that the doormen had already refused admission to their brother, John. He had joined the queue in front of them with his friends but was refused entry. His sisters were still enjoying the good mood of the crowd as other relieved young men and women congratulated themselves for making it past the bouncers. At this early stage in the evening there was very little drunkenness evident among the queuing patrons; the Keegan girls and their pals were sober going into the Stardust.

Antoinette noticed that they were among the first people to enter the cavernous nightclub and the girls had no difficulty securing seats in the first row, closest to the dance floor. They put their coats and bags at their feet, as they preferred not to leave their belongings in the cloakroom. Antoinette made her way over to one of the bars where a member of staff had just opened the shutter. She bought a pint of Harp for herself and ordered a Babysham for Martina, who was already moving across the floor to speak to some friends.

Mary joined them at their table soon after. She had failed to find her ginger-haired date in the Silver Swan pub, which was located beside the Stardust disco. She had made an arrangement to meet him in the bar but was now anxious to rejoin Antoinette and Helen Henvey, who were both without dates. Meanwhile, Martina met her boyfriend, David Morton, and the young couple joined the growing numbers on the dance floor. The music was getting louder as the place filled up and the girls took it in turns to dance to the tunes – somebody had to remain behind to keep the table and an eye on their bags and coats.

At 1.30 a.m. the DJ called out the names of the twenty-four competitors who were to take part in the final of the disco-dancing competition. Everyone else sat down or rejoined friends back at their tables. Antoinette remembers that Martina and David were particularly close that night. She could see them sharing a table nearby where they were both reading the Valentine's Day card Martina had made for him earlier in the week.

As the excited crowd gathered to watch the finalists go through their paces, Martina came over to Antoinette and told her how much she loved David. She handed her older sister the Valentine's Day card that she had made for her boyfriend and asked her to mind it for them. Antoinette hugged her and they got up to join the others on the floor as the names of the winners were announced. Antoinette's two sisters, their close friend Mary Kenny, and David Morton had just moments to live.

* * * *

With a happy shrug, 17-year-old Jimmy Fitzpatrick kissed Martina Keegan on the side of the face and watched her as she made her way back to her boyfriend, David. He recalls her looking particularly attractive that night. "She was a beautiful girl, a lovely person," he says today. Jimmy was a little jealous that David ended up with her because he had dated her for a while before that and still thought she was a great girl. "She had a beautiful face and was quite petite. But herself and David were meant to be . . . At the start the pair of them were very shy and even though they both liked each other, they wouldn't dare approach one another or let each other know how they felt. So I went out on a date with Martina one night and told her that David really fancied her. She said she felt the same way about him and that was that. They were the loveliest looking couple that I knew."

Pleased with the result of his matchmaking, Jimmy turned around to look for his mates, Liam Dunne, Paddy Coates, Joe Thompson and George O'Connor, who were sitting somewhere in the banked seating behind him. The gang of them were having a great time. Most of Jimmy's friends were co-workers he had met while training as an apprentice butcher at Superquinn in the Northside Shopping Centre. Some of the lads worked part-time in the grocery aisles. What had started out as an after school job for Jimmy was developing into a possible career. He displayed remarkable skill behind the meat counter and was asked by his manager to stay on and train full-time. He was pondering his next move – whether to stay on at Superquinn or go back to school – when the Stardust tragedy occurred. It was a night that would re-shape the rest of his life.

Just as important to Jimmy as his career, however, were the friends he had made working in the supermarket. Joining Superquinn opened up an entirely new and exciting social life for the young apprentice. The company regularly organised outings for their workers and everyone would be encouraged to mingle with their colleagues. Jimmy became very close to Liam Dunne, who also worked on the butcher's counter. They quickly developed a strong friendship and hung out together after work. The two jokers with the constant grins rapidly became the central figures of their ever-expanding social circle.

The Stardust became the focal point of that hectic social life as workers, after finishing up at 9 p.m. on Fridays, would head down to have a few pints in the Black Sheep pub. They would knock back a couple of beers before heading off to the disco in Artane. Jimmy lived with his parents in Kilmore, a stone's throw away from where he worked. He would first stroll the few yards home to get washed and changed before he went out. His friend, Paddy Coates, would stay over in Jimmy's house every Friday night because he lived in Finglas. The lads would drop into Jimmy's parents' house at lunchtime on Fridays to leave their wages in his bedroom and prepare their clothes for the night ahead.

As the last-minute shoppers queued in Superquinn before it closed, Jimmy made his way down to the busy checkout where the girl he was dating worked as a cashier. He was trying to make an arrangement to meet her in the Stardust after work but sensed that he was in the doghouse for some reason. Jimmy later found out that she had to baby-sit that evening and was expecting him to join her for a quiet night in. But Jimmy had made other plans with the lads and he left her to deal with her bad mood as he clocked-off work and headed home with Paddy.

His mother had left his favourite "disco suit" on his bed. Like many other young men at the time, Jimmy's prized possession was his three-piece, navy wool suit. At lunchtime he had asked his mother to iron his red shirt, which he would wear with a navy tie. Jimmy called it his "disco suit" because he wore it every time he went to the Stardust. To the teenager it made all the right fashion statements of the day. This suit would soon play a much larger role in Jimmy's life than he could have ever imagined.

Jimmy and Paddy made their way down the Kilmore Road where they met up with the rest of the Superquinn crowd. The arrangements every Friday night were the same: everyone would meet up near the flats in Kilmore before heading off to the disco. The Stardust had become the epicentre of a close community network of friends and work colleagues who all knew each other from going there every weekend. Jimmy feels today that this may have been a factor in the relatively peaceful atmosphere at the disco, where trouble rarely broke out.

Jimmy's friends were also very aware of the predicament posed by the selective doormen. Because they hung out in a big group, they were prime targets for refusal. This had happened on previous nights and it wasn't unusual that some of them wouldn't be allowed inside. On this fateful night, however, all of Jimmy Fitzpatrick's young friends, whose average age was just 17, were admitted without any problems. By the end of the night most of them would be dead and the rest horribly scarred.

Jimmy was stone-cold sober as he walked through the doors of the Stardust just after 10 p.m. Some of his friends had ducked into the Silver Swan pub next door to get some Dutch courage into them before the night's fun started. Because his house was a good fifteen to twenty minutes' walk from the Stardust, Jimmy never had time to grab a quick drink. By the time he managed to get into the Stardust, the place had already filled up and the prime seats next to the dance floor were taken. Instead, Jimmy made his way to the rows of banked seating at the back of the club to get a good vantage point from where he could spot his mates as they came in through the main door. He remembers that this set-up was unusual; the seats were usually sealed off unless there was a particularly big concert on. Jimmy and his friends would sit in the west alcove, which was normally open. However, he noticed that these seats were sectioned off this night. It struck him as peculiar.

As the lads gathered on the seats at the back, the slagging and banter got underway. They playfully tipped cigarette ash onto George O'Connor's hair as he sat in front of them. George had a self-deprecating sense of humour and he took the lads' horseplay in good spirits. Some of the others had a tendency to get a bit carried away, however. Jimmy recalls that, on the Christmas before the tragedy, they all decided to go to the annual Funderland carnival in the RDS. Jimmy reluctantly got on one of the rollercoasters with perhaps the biggest messer of the group, Paddy Coates. As the rollercoaster started its slow ascent to the top of the ride, Jimmy begged Paddy not to act the maggot. Paddy promised he would behave. As the car tipped over the sickening height, both lads stood up to prove their bravery. Paddy quickly ducked under Jimmy as he stood in the car. The coaster shot down the slope with Jimmy screaming his head off, unable to sit down.

It was pranks like this that made it a fun group to be with. On this night the jokes were flying thick and fast. The lads knew that there was a disco-dancing competition on, but they had little interest in it. They were more concerned about getting the pints in. After a while, another of Jimmy's close friends, David Morton, came over to him and asked him for a delicate favour. He wanted his trusted friend to go over to Martina Keegan and dance with her. An awkward scene was developing because David's ex-girlfriend had just walked in and spotted him with his new date. David asked Jimmy to look after Martina while he went over to his ex to try and defuse the situation.

During one of the slow sets, Jimmy gently teased Martina as they danced together. "She looked radiant that night, she really did," he says. "I remember her shoulders were bare because she was wearing a strapless top that had giant shiny sequins on the front of it. I slagged her off, saying I would have to wear sunglasses to look at it. But I still had a soft spot for her and I was just half joking when

I was telling her to stay with me and not mind the other fella. What did he have that I didn't, I asked her."

The pair danced together until the winners of the dancing competition were announced. The crowd cheered and clapped wildly and Martina turned to go back to her boyfriend. It was only while Jimmy was dancing with Deborah and Loretta, two girls he knew from Superquinn, that he sensed a commotion of some sort to his right. The next ten minutes would change his life forever.

Three

February 14, 1981
(1.40 a.m.–1.50 a.m.)

"It was only a small fire – easy to handle if you knew what you were doing."

– eyewitness account of the first sign of the flames.

The clock had just ticked over to Saturday, February 14, 1981, when the renowned jazz singer, Honor Heffernan, thanked her audience and walked off the stage in the Lantern Rooms. Heffernan had established herself in the 1970s fronting rock groups and had also acted in various Abbey Theatre plays. However, as the life of a musician or actress in Ireland was not always lucrative, she sometimes performed on the cabaret circuit to pay the bills. As she chatted with the other members of the band, she was completely unaware of the drama about to unfold just feet away in the adjoining Stardust ballroom.

After changing from her stage clothes, Heffernan decided to drop into the disco next door. She could hear the music pumping throughout the building and it sounded as if the crowd was having a lot of fun. By the time she walked down the corridor connecting the two parts of the complex, a disco-dancing competition was underway. As she stood against the counter at one of the bars, she could see that the young revellers were really enjoying themselves. "They were having a ball," she recalls. "If I had had a few drinks on me I would have been up there dancing away with them. There was a fantastic atmosphere."

The excitement in the Stardust was reaching fever pitch. Hundreds had gathered around the dance floor to see who would win the competition. Albert Buckley joined his sister-in-law,

Christine, on the floor. Together they watched Albert's younger brother, Errol, going through his moves. He was getting the loudest cheers from the crowd and easily stood out from the other competitors taking part in the final.

Just after 1.30 a.m. DJ Danny Hughes stopped the music momentarily to announce that a boy and a girl had been selected as the winners. The Buckley brothers were ecstatic when Errol was announced as the best of the men. The girl chosen from the three dozen hopefuls was 15-year-old Paula McDonald from Coolock.

Errol had brought the house down with his fantastic dance routine to the Patrick Fernandez disco hit "Born to be Alive". He punched the air as he stepped up onto the stage to be presented with his prize by Hughes – a £25 K-Tel record voucher. The winning couple was invited to perform a victory dance on the stage and the large crowd of onlookers gathered to clap along to the song. Another DJ, Colm Ó Briain, took the microphone and encouraged the audience to join in on the dance floor. Hundreds took him up on the offer and danced to what was to be one of the last songs of the night. It was now 1.41 a.m.

At the western side of the ballroom approximately fifty people were sitting or standing around five tables. Behind them was a roller blind made from a PVC-coated, polyester fabric. Split into five sections, the curtain was lowered to partition off an alcove of banked seating stretching to and along the side wall. The west alcove itself was the smaller of two such sections in the Stardust. It measured over seventeen metres in length and ten metres in depth. There were eight tiers of seats, with each tier containing fifteen units of double seats. Some of the regular patrons of the Stardust remember being surprised when they arrived at the disco that night to find that the west alcove was sealed off and the larger north alcove was open. Usually the reverse was the case, with the north alcove only open if the numbers warranted it.

Some of the people in this area were standing on tables and chairs to get a better view of the disco competition. A couple of girls stood on the ledge where the curtain came to the floor and were resting their backs against the partition. While the attention of most people was directed towards the dance floor, those standing against the curtain started to notice the smell of something burning. Linda

Bishop was sitting at the first table in front of the blind, next to the main bar. As she was watching the end of the competition, she noticed a sudden rise in temperature. This surprised her because she had spent most of the night feeling cold. She mentioned to her friend, Sandra Hatton, that she thought the management had switched on the central heating. They both wondered why anyone might have done that, considering it was close to the end of the night. The girls shrugged their shoulders and got up to dance to one of their favourite songs, "Lorraine", by Bad Manners.

Those remaining at the tables also started to smell smoke and they, too, felt a surge in temperature. Moments later, others sitting or standing in the area noticed a glow behind the curtain. Jacqueline McCarthy, from Kilbarrack, had just returned to her seat when she caught a strong smell of smoke. Suddenly, she felt a blast of heat. More curious than her friends, Jacqueline lifted up the curtain beside her to glance underneath. What she saw filled her with instant dread. She ran past groups of people and rushed towards the main door. She grabbed the arm of a bouncer standing inside the foyer and shouted at him: "They've started a fire up in the corner."

More people peered behind the curtain as the glow behind it intensified. On top of three seats in tiers seven, eight and nine of row A, they could see a small fire. One girl described it as "quite small". An eyewitness later told police that the back of just one seat was on fire and "it could easily have been put out if somebody had thrown a coat over it". Gerald Quinn said he thought there was something in the shape of a coat lying on the seat in flames. By now, most of the people sitting in this area could smell what they would later describe as "burning tyres". While hundreds still danced away to the music, people standing at the side of the dance floor sensed a commotion and turned around, thinking that a fight had broken out behind them.

One of the waitresses on duty, Elizabeth Marley, was serving meals to patrons that night. She was presented with a ticket stub by someone sitting in the north alcove at approximately 1.20 a.m. Although it was quite late, she returned to the kitchen area and asked her mother, Teresa, if she could get another meal for a customer. Her mother, who was working as the catering manager at the Stardust, told her to go ahead. Liz went back to the north alcove and gave the ticketholder the last meal served in the Stardust. She collected some plates from tables in this area and was walking along the aisle in front of the western alcove when she noticed a heavy smell of smoke. Alarmed, she walked quickly into the kitchen and told her mother about it. Both women immediately put down the plates they were holding and ran back into the Stardust. They looked up and could see the fire through a gap in the blinds. As they watched, people drifted over from the dance floor to see what was going on. Teresa Marley told her daughter to go back to the kitchen and alert the rest of the staff.

On stage, the assistant DJ, Colm Ó Briain, was sifting through the record collection to select the final track of the night. He put a popular Adam and the Ants song on the turntable. The attention of some of the dancers facing the stage was now drawn towards the curtained-off area to the right-hand side. At first all they noticed was a small, flickering glow behind the curtain. However, as they turned around to get a better look, some light smoke appeared to slowly rise over the partition and drift across the ceiling. Most of them thought it was a special disco effect that the DJ had set off to coincide with the end of the competition. They ignored it and carried on dancing.

* * * *

Patrick J. Murphy, 35 years of age, was a part-time doorman who had been employed at the Stardust club for just three weeks. He took up duty on the night of Friday, February 13, with other doormen at the main entrance and checked patrons as they entered the premises. He remained at his post until the doors were finally closed at 12.30 a.m. Later he moved into the disco and carried out an inspection of the sealed-off west alcove, where he discovered three female staff members having their break. He spoke briefly to the girls and, not noticing anything out of the ordinary, carried on with his inspection of the rest of the club. He returned to the main door at 1.40 a.m. and was standing there when Jacqueline McCarthy ran towards him, screaming that there was a fire.

Noel Quigley had also been employed as a doorman at the

Stardust. This night he was attending the disco as a patron and had decided to go home just after 1.30 a.m. He went to the double outer doors of Exit 2, which he discovered were locked. He turned back to walk towards two doormen who were standing at the inner doors, assuming one of them would have the key. As he asked them to let him out, he saw a girl running into the foyer yelling something about a fire. He heard Patrick Murphy shouting over to a colleague, Leo Doyle, that there was a report of a fire and to telephone the fire brigade. Murphy then tried to catch up with the girl as she disappeared back into the crowd.

Across the disco, other bouncers started to notice large sections of the audience turning away from the dance floor and towards the west alcove. The security men thought they must be crowding around a fight and moved quickly towards the scene to break it up. When Murphy reached the alcove, he crawled under the curtain and glanced to his right. In the furthest right-hand corner he could see a small fire on a seat at the back. Most of the people who were sitting at the tables beside the west alcove also later described the fire as quite small at this stage and insisted that it could easily have been put out. However, the inability of staff at the Stardust to deal with such a situation was about to be exposed with horrific consequences.

After glancing at the fire, Patrick Murphy rushed back to the foyer to grab a fire extinguisher. In the hallway, a young man, Peter O'Toole, was on the telephone, reporting the theft of his girlfriend's handbag to gardaí. His girlfriend, Ann Roe, a manager at Northside Shopping Centre, was standing behind him. As O'Toole was on the phone, Murphy approached, shouting that there was a fire. Doorman Leo Doyle grabbed the telephone from O'Toole to call the fire brigade. Doyle dialled 999 and handed the phone to another doorman, Frank Downes, telling him: "Frank, ring the fire brigade. There is a slight fire under the screen on the left."

Meanwhile, Patrick Murphy had grabbed a fire extinguisher from the wall and was trying to get back to the alcove. His way was obstructed by dozens of people who had walked across to the curtain to see what was going on. Frustrated, he ducked under the curtain nearest to the kitchen and ran along the alcove to where he could see the flickering of flames, about three inches in height. He aimed the extinguisher at the back of the seats, which he thought was the source of the fire, and hit the release valve. A spray of water engulfed the flames but, to Murphy's horror, had absolutely no effect.

Even though the fire at this stage was still confined to the back of three seats, Murphy could feel intense heat wafting down from the suspended ceiling above his head. Momentarily surprised, because the fire seemed nowhere near the ceiling, he stepped back. His hair started to singe and his face and the backs of his hands began to burn. Before he retreated from the boiling air, Murphy looked once more to make sure that the ceiling had not caught fire. However, it was unmarked and the carpet tiles on the wall were also intact.

Other doormen who tackled the fire in its early stages described an intense heat coming from the ceiling. Leo Doyle experienced a similar sensation as he arrived to help fight the blaze. Having pulled the pin from the fire extinguisher he was carrying, he pressed the grip and sprayed the water on the seats which had caught fire in Row C. The jet of water had little or no effect. As he was directing the spray of water, he, too, became conscious of heat coming from the ceiling. He described the heat on his hands, forehead and the back of his neck as similar to getting sunburned.

Another doorman, Michael Kavanagh, noticed waves of heat washing over his head. After taking a fire extinguisher from one of the waitresses, he joined Doyle and Murphy in the alcove. He could see that the fire was now travelling quickly along the carpet tiles on the walls and towards the ceiling. As it reached the roof, thick, black smoke started to envelop the area. He tried to get near the fire but was forced back by the intense heat emanating from above him. Realising that the water from the extinguisher was proving useless, he retreated back down the steps. As he did so, Kavanagh noticed portions of the ceiling appearing to melt and fall in the area where the other doormen were still fighting the blaze. He turned to leave the alcove and saw dozens of curious youngsters staring at him. Desperately, he yelled at them: "Get the hell out of here!"

* * * *

The head barman of the main bar, located beside the west alcove, was Gerry Guilfoyle. Just after 1 a.m. he closed the bar and started counting the takings. He was finishing some cleaning duties when a colleague told him that a fire had broken out in the alcove next to the bar. Guilfoyle ran through a set of interconnecting doors and into the Silver Swan bar where he met the owner of the Stardust, Eamon Butterly, and the assistant manager, Jack Walsh. As they conversed, one of his barmen, Lawrence Neville, rushed in and told them the fire was getting out of control.

It was at this point, according to a Garda report, that valuable time was lost because all four men went to the scene of the fire to look at it for themselves. Only after witnessing the flames rapidly spreading across the seats did they take action. By the time they returned through the crowd with extinguishers, they saw that the water that had already been sprayed had not had any discernible effect on the blaze. Neville described the fire as "jumping from row to row" and said it was "shooting like a fireball" across the seats. He could see that it was getting steadily out of control.

Another barman, John Andrews, noticed a smell of burning after 1.30 a.m. but passed it off as a cigarette. Seconds later he was forced to change his mind when he saw a waitress, Liz Prizeman, looking under the curtain. Through the gap he saw a very small fire on two seats. "The flames were about one foot in height, glowing but not blazing, with very little smoke," he told investigators after the fire. He ran immediately to Exit 1 and took a large extinguisher off the back wall. On his way back he was met by a colleague, Colm O'Toole, and they both carried the extinguisher to the west alcove. By the time they reached the area, a section of the blind nearest to the main bar had been fully raised by other members of staff. Andrews cautiously approached the fire. It was still small, but giving off intense heat that scorched his face. Unfamiliar with the operation of the extinguisher, he failed to get it working and dropped it in frustration. He rushed back into the main bar and met other staff, including Eamon Butterly and Jack Walsh, running towards the blaze.

Lawrence Neville had accompanied Butterly and Walsh from the Silver Swan. After looking at the fire for a few seconds, Neville told them he was going to call the fire brigade. He ran back through the main bar and into the Silver Swan. He grabbed the extension telephone at the back of the bar and dialled 999. The line was dead. He tried it again but to no avail. He realised he couldn't get a line out because it was not switched over to the public phone system.

As vital seconds ticked away, he ran back into the main area of the Silver Swan, where he saw Danny Hughes. He yelled at the DJ to switch over the public phone so he could call the emergency services but Hughes could not locate the switch. Finally, another barman, Cormac Rose, found it and Neville made contact with the fire brigade. His strained voice was recorded as saying: "Would you come down to the Stardust club in Artane as fast as you can? There is a large fire [and] there are over eight hundred people in the place. For God's sake, come quick, it is getting out of control."

The calm voice at the end of the line asked for his telephone number and then said: "We're on our way."

By the time Lawrence Neville got back to the alcove, the fire was well advanced. Some of those watching the blaze threw pint glasses of beer at the flames. One brave 15-year-old lounge boy grabbed an extinguisher and aimed the nozzle at the growing wall of fire. A 16-year-old colleague grabbed a waitress who was starting to panic and guided her to safety through a nearby exit door. Neville watched as the flames leaped across the tightly packed rows of seats "as if they had petrol on them".

The plastic seating was stuffed with polyurethane. When ignited under certain circumstances, this material can raise room temperatures to over 1,500 degrees Fahrenheit in less than a minute. The burning polyurethane emits thick, black clouds of hydrogen cyanide. A significant level of this deadly poison can kill a human being in seconds but it only takes a small amount to cause immediate respiratory failure.

Neville could see smoke drifting towards the dance floor. Within seconds it filled the entire ballroom. The fire itself was completely out of control, engulfing about one quarter of the alcove and flowing across the ceiling. "The smoke was very thick and choking and was going like a tornado across the whole disco," he remembers. At this stage there were almost ten people trying to fight the blaze. Colm O'Toole noticed one person, who was obviously drunk, stumbling towards the fire. The man was dragging an extinguisher across the floor. While attempting to operate the bulky apparatus, he dropped it on the ground. O'Toole grabbed him around the chest and dragged him back down the steps to the main bar. He wrestled the extinguisher from him and managed to get it working. He turned it on the flames and directed most of the blast of water at the centre of the blaze for over a minute. The fire was growing in intensity and O'Toole's heart sank as he watched the flames climbing inexorably towards the roof. As he was driven back by the heat, he tried to warn those who were watching the fire to leave by way of the main bar. Incredibly, few paid attention to him.

Just over two minutes had passed since the fire was first noticed by the people sitting beside the west alcove. In this short space of time, the flames grew until the entire alcove was ablaze and flames soared across the ceiling. Less than a minute later, a roaring curtain of flames spread along the entire width of the western alcove. By now the ceiling had started to melt and drip onto the remaining chairs that were not yet on fire. Patrick Murphy said that a "jelly-like" substance fell onto the cuff of his shirt, leaving a strawberry-red stain. Other particles were falling from the ceiling. With a sudden crash, a massive section fell in flames.

As soon as this part of the ceiling landed on the seats, a huge volume of thick, black smoke billowed out into the ballroom. The men fighting the blaze looked nervously at the remaining sections of suspended ceiling, afraid it would come down on top of them. Some directed their extinguishers at the blaze creeping over their heads, but by this stage the water from the extinguishers was just a small drop in an ocean of fire.

Eamon Butterly stood watching the ineffectual attempts of his staff to get the fire under control until an explosion ripped through the area and another part of the ceiling collapsed. He then ordered his men to abandon the fight and concentrate on getting people out of the building. As they dropped the extinguishers, the bouncers pleaded with the expanding crowd of onlookers to evacuate the Stardust. The majority largely ignored these warnings.

On stage, Colm Ó Briain glanced nervously at the flames shooting high into the air. The fire was spreading in the direction of the main bar and smoke was flowing across the room towards him. "At that stage people were beginning to panic," he said. "I started into another record and they were moving off the floor so I asked them not to panic. Just after that, I stayed on the stage for a while and some people sat down. When they noticed the fire getting bigger, they just started to panic and moved out – some people moved up on to the stage from the floor."

As confusion descended on the Stardust, Ó Briain picked up the microphone and said: "Don't panic, everything is under control. Move quietly to the exits." In reality, the situation was deteriorating rapidly.

* * * *

Next door, in the Lantern Rooms, the staff were cleaning up after the function, completely unaware of events in the Stardust. The head barman, David Rynne, was enjoying a quiet drink after work when a staff member, Elizabeth Marley, came in and said: "Dave, there's a fire in the Stardust, get everybody out." He remembered there was a fire extinguisher located in a cloakroom beside the exit in the Lantern Rooms. He lifted it off the wall and made his way through the kitchen corridor and stopped in front of the west alcove.

Rynne could see that the fire was dangerously out of control. He sprayed water at the inferno for about a minute until the heavy black smoke made it increasingly difficult to breathe. He was eventually forced to drop the extinguisher and ran back down the corridor to the Lantern Rooms. He held his head over one of the wash basins and suffered a fit of retching brought on by the fumes. As he was getting sick, he noticed the lights flickering in the bar. He turned to the band leader, Mick Morrissey, who had come over to see if he was all right, and said: "This is very serious, get everybody out."

Honor Heffernan was back in the Lantern Rooms after soaking up the atmosphere in the Stardust. She was looking forward to getting out of the club and going home. As she waited, a bouncer ran past her in a panic. He told her and the band to get their gear together quickly. "He said there was a fire inside," she recalls. But the next thing he said stuck clearly in Heffernan's mind.

"He said, and I'll never forget this: 'Get your gear together while I find the keys to unlock the emergency doors.' "

Even then, Heffernan thought it was a very strange thing to say. "I mean, it occurred to me, 'Why does he need keys to unlock the emergency doors?' But I just assumed, I suppose, that the fire he was talking about was very small and they would be able to put it out."

It took Heffernan and the band just over four minutes to get out of the Lantern Rooms after the bouncer returned with a key to unlock a chain draped over the exit door there. Outside, they noticed the first traces of smoke drifting down from the roof. Apart from that, there was very little indication of what was going on inside. It was only when people started to gather at the front of the building that the band decided to leave because bouncers were pleading with the growing crowd to go home. Heffernan got into a car and drove away. She had no idea of the horrific scene unfolding inside.

* * * *

The three Keegan sisters were dancing together with their friends, Mary Kenny and Helen Henvey, when they noticed smoke rolling across the ceiling. They thought it was some sort of special effect, until the DJ stopped the music. He announced that there was a small fire and asked everyone to remain calm. By now, many other dancers were turning around as the first wave of heat spread out from the alcove. Ó Briain again picked up his microphone and told everyone to hold hands and make their way slowly to the exits. The girls decided to go back to where they had been sitting to get their coats and bags. This took less than a minute, but by the time they had collected their possessions, a black wall of smoke had enveloped them. The girls started choking as they gasped for air. As they struggled blindly, a mass of people pushed them towards one of the exits.

Antoinette clearly remembers the carpet tiling on the walls shooting off in flames as the girls were pushed to within six feet of one of the exits. Screams shattered the air as those at the back of the crush were engulfed by the flames. "Some of those at the front were pinned against the walls, while others were pushed to the floor," she recalls. Those trying to escape the fire behind them desperately pushed forward and stumbled over the bodies struggling on the ground.

The Keegans were caught in the crush. The girls held onto each other as, one by one, they were dragged to the floor. Flames were soaring over their heads, fuelled by the rows of plastic seating and tabletops around them. Antoinette was lying on the floor, her face pressed into the carpet as feet stampeded over her back and neck. She clenched her eyes in pain and tried to hold onto her sisters' hands. Antoinette could hear a sickening sizzle as the roof melted and poured a river of fire over the heads of those around her. She found it impossible to breathe as the crush of feet expelled the last gasp of oxygen from her lungs. She took one last breath. Her final thought before passing out was: "Oh, please God, help us." Then the ceiling collapsed in flames on top of her.

* * * *

Albert Buckley was congratulating his brother, Errol, on winning the competition when he noticed a commotion at the far side of the ballroom. He saw a bouncer running towards the west alcove. "As soon as that man pulled up the curtain, I saw flames shooting up to the ceiling," he remembers. "I was thinking: 'What the hell did he do that for?' It just made matters worse."

At first, only one section was lifted, directly opposite the place where the fire had been first spotted. It was not until the remaining sections were raised, as the bouncers attempted to tackle the rapidly expanding blaze, that widespread panic swept through the crowd. The effect of the curtains being raised and the subsequent outbreak of hysteria left a strong impression on the minds of survivors. To this day, many are convinced that the raising of the partitions contributed to the sudden spread of fire. Some described the flames as "fanning out" from the alcove as the blinds went up. Others said it seemed as if a breeze had pushed the flames towards them.

As the DJ was telling everyone to stay calm, Albert grabbed Christine and Errol. Without ceremony, he pushed them roughly towards one of the exits which he knew was located behind them. Full-scale panic broke out behind Albert as he herded Christine and Errol towards the exit. Albert shouted over his shoulder for his older brother, who was still somewhere inside the inferno. As Albert reached the door, he felt a hot draft sweeping over them. He turned once more to look for Jimmy, but was pushed outside by the crowd scrambling for safety.

* * * *

Jimmy Fitzpatrick was one of the first people to get out of the Stardust that night. Seconds after he noticed a commotion near the partitioned-off alcove, he was out the door. Before leaving, he clearly saw the fire streaking up the wall and across the ceiling. In a matter of seconds, the flames spread across the roof of the dance floor, just feet above the heads of the dancers below. As the DJ urged people to stay calm, Jimmy thought, "Feck that," and ran for the main door. "Call it instinct, call it whatever you want, but as soon as I saw that fire I knew it was serious," he says.

Jimmy made it out of the front door before the first wave of panic hit those still watching the flames. In fact, he was rushing out before the security staff stationed there even realised what was going on inside. Jimmy was safe, but there was one problem. As he reached the foyer, he passed two girls he knew who were clutching each other in fear. To Jimmy, their screams seemed to herald the disaster about to happen. The look of fear on their faces as they clung to each other made an uncomfortable impression on the young man. He knew he couldn't remain outside while they stood inside the door crying. If he survived and they died, their broken faces would haunt him for the rest of his life. As he stood outside the door, he knew they would not make it. Realising that he couldn't leave them there, he braced himself and ran back inside the disco.

As he approached the girls, Jimmy knew that offering them practical advice was not an option. There was simply not enough time to explain to the two girls what they must do to save their lives. They were in such an obvious state of paralysed fear that they could not move. Having trained hard as a boxer in Kilmore West, Jimmy had the power and strength to grab both girls and throw them towards the door. There was no polite request. He simply picked both of them up at the same time and propelled them in the right direction. Jimmy saw them stumbling towards the exit and, satisfied, he turned to follow them.

He had taken two or three steps towards the open doorway, just feet away, when he tripped. It was a casual fall that in any other situation would have caused nothing more than slight embarrassment. This stumble, however, would almost cost him his life. Jimmy is convinced that he tripped on a handbag lying on the floor. He remembers straps wrapped around his feet before falling down heavily. This minor upset was not enough to keep a strong man down for long, but at that moment circumstances conspired against him, transforming a simple stumble into a fight for life.

As he was lying on the floor, hundreds of screaming people pushed and shoved their way towards him, running in the direction of the main door. Jimmy lay between them and safety. As he huddled on the ground, dozens of feet pummelled his back, legs, arms and head; he tried desperately to roll himself into a protective ball. The next rush of bodies reached him as he tried to get on his feet and the same punishing routine was repeated. Jimmy was now thinking to himself: "If I don't get up here, I'm a dead man."

* * * *

As the fire raged, hundreds of people still remained inside the Stardust. Although some left as soon as they saw the flames, eyewitnesses claim that there could have been as many as five hundred people still converging near the west alcove. Despite the black clouds of smoke rolling across the dance floor, others appeared completely unconcerned and were still dancing away.

Paula O'Connor was dancing when she thought she could smell smoke. Then she heard somebody say there was a fire. She turned and saw that the flames were already lapping across the ceiling. Paula made a run for Exit 5 but encountered crates of bottles stacked against the door. She then turned in the direction of Exit 2, the main door, but was blocked by the roaring sea of flames. Terrified, she ran back to Exit 5, which had been opened in the meantime, and managed to escape. All during this time, she saw people who were blissfully unaware of the chaos. The music was playing and some were still dancing, completely oblivious to the fire. At least six people remained asleep at their tables, having had too much to drink.

At approximately 1.45 a.m., just four minutes after the fire was first discovered, the final instalment of pain was visited upon those still inside the Stardust. On learning of the fire, doorman Phelim Kinahan pushed his way through the crowd and went into the lamp room where he turned all the lights in the Stardust up to full strength.

As he came back down the steps to the main bar, he saw a thick, black cloud of smoke making its way across the ceiling in front of the north alcove. He heard a loud bang and the lights suddenly went out. The sound of music was replaced with deafening screams as the ballroom was plunged into darkness. Over five hundred people were left fighting for their lives with only the light from the flames to guide them through the mass of frightened bodies.

Frank Downes was on duty at the outer door of Exit 2 when he saw the first sign of grey smoke drifting past the inner door and into the foyer. He immediately unlocked the outer door and stepped back to fold both leaves towards the ballroom. He secured the right-hand side door by lifting up the edge of the mat. He then secured the left-hand side by putting the bolt down into the gap between the mat and the well, leaving one leaf of the door partly jutting out into the doorway. He did not realise that this action would cause serious congestion within a matter of minutes.

As Downes opened the doors, he heard a scream from the ballroom; suddenly, a wave of people flooded into the narrow foyer. As the lights went out, Downes remembered, "complete panic" ensued. People were knocked to the ground and for the next four to five minutes the tiny foyer was transformed into a seething mass of people, all kicking and yelling to get out through doors they could no longer see. Smoke soon filled the narrow space and people fell to the ground, hands clasped over their mouths in a desperate effort to keep out the choking fumes. Concern for friends and family was replaced by a battle for personal survival.

By far the most distressing scenes were played out at this door. Experienced firemen explain that when people panic, they instinctively try to leave a building the same way that they entered it. As the majority of patrons had queued at this door to gain admittance to the Stardust earlier that night, this was where they ran to escape the inferno. Gardaí later reported that almost three hundred people got out through this exit on the night.

Survivors later described the great confusion and blind panic in the foyer, particularly after the lights failed. Some young people started punching and kicking those around them in an effort to get out. People were pushed to the ground in the rush and many more were trampled where they fell. Others were shoved and forced to the sides of the exit, and into the next-door bar and toilets. Deirdre Dames was running towards the main door when the lights went out and she was pushed to the floor. When she got up she couldn't see where she was going and found herself trapped in the ladies' toilets. Smoke poured in from behind her and she vomited as it filled her lungs. As she tried to breathe, she could see other figures, a man and a woman, screaming and banging on the tiled walls with their fists.

Jean Hogan ran into the back of the crowd as she fled towards the main door. At this point, people were backed up as far as the corner of the stage. A girl grabbed her and pulled her through a doorway which she thought was the main door. Instead, they found themselves in the men's toilets where almost a dozen other people were crammed against the windows. The sound of the fire approaching behind them was muffled by the noise of coughing and retching. As thick smoke flowed into the toilet, those trapped inside started screaming and crying hysterically. Jean hammered on the wall and beat the small windows at the top desperately with her fists. The windows were broken; the people inside pressed their hands between the jagged glass and screamed for help. More smoke filled the tiny space as flames entered the room. Some of the sobbing youngsters collapsed on the floor, helplessly resigned to their fate.

Outside in the foyer, people were kicking at the main doors, which appeared to be shut. In the aftermath of the fire, survivors would tell that that they were forced to kick at the door for as long as seven to eight minutes after the DJ announced that there was a fire. The doorman, Frank Downes, said he was wedged into a corner of the wall by the sheer press of bodies against him. When he eventually got out, he spent a number of minutes wrestling people to the ground who were trying to get back inside the building. When he looked back at the main doors, he saw they were closed. He later told gardaí that he didn't know how this had happened. He described the sight, after a few minutes, of the doors bursting open and dozens of blackened figures falling out onto the steps.

Inside, those stuck behind the mass of bodies in the foyer turned to fight their way through the billowing smoke in a frantic attempt to find another exit. Many paid for this decision with their lives. At the same time, scenes of sheer pandemonium were breaking out at the other fire exit doors. Dozens of witnesses would later report to gardaí that they had seen six or seven men kicking furiously at the doors of Exit 5 as the ballroom erupted in flames behind them.

One eyewitness, Adrienne Evans, saw a man kicking at a padlock that was locked on a chain wrapped on the inside of the door. She told gardaí that it took this man over three minutes to break the padlock and get the door open. During these short minutes, more desperate teenagers were pushing up against the backs of others crushed near the exit.

One man, Raymond English, said he tried to lift the emergency push bar but the door remained shut. "I messed around with it and I wasn't sure whether to open it or not," he stated. "A girl behind me started to scream and shouted: 'Let me out, mister!' I then succeeded in opening the door and two sides of the door opened outwards."

One of the bouncers, Gabriel O'Neill, told police that when he was informed about the fire by a waitress, he went to Exit 5 to open it. "I pulled the chain that secured the door and when I saw that the chain was locked, I pulled the chain a couple of times but it did not give way and the doors did not open. I assumed that the door was locked." Peter Griffin was sitting at a table across from that door when he saw a bouncer running towards it and kicking out at it. He saw a number of people running across the hall towards the door but he didn't move because he "didn't appreciate the seriousness of the situation". He was eventually pulled towards the door by a friend and was forced outside by the pressure of the crowd pushing to escape.

Martin Quinn remembers escaping through Exit 5 while the lights were still on. After getting out safely, he desperately searched for his sister but could not find her. He ran back into the blaze through the same exit. He helped one girl whose skirt was in flames and put his jacket around her to quench the fire. After ensuring that the badly shocked girl was safe, he ran again towards the flames but was forced back by the heat. Before he reluctantly turned away, he saw bodies burning on the floor near the stage.

Harry Mahood also got out through Exit 5, along with thirty or forty others in front of him. He then turned back and helped pull people out through that exit. As he stepped back into the furnace, he saw a girl moving slowly through the fire towards him. "She just went up in flames," he recalled. "She just hit the ground and then she stopped moving."

* * * *

Jimmy Fitzpatrick was one of those who escaped through this door. He had fought his way off the floor and was struggling towards the main door, which he thought was only a few feet ahead of him. He struck out to clear a way for himself but he was making poor progress. "A sickening thought occurred to me that I should have got out by this stage," he says. "A gust of air swept over my head and I tried to protect my face with my hands. Then I fell a second time."

Blindly reaching out with his hands, he could feel the wooden floor of the dance area under his splayed body. He almost vomited with shock when he realised he had gone the wrong way. "While I was fighting my way onto my feet I had become badly disorientated. When the lights went out I was totally lost and it turned out that I ran in the opposite direction, towards the heart of the fire."

Jimmy took a deep breath of air and then stood up. For years after the disaster, experienced fire officers would try to explain to Jimmy that flames cannot exist in smoke because there is no oxygen, but Jimmy maintains to this day that the black clouds of smoke that formed over his head contained flames that burned both his hands when he raised them to protect his face. "I was swallowing lumps of thick black smoke and chewing it like it was tobacco," he remembers. Long, flowing rivers of fire ran from the ceiling and poured over his head. His hair burst into flames and his favourite red shirt, so carefully laid out by his mother just hours earlier, started to run down his back. Jimmy Fitzpatrick was being burned alive.

As his body raged in pain, he sensed his consciousness starting to slip. His mind was telling him that he didn't want to die like this. Over the screams and shouts of those dying around him, Jimmy could hear frantic pounding as he lay suffocating on the floor of the Stardust ballroom. He stumbled towards five or six lads battering themselves against Exit 5 in an effort to get out. Frantically, they threw everything they had against the thick wood. They kicked, punched and slammed their bodies against the door as the fire approached them. For an immeasurable amount of time, Jimmy rammed his burnt body against the door with the others until it fell open and they stumbled out into the saving grace of the cold night air. As he was pushed through the exit, he remembers a locked chain sounding like a death knell as it swung from one of the doors.

Outside Exit 5, those within inches of safety found their progress severely impeded by others trying to get back in. People fell on bottles which were lying scattered on the ground outside the club. It would later emerge that the first panicked youngsters to get out found their way blocked by two plastic skips positioned outside the door. They pulled one of the skips away from the exit and threw it to the side. Hundreds of bottles spilled onto the ground where people slipped on them and suffered nasty cuts as they fell.

Meanwhile, at Exit 6, the orderly evacuation contrasted sharply with the panicked struggle taking place just a few feet away at Exit 5. Few used this door as their escape route, most probably because it was located at the north-east side of the building, and customers were unaware of its existence.

* * * *

Three friends – Joan Flanagan, Maureen Brazil and Christina Fullam – were standing outside the ladies' toilets, near one of the bars, when they first saw the fire. They ran down a narrow corridor through the open inner doors and were confronted by two closed outer doors at Exit 3. Flanagan remembered Fullam fumbling with a chain and lock and saying: "The bloody door is locked." As they tried to unravel the chain, three young men ran down the corridor towards them, shouting: "Don't panic, don't panic!"

Patron David Weldridge claimed he was the first person to arrive at this door. He said that he and his friends took turns kicking at the door in massive co-ordinated strikes. After a minute, the doors finally opened and the relieved crowd ran for the outside. They were blocked again, this time by the chain which remained intact, holding both doors together. Relentlessly, they lashed out at the doors for a full minute until they finally burst open completely.

Their desperate efforts to get out attracted the attention of survivors who had already reached safety through Exit 2. They could see the door bulging outwards as those trapped inside pressed against it. Finally, the doors opened a fraction. "It only opened a small bit and smoke bellowed out," said eyewitness Andy Boylan. "I could see a chain and lock keeping this door from opening fully."

When this door finally burst open, survivors who managed to get out found their escape hampered by a large, white van parked close to the steps. As a result, they were forced to jump and scramble over a low rail at the top of the steps to get away from the door. The Mercedes van had been parked there by one of the disc jockeys. Earlier in the evening, projectors, amplifiers and other equipment had been brought in through this door from the back of the vehicle. This van presented "a great hindrance", according to later Garda reports. A number of patrons standing outside, who were trying to help people get out of Exit 3, eventually smashed the windows of the van and managed to steer and push it away from the door.

People scrambling for safety through Exit 4 ran into other obstacles during the evacuation. On the night of the fire, a portable platform was placed near the exit. This platform was on wheels and could be raised or lowered during cabaret shows to extend the stage. There were also tables and chairs stacked on either side of the door. This left a gap of less than three feet for the crowd to get out through. Doreen Desmond said the lights failed as she was just feet away from the door. There were about a dozen people in front held back by some obstruction she could not see. Margaret Lynch remembered tripping over someone as she made it to Exit 4. As she struggled to get to her feet, others fell on top of her and she was pinned to the ground. Through the thick smoke she could hear people screaming: "Please open the door!" She managed to crawl towards the sound of someone banging their shoulder against the door. Within the space of a minute, she felt a breeze and crawled towards it to safety.

Outside, panic reigned as desperate attempts were made by survivors to get their friends out of the burning building. There were scuffles on the grass verge at the front of the complex as hysterical youngsters were pinned to the ground by friends trying to stop them rushing back inside. Although some fled the scene in fear, hundreds stood at the front of the building. Many were badly burnt and were urged to sit down on the grass as skin fell away from them in strips. Young men and women were indistinguishable from each other as their blackened faces stared blankly at the scene around them. The number of people gathered in the vicinity grew as local residents and passers-by hastened to the scene.

At the front of the building, desperate attempts were being made to get steel plates off the windows of the toilets. These had been secured two weeks earlier on the instructions of Eamon Butterly to prevent alcohol being smuggled into the Stardust. Dozens of voices shrieked from the darkness as those outside ripped at the steel with their bare hands. Patrons trapped on the landing over the main door could be seen breaking the glass in the windows and climbing out onto the canopy. The fire was now reaching its peak of intensity.

This was the scene that greeted the first unit of the fire brigade as it screeched to a halt outside the Stardust just after 1.50 a.m. on St Valentine's Day, 1981.

Four

The Emergency Response (1.42 a.m.–2.54 a.m.)

"The shit has hit the fan."

– Dublin fireman to Garda Control,
2.12 a.m., February 14, 1981.

At 1.42 a.m. on Saturday, February 14, 1981, an officer on duty at Central Garda Control in Dublin Castle received a call from a public payphone in the Stardust disco. A young man wanted to report that his girlfriend's handbag had just been stolen. As Garda James Gallagher was taking down the details of the theft, he thought he could hear screams and shouting in the background. The voice at the other end of the telephone became distracted and the Garda could not get answers to his questions. Suddenly, there was click and the line went dead.

Concerned, the officer radioed Garda Bartholomew Doherty, who was patrolling the Coolock area in car Romeo 1, based at the local station. Garda Doherty was directed by Control to go to the Stardust disco to investigate the alleged larceny of a lady's handbag. However, as he was dealing with another matter at the time, he did not respond immediately to the call.

Garda Doherty was having a busy night. He had already responded to a call from Garda Control at 11.40 p.m., directing him to go to the Stardust to investigate a report of intruders on the grounds. He had arrived at the security office at the eastern side of the building ten minutes later and spoken to the security man on duty. The security man, Mr Holt, told Doherty that he had been patrolling at the east side of the Stardust premises at 11.30 p.m. when he saw a gang of youths acting suspiciously near Exit 6, located at the back of the premises. He had informed the other security men on duty inside the club and then alerted gardaí.

After speaking to Holt, Doherty decided to carry out an inspection of the grounds surrounding the Stardust. He walked around the outside of the building and examined the tractor and oil tank on the eastern side where the security man claimed the youths had been hiding. However, Doherty could not see anybody in the vicinity. He finished his search, but before he left, Doherty noticed that a simple steel barrier was locked in position to prevent vehicular traffic access into the grounds. In less than two hours, this barrier would cost the Fire Brigade vital time as they tried to manoeuvre their trucks and equipment into position to fight the Stardust blaze.

As Garda Control finished alerting Doherty to the theft of the handbag, a 999 call was logged at Dublin Fire Brigade Headquarters in Tara Street at 1.43 a.m. Fireman Rory Glover answered the phone. The caller told him: "The whole place is on fire." After getting the telephone number for the location, Glover turned to his superior, Sub-Officer Hughes, and passed on the details of the call. In Dublin in the early 1980s, the set procedure was to mobilise two engines at the first report of a fire. Hughes dialled the number for Kilbarrack Fire Station and told the officer in charge to turn out the first crew. He then called the North Strand station and gave the same order.

Sitting around a game of cards in the station at North Strand, a 41-year-old veteran with sixteen years of experience under his belt heard the first ring of the telephone. Paul Shannon, from Finglas, could hold his own in the regular card games the crew played to alleviate the boredom between call-outs. It had been an average night for the men in North Strand, with the usual calls to a car accident, a stuck elevator, a report of a skip on fire and a false alarm. Having dealt with the Dublin bombings of 1974 and the serious fires which tore through the city's docklands on a number of occasions during the 1970s, Shannon was having a comparatively quiet time. However, the call he heard ring through as he sat playing cards was to signal the start of a night unlike any other he would experience for the rest of his career.

Shannon had spent the previous three years in North Strand, having served his time at Tara Street Fire Brigade Headquarters. He was the elder lemon among the young fire-fighters based at the station. Shannon was a popular fireman who was affectionately called "The General" by his colleagues.

As Shannon got up to answer the call, the bells were ringing and lights were flashing in Kilbarrack Fire Station, five miles away. Within forty seconds the first fire engine was on its way to Artane. The crew busied themselves preparing their equipment as the engine roared along Tonlegee Road, up the Malahide Road, across the Artane roundabout and finally along the Kilmore Road. Just two minutes into their journey, the firemen could see clouds of smoke rising into the air in the distance. They knew instantly that they were in for a long night.

As he climbed into the back of the fire engine, Shannon glanced at the colleagues who were settling themselves around him. The others had accompanied him on many previous occasions into scenes of death and destruction. In a vocation as challenging as the fire brigade service, the bond between these men was as strong as any brotherhood. Their union would be tested to the extreme this night. The continuous and tough training had prepared the men for almost any situation, but the Stardust disaster would illustrate just how badly under-resourced the fire service was at the time.

There was little talk between the men as they approached the scene of the fire. Shannon ran through his mind the drill he would be carrying out as the "number five" man on the team. Shannon's role was that of a "make-down" man. In civilian terms, he was one of two men responsible for identifying vital water access points in the vicinity of the fire. All engines were supplied with limited water reserves, but it was down to men like Shannon to find the hydrants that were located on almost every street in Dublin. Just as the engine turned the last corner onto the Kilmore Road, the firemen saw the first streaks of flames shooting into the sky. Rows of houses still blocked their view and, at first, one of the men thought the fire was in McMahon's timber yard, located next door to the Stardust. "Holy fuck!" he exclaimed to his colleagues. "We'll be here all night if that timber yard is on fire."

As the first fire engines screamed towards Artane, the radio in Garda Doherty's car again crackled. He was responding to another matter when the call came in from Central Control telling him to proceed immediately to the Stardust. The Garda told him to drop what he was doing and investigate a report of a fire on the premises. Garda Doherty jumped into the car and drove quickly towards the Stardust, just three minutes away.

Meanwhile, Garda Willie Staunton, driving patrol car Romeo 2 from Coolock, was passing through the area when he heard the first message relayed on his radio from Garda Control to Romeo 1 regarding the theft of the handbag. He heard the call being acknowledged by Romeo 1. Four minutes later he heard the second call directing Romeo 1 to the Stardust to check out a call about a fire. Staunton decided to investigate the fire report and drove towards the Stardust. As he did, Romeo 1 roared past him with blue lights flashing. Romeo 2 then passed a unit of Dublin Fire Brigade as he turned onto the Kilmore Road. Now the officer was driving towards an ominous glow which lit up the sky behind the houses in Artane.

The firemen sitting in the back of the engine could see crowds of distressed people on the road, frantically waving their arms to get the brigade's attention. Some screamed as the fire engine flashed past them and the lads inside knew immediately that this was no timber yard fire. People were stopping cars on the road and pulling doors open, trying to push injured friends inside. An ambulance had pulled over to the side of the road, still a small distance from the entrance to the complex. It was completely surrounded. People pushed and shoved the ambulance men as they tried to get their injured friends on board.

This was the Dublin Fire Brigade ambulance from Tara Street. Firemen Earley and Daly had received a call from HQ directing them to the Stardust at 1.45 a.m. Their ambulance was the first to arrive at the scene. It took eight minutes to get to the Kilmore Road, where they were swamped by a crowd of injured and hysterical youngsters. The two men got out of the ambulance and were immediately encircled by frantic people trying to get into the back. With a capacity for holding six people comfortably, at most, Daly radioed the Mater Hospital and told them he was bringing in fifteen casualties, all crammed inside his ambulance.

Crowds streamed onto the road in ever increasing numbers, blocking the emergency services and causing chaos. Stunned drivers stopped their cars and craned their necks to have a look. Sean Gilroy, from Clontarf, was driving friends home when he spotted a girl and a boy staggering along the Kilmore Road with their clothes aflame. "I stopped the car, put the two of them in the back seat and drove them to Jervis Street Hospital," he later told reporters. "The girl was screaming and the fellow seemed to be semi-conscious."

He left the pair in the casualty department of the hospital. He returned to the fire after 2 a.m. where he saw fleets of ambulances and cars departing with the dead, dying and seriously injured. Taxi drivers also played a vital role in the rescue operation by selflessly giving up their night's work to ferry the injured to hospital.

Paul Shannon's fire engine was the second to arrive on the scene. His immediate first reaction to the blackened figures streaming onto the road was: "It's a little bit early for a Halloween party." He didn't fully realise until he got out of the vehicle that these people were seriously burned. "It never dawned on me what we were about to be hit with," Shannon recalls today. The Kilbarrack unit had arrived moments before and was greeted by similar scenes of chaos. Station Officer Mooney, who was in charge, noted that many people he first saw on arriving at the Stardust were in a hysterical condition, some suffering from horrific burn injuries.

Mooney directed the driver to park the vehicle at the east side of the blazing building, but one of the steel barriers erected across the front entranceway to the complex stopped the fire engine in its tracks. A couple of men jumped down from the truck to try and get the barrier out of the way. A crowd of people standing nearby joined in the effort. Together they managed to bend the barrier back towards them. The driver, Vincent Keane, had to reverse a few feet in order to let the barrier swing around. All this time, valuable minutes were lost as the flames crept closer to those still trapped inside the burning building.

The engine finally parked between Exits 4 and 5 on the east side of the complex. As Mooney stepped down from the vehicle, he registered the scene before him and made an immediate "district call" to Tara Street headquarters. This level of emergency can only be declared by an officer at the scene of a blaze. On receipt of this type of call, headquarters will respond by sending two more fire engines, an ambulance and an emergency tender stocked with additional items of equipment.

Each fire engine carried twenty lengths of hose and three branch pipes which were fitted to the hoses in order to direct the jets. Reels of first-aid hose were also carried on board. These secondary hoses were smaller in diameter and therefore easier to handle. Some of the engines, including FB 61 from Kilbarrack, carried a portable pump that enabled the crew to access a source of water other than the mains supply, such as a river or a water tank. In the case of the Stardust fire, the existence of a thirty-thousand gallon static tank located under the club proved crucial.

The initial burst of water from the hoses operated by the crew of FB 61 was fed from the four hundred-gallon tank attached to the fire engine. They directed the first gush at the entrance to Exit 6 where firemen had found it impossible to get near the doorway because of the intense heat. After about seven minutes, Fireman Keane realised the tank was emptying. For a number of minutes, there was no water supply to fight the biggest blaze these firemen had ever experienced. At that moment a man, who Keane assumed was a member of the Stardust management, approached the crew and told them of the existence of the underground water tank. Station Officer Mooney directed three firemen to bring the portable pump to the tank and effect the connection immediately. Together, the four men grappled with the hoses and connection points. Finally, the hoses burst into life once more.

The mechanics of getting the supply reconnected by setting the portable pump to the static tank had cost four vital minutes. It would be argued that because the firemen were initially unaware of the existence of the tank, this led to an interruption in the vital water supply, for however brief a period, at an important stage in the rescue operation. Eamon Butterly would later tell the tribunal of inquiry into the fire that he had informed a member of the first crew to arrive of the underground storage tank.

As Mooney radioed back to headquarters for reinforcements, he was unaware that a district call had already been made to Tara Street before he had even arrived on the scene. This call was made by one of the doormen in the Stardust, John Fitzsimons. As was usually the case in the fire service, many members had second jobs. Taking up a bit of extra work as a bouncer at a nightclub was a logical part-time occupation for many firemen.

John Fitzsimons was a 34-year-old Dublin Fire Brigade officer from Grace Park Heights in Drumcondra. He had been employed as a doorman at the Stardust for six months but already had ten years of broad experience as a bouncer at other venues. On the night of Friday 13, 1981, he took up duty as the ticket collector at the main entrance until after midnight when the doors were closed to the public. Just after 1.30 a.m. he relieved a colleague, Frank Furley, who was on duty in the Lantern Rooms. He had just taken over monitoring the bar when a waitress ran in from the Stardust saying there was a fire next door. Fitzsimons ran to the west alcove, where he saw a couple of fellow bouncers attempting to fight a small fire with extinguishers.

When he learned from a member of staff that nobody had called the emergency services, he decided to do it himself. He ran into the Silver Swan Bar and dialled the fire brigade. He spoke to Officer Dowdall in Tara Street Headquarters and told him there was a fire in the Stardust that should be classified as a district call. The fireman reported to Sub-Officer Hughes that Fitzsimons, who was known to both of them, had made a district call. Officially, a district call can only be made by an officer on duty at the scene of a fire. However, Hughes decided that Fitzsimons' warning should be taken seriously and he gave word to send out the district call, alerting the second crew standing by in North Strand. An emergency tender and an ambulance crew were mobilised in Tara Street. A third crew was put on stand-by in North Strand. More calls flooded into Dublin Fire Brigade HQ, as neighbours living close to the Stardust were awakened by the chaos.

Garda Doherty and Garda William Staunton stood in shock outside the main front door of the Stardust. They would never forget the scene for the rest of their lives. The area was in darkness, with only the headlights from their vehicles lighting up the front of the building. From the second he jumped from his car, Doherty realised the fire was seriously out of control and that many people were injured and dying inside the blazing building. He attempted to get in through the main doors but was driven back by the intensity of the heat. He sent an urgent radio message back to Garda Control, requesting that ambulances be dispatched to the scene. As he was radioing for support, the Kilbarrack tender pulled into the car park. Seconds later, the North Strand engine, with Paul Shannon sitting in the back, also arrived at the scene.

On their arrival, the firemen could hear dozens of desperate voices screaming from behind the blocked windows of the toilets at the front of the building. Some members of the crowd ran over to the fire engines and pulled heavy sledgehammers from the lockers. One man attempted to batter down the steel shutters on the windows of the toilets. Others jumped on top of the window ledges and made vain attempts to kick the windows open.

Against the odds, the firemen tried to concentrate on the job in hand. There was no banter between the crews as they carried out their various duties. Each of them knew they were up against it tonight but, as professionals, they kept their thoughts and fears to themselves and got on with the job. The first two men had the daunting task of running through an exit and into the heart of the blaze with hoses attached to the fire engine's water supply. The driver of the vehicle remained at the pumps to monitor the pressure and flow while the officer in charge supervised and assisted with the rescue of the injured.

Paul Shannon ran to the side of the vehicle. He grabbed the heavy standpipe key and bar in one hand and looped a reel of hose around the other arm. The tools were used to access the main water supply through the hydrants located on the street. However, no full plan existed at the time to indicate where exactly the hydrants were positioned. Shannon and his colleague ran in opposite directions on the Kilmore Road to find them. As Shannon ran towards one end of the road, he passed another fire-fighter from the Kilbarrack unit who was trying to find water for his team. Together, they ran down the street, now filling with scores of onlookers as the sirens drew attention to the fire. The two men ran past the first hydrant, hidden under a parked car. They reached a second hydrant and Shannon told the other fireman to attach his hose to it.

Shannon ran on further for another frantic two minutes. He was sweating profusely under his thick uniform and his heavy boots thudded on the pavement. He finally stopped and crossed the road, running back towards the Stardust. He scanned every inch of pavement, desperately trying to find a hydrant in the dark. Finally, he saw a water mains sign on the ground which indicated that the next one was located across the road from the Stardust, back where he had started. He followed the directions and found the hydrant – buried under a bank of earth. He groaned out loud and made his way back to the fire.

Meanwhile, Shannon's team-mate was being attacked by a crowd of youths as he ran in the opposite direction to look for a hydrant. The angry mob had turned on the fireman because they thought he was running away from the fire. In desperation, he shouted at them what he was trying to do. At this moment, another fire engine, one of the reserves from North Strand, arrived on the scene and two firemen jumped out to go to the assistance of their battered colleague. The three men managed to fend off the crowd and turned their attention back to finding the elusive water supply.

Other fire units arrived as the gardaí radioed for more assistance. Terse messages came flooding into Garda Control: "There's a full scale emergency out here. There's a lot of people trapped and many more burned." In fact, there was serious disorder as the panicked crowd attacked firemen and gardaí. Ugly scenes of violence erupted. Young men, many of them inebriated, took out on members of the emergency services the frustration of watching their friends die. One Garda was dragged to the ground, punched and kicked as he tried to maintain order. He battled with his attackers until colleagues came to his assistance. One young man was arrested and brought to Coolock Garda Station.

Sergeant Michael Duggan, who was attached to the Crime Task Force at the time, remembers the rescue operation being seriously hampered by hysterical survivors trying to get back inside the burning complex. He assisted in the desperate attempt to disperse the crowd that had gathered in front of the main entrance. There were violent scenes as some of the youths made physical contact with Duggan and his colleagues. Duggan, now retired from the force, believes that drunkenness certainly contributed to the levels of panic. "I've no doubt that alcohol heightened the hysteria," he says. Duggan would later have the gruesome task of overseeing the removal of dead bodies from the scene to the City Morgue.

Paul Shannon was taking no prisoners as he made his way back to the front of the Stardust. "Anybody who got in my way got a whack of the standpipe and the weight of that thing would flatten you," he recalls. By the time he pushed his way back through the throngs of people, senior fire officers at the scene had realised that a great number of patrons remained trapped inside the building. They decided to direct their energies away from bringing the fire under control and towards saving as many lives as possible. This became the priority for the rescue personnel and the order went down the line accordingly. Shannon's commanding officer met him at the front gate and ordered him to abandon the water search. "He told me that this was no longer a firefight – this was a major rescue operation," says Shannon.

As Shannon pushed his way through the gangs of people shouting and screaming in front of the building, Garda Staunton was trying to help a man who was aiming heavy blows at the windows of the toilets with a sledgehammer. The officer grabbed the tool from the man's hands and launched a succession of blows at the windows. He smashed through the glass but made little impact on the steel shuttering. People's faces were pressed against the steel, screaming for help. Others gathered outside the ballroom tried to get through the metal with any implement they could find. Some tore at the steel with their bare hands, as the screaming and banging from inside became more frantic.

From the steps leading up to Exit 3, Shannon could hear the screams coming from the windows of the toilets to his left-hand side. He climbed on top of some railings that were outside the fire exit and peered through a small gap in the window, but his view was blocked by steel plates. From his vantage point, Shannon could just make out the cowering bodies through the coils of black smoke that poured through the ten-inch gap over the steel plate. He shouted into the darkness, asking if everyone was all right. Above the roar of the fire, he could hear them yell that they were dying from the smoke. "I told them to get down on the floor to escape the smoke and we'd be in to them in a minute," recalls Shannon. " I told them if they lay on the floor, the smoke would rise over them."

Shannon directed a stream of water from one of the hoses through the window to cool the intense heat inside the toilet. Meanwhile, desperate attempts were being made by the firemen to pull the bars from the windows. They tied steel hawsers to the bars and attached the other end to the fire tender. The engine was driven away from the windows at speed. The first attempt made no impression on the thick steel bars because the vehicle could not move forward over a slight bank located in front of the building. Another attempt simply resulted in the bars becoming bent together, which made matters worse.

Shannon spotted John Fitzsimons, the off-duty fireman who had made the first district call to Tara Street HQ. Fitzsimons had been helping people out of the front door since discovering the fire. Now he was assisting the fire crews by briefing them on the layout of the disco before they went in. Shannon grabbed his fireman colleague, tonight dressed in a bouncer's tuxedo, and asked him what he would be up against as he prepared to go in through Exit 3.

One of the many acts of individual bravery had already been played out at this door earlier in the night. Before the first fire engine arrived at the Stardust, a number of local people had left their homes and arrived at the scene. One local man, Michael Kelly, was praised by firemen for saving numerous lives, clearly putting himself at considerable risk. Kelly had been disturbed from his sleep in nearby Ardmore Drive by the sound of loud crackling at approximately 1.45 a.m. When he went into his back garden to investigate, he could see the massive clouds of smoke coming from the direction of the Stardust. He immediately jumped into his car and drove to the west entrance, where he parked. He ran through the door in the Lantern Rooms, behind the kitchen area, and tried to get into the Stardust. He was prevented from doing so by an entrance door that was in flames.

Kelly then ran back outside and around to the front of the building where he saw people starting to break the windows of the front door. He noticed that the doors to Exit 3 were open. Without any protective equipment, he ran in through the entrance and along the corridor, feeling his way with his hands. Soon he was choking on the thick, black smoke that had already killed scores of young people inside. As he reached the main part of the ballroom, he could see that all the tables and chairs on the dance floor area were in flames. Using a small torch he had brought with him, he could just make out bodies slumped near the entrance to the men's toilets to his left. He found a number of people alive and assisted them out through the door.

Paul Shannon was one of the first firemen through this door. He kicked through the inner doors, which were now in flames, and hosed down the blazing walls and floor as far as the stage area. He had not walked far when he stumbled over the first of the dead he would see that night. The body was rammed in behind the door, an indication that the victim had almost made it to safety. Shannon could not make out if it was a man or a woman because the flames had stripped the body of any obvious features. He couldn't hesitate and proceeded to move forward against the flames. The water was starting to have some effect on the fire in the immediate area and he made his way slowly over the smouldering dance floor. Behind him, other firemen were clearing the first escape routes for those choking on the floor of the toilets. One by one, they guided the trembling teenagers out. Shannon says he rests easy today in the knowledge that nobody died in those toilets after the arrival of the fire brigade.

However, people trapped in the toilets on the east side of the building, between Exits 5 and 6, were not so lucky. Some had run blindly past the open door and had mistaken the toilets for an exit door. They found themselves trapped in a similar fashion to those at the front of the building. The fire was worse here, the tightly packed rows of banked plastic chairs and tables providing a mass of fuel for its deadly progress.

Other firemen had attempted to get in through Exits 5 and 6, but the heat had driven them back. Few of them had any breathing equipment, as there were not enough sets available in the fire engines. Taking huge gulps of air, they crawled on the ground to try and escape the worst of the heat and smoke as they directed water at the blaze. Some angry youngsters launched a frustrated attack on the vulnerable firemen. Shannon remembers the crowd kicking the firemen on the ground as they wriggled backwards to avoid the flames.

When the first crews finally managed to get inside, they were greeted with scenes reminiscent of a battlefield. As they made their way towards the toilets, they were forced to step over burning bodies lining the route. Just inside the exit doors, corpses were heaped on top of each other. As the firemen dragged the bodies towards the exits, they realised there were people still alive among them. On their way back out, the firemen noticed more blackened shapes lying just inside the door. These people had made it to within inches of safety but were now burnt beyond recognition.

The full extent of the tragedy was now becoming apparent. Third Officer Joe Kiernan arrived at the blaze after receiving a telephone call at home. He rushed immediately to the Stardust when headquarters informed him that a district call had been put into action. His first order as he arrived outside the Stardust was to stop the attempt to pull the bars from the windows at the front of the building. He inspected the toilets and was satisfied that there was nobody left inside. He then made a "brigade call" to Tara Street, calling in all reserve engines on alert in the Dublin area.

By now the fire was showing the first indication that it had passed its peak. Fire crews could see that a major portion of the roof had caved in. Firemen call this process "venting", which means that the heat and fire rise up through the disintegrated roof instead of increasing temperatures inside the building. This made rescue attempts manageable within the sweltering inferno, but most of the firemen had now resigned themselves to retrieving the dead rather than the living. It was now just over an hour since the fire was first spotted.

Psyched-up on adrenaline, Paul Shannon rushed back to his post after taking a quick breather and splashing water on his face. Joe Kiernan grabbed him by the arm and motioned towards the doors. Kiernan issued his instructions as both men watched their colleagues dragging blackened bodies outside and leaving them scattered on the ground. Some of the men were dropping the bodies as soon as they got outside before rushing back into the building. Others were kneeling over smoking corpses giving them the kiss of life. Some refused to give up, pressing their lips against ruined faces, even as smoke poured out of the victims' lungs. Kiernan told Shannon to gather up the dead and line them against the wall between Exits 5 and 6. As he commenced his unenviable task, Shannon noticed that some of the bodies were still burning. He turned a jet of water over them to quench the flames.

Despite the gruesome ordeal, Shannon never baulked. "It was preferable to going back inside," he says. "Some of us didn't even have gloves, for God's sake. Having to pick up scorching bodies with bare hands was absolute torture." The stench of burnt flesh is something Shannon still finds difficult to forget. "It sticks to your clothes, your hair and your body. It lingers for days and there is no mistaking it. Experienced firemen can smell a burnt human in the remains of a fire when they first reach the scene. They can instantly tell if somebody has died."

As the bodies mounted up outside the still-smouldering shell of the Stardust, Kiernan decided that Stage 1 of the Major Accident Plan should be implemented immediately. This plan had been drawn up by Dublin Corporation, which defined a major accident as any serious incident involving twenty-five or more seriously injured casualties. The plan was divided into two stages, the first to be implemented by the Senior Fire Officer in Dublin Fire Brigade in consultation with the Senior Garda Officer in Dublin Castle. Stage 1 involved the dispatch by the Fire Brigade of all their available ambulances and the notification of the "first line" hospitals. The Eastern Health Board Ambulance Control centre and private ambulance services were also called in, as were the Civil Defence. The ambulance control centre then took action and ten beds were immediately made available in each of the front-line hospitals, which included the Mater, Jervis Street, St Lawrence's, St James's, the Meath, Dr Steeven's and St Vincent's.

As the line of the dead continued to stretch across the ground, Officer Kiernan asked a Garda with a walkie-talkie to send instructions for the implementation of Stage 2 of the Major Accident Plan. This alert put all the hospitals on emergency footing to receive numerous casualties. It also notified the morgue in Store Street. The Eastern Command of the Army was contacted, as was Dublin Airport and the Air Corps in Baldonnel. Meanwhile, the Order of Malta and the St John's Ambulance Brigade were called out by the Civil Defence to assist in the rescue operation.

The Minister for Health, Michael Woods, would later say that the Major Accident Plan had worked well in relation to the Stardust. A weakness in the plan, however, would be exposed by an exchange between Garda Control and Dublin Fire Brigade. The following transcript of this exchange clearly suggests that Garda Control did not know what the Major Accident Plan involved.

Garda unit (at scene): I have been talking to the Fire Chief and he says that there is a major accident, Stage 1, over.
Garda Control: Roger.

Garda Control (to Fire Brigade): Guards here again, one of our units came in to say that one of your chiefs said that this is a major something... Phase 1... Major Accident Plan.

Fire Brigade: Major accident?

Garda Control: ...Plan.

Fire Brigade: Phase 1?

Garda Control: Yes... Hang on just a second, will you? **(aside, to Garda unit at scene)** Hello? **(to Fire Brigade)** Yes, the guards here, we have word back through our car from one of your chiefs that this is a major accident, Phase 1... What does that mean in our language?

Fire Brigade: It means that you will have a list there. You are in control, aren't you?

Garda Control: Yes...

Fire Brigade: You have a list there: who to notify, all the hospitals, dangerous buildings. We'll do most of it anyway.

Garda Control: All hospitals?

Fire Brigade: Yes, now the only thing, the only way you can help us out is if you get CIE with the single-deck buses for the non-urgent cases up there or any of your cars that are available to shunt them into some of the hospitals.

Garda Control: Yes, we have all our mobiles on the way out there to get them in.

Fire Brigade: Yes, we've had ten ambulances; that's the best we can do.

Garda Control: We have our cars taking them in also.

Fire Brigade: Yes.

Garda Control: But all we have to do is... you have notified the hospitals, is it?

Fire Brigade: We are looking after that end of it.

Garda Control: And we've got to contact CIE to see if they can produce any single-deck buses?

Fire Brigade: Yes, and if you can... have you got a direct line to any of the Army barracks there?

Garda Control: To where?

Fire Brigade: To see if they can help with any of the ambulances. Any of the Army barracks.

Garda Control: What's stage 2? Now he says Major Accident Phase 2.

Fire Brigade: That's it: the shit has hit the fan, so.
Garda Control: What?
Fire Brigade: The shit has hit the fan.
Garda Control: Is that right? What does that mean?
Fire Brigade: It means everything is notified – the Army, the whole lot. That's everyone notified, right?
Garda Control: You want everyone notified?
Fire Brigade: Yes.
Garda Control: Right you are, thanks.

While the emergency services struggled to deal with the mounting catastrophe, the numbers fleeing through the emergency exits had reduced to a trickle. By 2.12 a.m. most of those being brought out of the Stardust were unconscious or dead. Furious battles for life took place in pockets around the fire exits where firemen tried to resuscitate the figures curled up on the ground.

* * * *

Antoinette Keegan's next memory after blacking out was lying on her side outside the Stardust. Her first thought was for her two sisters, who had been beside her on the floor of the disco. The three sisters had almost reached Exit 6 together. They were within six feet of safety when the ceiling collapsed in flames on top of them. "We were so close," Antoinette recalls, "but there were so many people in front of us. When the lights went out, I was still holding Mary and Martina's hands but we were pushed one way and then the other and we didn't know which way we were going." By the time Antoinette regained consciousness, her sisters had already died.

Days after the tragedy, as Antoinette lay in intensive care in Dr Steeven's Hospital, a man from the Kilmore Road area of Artane visited her father, John. The stranger told how he had arrived at the scene of the tragedy after noticing the black clouds of smoke rising into the air near the Stardust. According to the man, he had made his way to the side doors of the complex to try and help people who were making their escape. Antoinette's bright white disco blouse caught his eye; it was glinting through the choking black smoke pouring from one of the exit doors. He ran through the door and grabbed the unconscious girl. As he tried to drag her out, he realised she was still holding her sister's hand. He was forced to kick Antoinette's hand to free her grip. Then he dragged her outside.

Lying unconscious outside the Stardust, Antoinette was just coming around when she remembered that her sisters were still inside the building. As she screamed for somebody to find them, she became aware of her body burning. Her blackened face, neck, shoulders and arms were still smoking, as skin fell from her body. However, the worst pain was coming from her hands. They were stinging so badly that Antoinette tried to cool them down by sticking them into the dirt on the ground.

A fireman lifted her up and pushed her towards a waiting ambulance. She refused to leave, yelling that she had to go home and tell her parents that she couldn't find Mary and Martina. Antoinette tried to explain that Martina was only 16 and that she was responsible for looking after her little sister. To calm her down, the fireman told Antoinette that everyone had survived and had been brought to hospital. It would be two weeks before Antoinette would learn the awful truth.

* * * *

As Jimmy Fitzpatrick escaped from the building, he was grabbed by a badly burnt figure whom he mistook for his friend, "Johnner" Lynch. The man insisted that Jimmy go with him towards the front of the building. Jimmy responded that he had to see his mother. "That's all that was going through my mind," he remembers. "I had to tell my ma and da. I knew I was hurt and I had to go to hospital, but I wanted to tell them where I was."

A wire mesh fence separated the two injured men from the rescue services parked at the front of the building. As darts of pain rushed over his burning arms, face and hands, Jimmy was forced to turn around and make his way back and around to the other side of the building. He made it half-way across to the other side of the Stardust before his strength gave out and he fell to the ground. His mysterious companion tried urging him to get to the ambulance, but Jimmy was staring, transfixed, at his destroyed flesh: the skin on his arms was rolling back, exposing the cooked muscle beneath. Jimmy felt hot fluid running over his face and dripping onto his legs. As his helper screamed at him to get up, Jimmy put his twisted hands to his head, thinking he could feel blood. He couldn't remember hitting his head at any stage, but the fluid continued to spurt out of his skull. He was told later by doctors that the reddish-white liquid was, in fact, pure adrenaline. It was pumping out of the holes burned into his skin by the fire.

Eventually, the two walking wounded teenagers made it to the front of the building. They stumbled past fire crews and gangs of screaming youngsters. Jimmy stared in cold horror at the injured thrashing in pain on the grass. Walking very slowly, so his clothes would not chafe against his burnt skin, he gradually made his way down to the Kilmore Road. As the level of pain threatened to send him into unconsciousness, his companion guided him to an ambulance which was already packed with injured youngsters.

"The attendant was trying to close the rear doors as we came along," Jimmy remembers. "This person I was with tried to push me into the back of the vehicle. The attendant was shouting at us to get back, telling us there was no room. He kept saying he was full but this lad I was with, whoever he was, dragged me around to the front of the cab and pushed me in the passenger door. Then he shouted at the attendant: 'Now you're fucking full!'"

The driver turned around, expecting to see his colleague clambering into the passenger seat. Instead, Jimmy slumped beside him. The ambulance man tried telling Jimmy that he couldn't sit there and he would have to get out but, suddenly realising the serious state Jimmy was in, he exclaimed, "Fuck this!", and got on the radio. Through a haze of pain, Jimmy could hear the driver screaming at the dispatcher: "Which hospital? Which hospital? Quick, tell me now!" The radio crackled with a response: "The Mater Hospital."

Shaking in the front seat of the ambulance, the memory of when the bouncer first pulled up the shutter in the west alcove was replaying in Jimmy's mind. "I was thinking: 'Why did he fucking do that?' If he hadn't pulled up the shutter, we might have had a chance." As the ambulance careered away from the scene of the disaster, it narrowly avoided crashing into a pole. Jimmy could not resist telling the driver to be careful. "The last thing I need right now is to go through the fucking windscreen," he told him.

As the ambulance pulled into the emergency yard of the Mater Hospital, Jimmy was wondering what had happened to his friends. He had last seen them laughing and joking on the banked seating in the north alcove, just moments before the fire broke out. It would be several weeks before he could be told that most of his closest friends were dead, and the rest seriously injured.

* * * *

Antoinette Keegan was forced into the back of an ambulance. A girl was pushed in behind her, smoke still wafting from her burnt clothes. As the ambulance pulled out of the grounds of the complex, she made a coughing sound and slumped, dead, against Antoinette's shoulder. There were twelve others in the back of the ambulance: some whimpering in pain, others crying out in agony, all of them suffering from horrendous burns. The ambulance team shouted back to the wounded that they would be at a hospital soon. However, the victims' nightmare was only beginning.

The first hospital turned the ambulance away because its casualty department was overwhelmed by the flow of injured. Through the windows in the back of the ambulance, the injured could see hospital staff at Jervis Street frantically waving their arms. They were telling the driver that they could not accept any more casualties. The pain of the passengers in the back steadily worsened as the driver turned the ambulance around and accelerated in the direction of the next hospital. Similar scenes greeted the anguished passengers at the Mater, the Meath and James's Street hospitals. The injured screamed at the driver to take them home. When they reached Dr Steeven's Hospital, the dead girl was finally lifted off Antoinette Keegan's shoulder.

* * * *

Meanwhile, Albert Buckley's search for his brother, Jimmy, was just beginning. He had made it out of Exit 4 with his younger brother, Errol, and his sister-in-law, Christine. Errol made desperate attempts to claw his way back into the burning building to get his older brother but Albert was having none of it. He forced Errol onto the ground and ordered him to stay where he was. He grabbed Christine and told her to keep Errol out of the Stardust. Albert felt that the best plan would be to check all the other exits to see if Jimmy was among those who got out. Frantically running between the fire exits, he spoke to survivors who knew Jimmy. Some said they had seen him assisting people at Exit 1 at the back of the premises.

As Albert made his way back around the building, he tried to calm himself with the knowledge that Jimmy was a regular in the Stardust and must have known the layout of the premises very well. This gave Albert some hope that his brother had made it out alive. But there was no sign of him at the rear door. Albert made his way back again to the other doors and briefly spoke with Errol and Christine. The three of them were in tears as they split up to search around each of the exits once more. Albert continued on his way, pushing through the onlookers and stepping over the figures lying on the ground. As the chaotic minutes ticked away, he was forced to consider the possibility that his brother had been hurt and taken away in one of the ambulances. He told Errol and Christine that he was going to start searching every hospital in the city. His last hope was that his brother was alive somewhere, either in a packed ambulance or in a hospital casualty ward. It would not be long before this desperate hope was cruelly crushed.

By 2.54 a.m. the fire had been extinguished. Just over an hour had passed since a small flame was discovered on a seat in the western alcove. Within the space of sixty minutes, the entire Stardust complex had been gutted. As word of the disaster spread, hysterical parents arrived looking for their sons and daughters. Many were still in their night-clothes, having been summoned from their beds by friends and neighbours or alerted by the distant sounds of sirens. The fire in the Stardust was out but the horror and heartache for hundreds of families was only just beginning.

Five

The Desperate Search

*"I anointed the charred bodies lying in the hospital.
People's flesh was burning off as I said some prayers.
One man's hair and flesh was completely removed from
his face. I was praying over a bare skull."*

– Fr Heber McMahon, parish priest.

Death hung heavily in the air over the gutted remains of the
Stardust. The stench of fire and death was like a funeral shroud
draped over the shoulders of the rescuers as they sifted through the
wreckage. Newspaper reporters dispatched to cover the tragedy
pursued firemen for comment until they, too, had seen enough.

A journalist for *The Evening Herald* described the scene: "The
ambulances poured in, their cruel sirens spelling out the message of
death. Firemen, their faces blackened by smoke, scrambled through
the darkness, their arms comforting the whimpering sobs of the
rescued. Teenage faces had aged in minutes. Tears rippled down the
smoke darkened faces as friends rushed over, calling out frantically
the names of those believed lost in the inferno."

On the steps of one of the exits, two half-empty pint glasses sat
unnoticed. A steel lock and chain hung from a panic bar on the inside
of a door. Exhausted gardaí and firemen wandered aimlessly through
the smoking ruins, so stunned by what they had witnessed that they
could barely speak. They stared in silence as the terrible realisation
of the carnage finally hit them. The horror of the Stardust experience
would haunt many of them for the rest of their lives.

Sergeant Michael Duggan made contact with the Dublin City
Coroner, Dr P.J. Bofin, at approximately 3 a.m. and received his
grim instructions. All the deceased were to be brought immediately
to the City Morgue on Store Street. The removal of the bodies

commenced half an hour later. Duggan recorded and controlled the operation as body after body was covered with a blanket and brought to one of the waiting ambulances on the forecourt. Duggan recalls that, although it was a gruesome ordeal, it was difficult to relate to the corpses as actual people because many were so badly burnt beyond recognition. "There was a sense of unreality about it," he says today.

As firemen sifted through the smouldering wreckage to "blacken down" the last flickering traces of fire, the dreaded order went down the line to conduct a "sweep". With most of the bodies outside on the ground or removed to the morgue, the final task for the firemen was a thorough search of the gutted interior. They were assembled at one side of the complex and ordered to walk slowly through the ashes to look for body parts. As they carefully made their way across the scorched dance floor, the firemen would pick up a leg, an arm, or a piece of torso. While some corpses remained relatively intact, others were incinerated, leaving only parts of limbs. The body parts were gathered in black tarpaulin and bundled into ambulances for transfer to the morgue. In the north alcove firemen found dead couples with their arms around each other. Others lay motionless on the remains of seats where they had fallen asleep or had been overcome by smoke and fumes earlier in the night.

One figure of the community who would bear huge emotional scars from his experience at the Stardust was the local parish priest, Fr Heber McMahon. He had taken up his position at Our Lady of Mercy Church in Artane just one year before the tragedy. His home was around the corner from the Stardust on the Malahide Road. On the night of the fire, Fr McMahon was awakened from his sleep by a phone call. He was told by a friend that something dreadful had happened at the Stardust. The priest got dressed immediately and walked the short distance to the nightclub.

After bravely assisting with the rescue operation, Fr McMahon was approached by a senior fire officer. "He told me they had done all they could for those who survived and now it was time for me to come with him into the building," Fr McMahon recalls. "For a few moments I didn't really know why." The priest was given a pair of heavy boots to put on before stepping into the dark shell of the former disco.

"My overwhelming impression was one of complete silence," he relates now. "It was an awfully sickly time. I can't recall how long I was in there but it couldn't have been more than ten minutes. The place was in utter darkness. As we walked, the officer shone a torch to guide us further into the building. Even through the heavy soles of my boots I could feel the heat coming off the floor. And there was this awful smell – an acrid stench that stuck in my throat."

Fr McMahon was in shock as he saw the first of the dead. "As the fire officer flashed his torch around, I could make out these black mannequins scattered in grotesque shapes all over the floor. On first impressions you wouldn't think it was a body. All the clothes and hair had been burnt off but on closer inspection you could see hands reaching up and you thought: 'Jesus, what sort of deaths did these poor people have?' Some of them were lying out flat but I distinctly remember those twisted forms who obviously died struggling. It was not a peaceful death, judging from some of the bodies I saw. It looked like they had been fighting for air or even trampled as they lay on the floor. That was truly a terrible moment. The real awfulness hadn't hit me until then. Up to that point, there had been a lot of action and excitement and, above all, hope for those people who could be attended to. But when you went inside and saw how they died, you realised that this was the worst possible scenario. All hope had fled that awful place."

After the final sweep, the exhausted firemen filed into the Lantern Rooms and the Silver Swan to rest. On their way into the Silver Swan they stumbled over yet another body, this one behind the main bar. Paul Shannon recalls looking around the Stardust on his way to the bar and thinking: "Jesus Christ, what a waste of human life."

The framework that had held the suspended ceiling in place was hanging in rows from the roof. Where the plastic tables and chairs were bolted to the floor, there remained a mesh of steel resembling a disorganised junkyard. Empty fire extinguishers littered the floor where pools of water collected in mounds of black ash. Blackened fire doors hung silently by the exits. Inside the Silver Swan, the fire crews sat in silence. Some bore superficial wounds from the battle with the blaze. They counted their blessings that just one of their number was slightly injured. William Redmond, a brave, young fire-fighter, had been overcome by smoke as he dashed repeatedly in and out of the building to drag people out.

RTÉ news teams arrived early in the morning. As a union representative, Paul Shannon was assigned to be the spokesperson for Dublin Fire Brigade. "All the press wanted to know was how it started, where it started, was it deliberate and so on," says Shannon. He started to get frustrated at the repeated questions. "I said, 'Look, there a number of homes in this area that have lost loved ones. I'm not interested in how it started or where it started.' All I cared about was getting those people out and caring for them. I told them it was not my job to lay blame on anyone."

By 4 a.m. the firemen had done enough and the order was given to turn off the hoses. As dawn broke, gardaí erected two steel barricades across the entrance to the complex. Onlookers watched as fireman and gardaí picked their way back and forth over the web of hoses that splayed across the yard. At the side entrances a body count was carried out as the last corpse was dragged from the ashes. The limp figure of a teenage girl, barely out of school, was covered with sheeting and given a number – another addition to the rising death toll.

The morgue had already received the majority of the dead. At one stage five ambulances were discharging bodies at the same time. At 4 a.m. thirty-five victims had been counted. Half an hour later this figure had risen to thirty-nine. By 5 a.m. another had been added to the list. As the death toll rose, a decision was taken to erect a temporary mortuary in the yard at the back of the Coroner's Court. Soldiers from the Army Medical Corps were dispatched to assist in the operation. By daylight, most of the dead had been laid out on stretchers under the canvas marquee. At 8.30 a.m. the known dead numbered forty-four. Forty bodies were laid out at the morgue; four others were brought to hospital for resuscitation but were found to be dead on arrival.

* * * *

Located just three miles from the scene of the disaster, the Mater Hospital bore the brunt of the casualties. At first the accident and emergency department had been relatively quiet for a Friday night in Dublin. Apart from treating the usual drunks with minor cuts and bruises, the staff were having an easy shift. Then, in the early hours of Saturday morning, the hospital was transformed into a scene of chaos as the first of the Stardust's dying and injured crashed through the doors. At first, the night staff expected a few casualties as news filtered in about a fire in Artane. Even experienced medical staff would be shocked at the scale of the tragedy as stretchers carrying writhing figures were rushed through the doors.

Victims prostrated on stretchers were followed by groups of smoke-blackened survivors who shuffled painfully after them. The hospital canteen was opened to make room for the endless stream of injured now starting to arrive. It seemed as if hundreds of youngsters were being admitted in the confusion that followed, but many were actually unhurt survivors. They were crowding into the hospital to search for the friends and relatives from whom they had been separated at the height of the blaze.

Jimmy Fitzpatrick tripped over a stone block as he was gently guided into the hospital. "For fuck's sake, who the fuck left that there?" he screamed in frustration. The seventeen-year-old was led into the casualty department where basins of water had been laid out on the floor. Mayhem ensued as cubicles were taken up and patients were moved from their beds to make way for the Stardust injured.

A week before the fire, Jimmy had been pre-packing rashers at the butcher's counter in Superquinn. He had touched his finger off a hot plate and was left with a painful burn. That night his father had playfully called him a big wimp because Jimmy had sat with his finger in a glass of iced water, trying to numb the pain. Every time he took his finger out of the glass, Jimmy would cry out as the burn intensified. Now a nurse tried to convince him to put both of his seared hands into the basins of water lying on the floor of the hospital. He tried telling her about burning his finger the previous week and how it hurt like hell when he took it out of the water.

As Jimmy was arguing with the nurse, a young man walked in holding his coat around his girlfriend. Jimmy stood up to let them sit down and another nurse, who was dealing with someone else, started staring at him. "I could feel her looking right at me until she came over and freaked me out by shouting: 'You better come with me right now – right now!' I must have looked an awful state."

Although Jimmy knew his injuries were serious, he never thought they were life-threatening. He assumed he would have to stay in hospital for about two weeks at most before he could go home. "I never thought I was dying," he admits. "It never crossed my mind. When I went back into the fire to get those girls, I knew there was a possibility I was going to get burnt, but I never thought I could be killed."

Jimmy had been transformed from a young, good-looking teenager into a shivering wreck. Clumps of burnt hair stuck to his head and his skin was peeling back from his face. The flesh on his arms and shoulders had burned away. However, his treasured disco suit had saved his back and legs – and probably his life – as it didn't catch fire. Every other part of his body displayed the terrible trauma he had endured. He was led into a cubicle and laid on a bed as his body began to swell from the burns. The nurse was taking his details when a doctor appeared and yelled: "Give him enough for an elephant!" His next memory was waking up in intensive care.

As Jimmy was drugged into unconsciousness in hospital, his parents were driving home along the Kilmore Road. They were deafened by sirens as ambulances raced past them in the opposite direction. Soon they came across a scene of outright chaos: the road outside the Stardust was filled with people. Jimmy Senior and Elizabeth Fitzpatrick parked the car on the pavement and met a girl they recognised as a friend of Jimmy's. With rising fear they asked her where their son was, but found her too shocked to speak. Jimmy's father made his way through the crowd until he saw a fireman he knew and asked him if he had seen his son. The fireman told him he had seen Jimmy taken away earlier in an ambulance. He lied to get the couple away from the scene in case their son was the next corpse dragged from the building.

Jimmy's parents drove to the Mater Hospital, where they found a nun carrying a list of those who had been admitted. They begged her for information but she could not find their son's name. In desperation, the Fitzpatricks pleaded with her to look again. The nun scanned the list once more while others frantically shouted names at her. The nun insisted there was no Jimmy Fitzpatrick from Kilmore on her list. However, she did have a Jimmy Fitzpatrick from Macroom Road, near Bonnybrook. It transpired that, as Jimmy lay unconscious on the bed in the cubicle, another injured young man recognised him from hanging out on the Macroom Road. This youngster told the nurse that he knew Jimmy and that he lived in Bonnybrook. Jimmy's parents shut their eyes and thanked God they had found him.

The couple's relief was to be short-lived. They were soon seated by a doctor and gently told that their son was in intensive care. Jimmy's condition was considered critical and there was little hope for his survival.

* * * *

Albert Buckley also arrived at the Mater Hospital on his first stop to find his brother, Jimmy. He was disappointed not to find him and would spend the next few hours frantically trawling around the city's hospitals. He quizzed dazed victims in waiting rooms and again heard how Jimmy had last been seen helping people from one of the exits. These accounts fuelled Albert's hopes that his brother had escaped.

In the chaos of the casualty department, gardaí tried to take statements from numbed survivors. A traffic cop in full helmet and uniform was attempting to direct people when he collapsed to the floor in front of Albert. "The guy was completely traumatised," he remembers. "I had to support him, get his helmet off him and open his jacket. He just couldn't cope with what was after happening."

Other anxious relatives and friends arrived and departed as the frantic search for the missing continued. Nursing and religious staff compassionately handled queries from worried parents. Sighs of "Thank God!" were whispered as the names of those who survived were read out. Parents huddled together in the canteen where staff dispensed coffee and consolation. In the wards behind them, around-the-clock efforts were made by surgeons to save the lives of the critically ill. As the night wore on, one young man died and little hope was held out for a girl in the intensive care unit. To their immense credit, hospital staff and gardaí dealt with the situation with calm efficiency, even though they were snowed under with enquiries.

There were many who could not be consoled. Mrs Margaret

Griffiths, from Kilbarron Road in Kilmore West, was sobbing uncontrollably as she tried to sip a cup of tea. She told *The Evening Press* how she had searched all the hospitals in vain for her 18-year-old son, Michael. "He and my 17-year-old daughter, Jackie, went to the disco and Jackie is now in Jervis Street Hospital but she is OK," she said. "But we don't know what happened to Michael. He has a big birth mark on his leg . . ." Michael Griffiths would soon be listed as one of the dead.

Other families were luckier. As nurses read out the names of those detained, relatives broke down with relief. Theresa Curley from Castlekevin Road in Coolock had three children in the Stardust that night but only one, her eighteen-year-old son Denis, had been injured.

Fr Heber McMahon arrived at the Mater Hospital, still in shock after witnessing the scene of the fire. "Somebody outside the Stardust, I don't remember who, told me they needed priests at the Mater Hospital," he says. "I was reluctant to go. I had seen enough and I didn't want anything more to happen to me. However, I eventually left for the hospital, although I don't even remember driving there. While the Stardust was dark, smoky and eerily quiet, the hospital was bright and noisy. And under those lights you could see the terrible devastation to the people. The cool professionalism of the doctors and medical staff struck me as they went about their business. They were moving calmly through the wounded, quietly saying things like: 'This one to the ward, this one for surgery, we may have to amputate here.'"

Fr McMahon did what he could to comfort the families and injured. "There was a huge room and the place was very busy but I just instinctively went where I thought I might be of some use. There were families gathered around victims who were shaking in beds and I approached them and asked if there was anything I could do. People were going through various phases of emotions but the overwhelming feeling in the hospital was one of quiet resignation. I don't want to glamorise the scene, but there was a quiet dignity or even an acceptance among those who were there. I suppose it's possible they had been given shots of morphine to deaden the pain but I suspect it may also have been the extent of the aftershock."

Similar scenes were repeated in Dr Steeven's Hospital, where

Antoinette Keegan was wheeled into a tiny cubicle on a trolley and left for what seemed like an eternity. "There was complete pandemonium while the doctors and nurses ran around all over the place trying to help everyone at once," she remembers. "They were obviously not prepared for this night. Nobody was prepared for anything like what happened after the Stardust fire. There were so many casualties – too many for them to deal with." Antoinette lay in the small cubicle, listening to the screams of the injured and dying around her. With the curtain pulled around her, the frightened 18-year-old thought she had been forgotten. Her face pulsated in pain but she was afraid to touch the damaged skin. Her shoulders flared and her arms glowed, but her hands were causing her the most anguish. It soon became too much and she smashed her bloodied hands against both sides of the cubicle.

"The pain was so bad that I just couldn't take it," she says. "I felt that I couldn't cause any more damage by hitting them against the wall. It was better than just lying there in agony." Eventually a nurse came in and told her she would be treated in a few moments. Soon Antoinette was wheeled into an operating theatre.

Nurses stood at each side of her, dressing her hands. They pulled her hair back and white cream was smeared over her face, arms and neck. Special dressing was applied to her shoulders, which were in a particularly bad condition. Tubes were inserted into her body as the doctors put her on a life support machine. All this time she was calling out for her sisters and asking the doctors where they were. The medical team tried to calm her; she would not rest until one doctor told her to stop speaking because one of her lungs had collapsed.

She was later brought into one of the wards where other victims of the fire were recovering. A girl there was bandaged from head to foot and lying on a waterbed. Antoinette lay in the dark, crying out for her parents, too frightened to sleep. Every time she closed her eyes, her mind replayed the experience of the fire. She drifted into semi-consciousness until she felt herself burning and snapped awake, thinking the hospital was on fire. She remained convinced that her sisters had escaped from the disco alive but worried that they, too, might have been badly injured. She was concerned that her parents would be angry when they found her, as she imagined trying to explain that she had lost her sisters. After hours of personal turmoil, Antoinette finally lapsed into unconsciousness.

* * * *

Later that morning, Fr Heber McMahon returned to his modest home on the Malahide Road. He remembers sitting down in his quiet, peaceful sitting room and turning on the gas fire. The stillness of the house after the traumatic events of the previous hours unsettled him. He sat staring at the gas flames, beginning to seriously doubt that the disaster had happened at all. "I remember taking off the anorak I had been wearing and sniffing the sleeve. I could smell the smoke and only then could I accept that it wasn't my imagination." Sitting alone in the house, Fr McMahon reflected on the loneliness of his vocation. "I remember thinking that it was at times like this that this celibacy lark wasn't a great idea. I needed someone to talk to or just hold."

* * * *

At Antoinette Keegan's home in Greencastle Crescent, her 13-year-old sister, Lorraine, waited anxiously. Her parents, John and Christine, had taken the car to search for the three girls who had failed to come home. Lorraine had passed the long hours frantically pacing around downstairs in the small family home.

As she got breakfast ready for the younger children, she glanced at her teenager brother, John Jr, who sat staring into space at the other end of the kitchen, quietly waiting for news. "He was in a world of his own," recalls Lorraine. "He didn't even look up when I came back from the shops with the papers and he wouldn't acknowledge one of the neighbours who came in to check if we were all right. I think he was taking it particularly badly because he had been refused entry into the club while the others were allowed in."

At 7 a.m. John and Christine arrived back at the house, exhausted. They had spent the past few hours driving from one hospital to the next, but nobody had heard anything of the Keegan girls. The couple's faces were etched with the pain of the terrible scenes they had witnessed in the various hospitals. As they stepped through the front door, they were praying that their three daughters had returned home while they were out searching, but a quick glance at Lorraine's expectant face told them that their girls were still missing. They all burst into tears as they finally accepted that something had happened to them. Quietly consoling John Jr, they switched on the television to see if there was a Keegan name on the first roll call of the injured. John and Christine had a quick cup of tea before leaving to recommence their search of the hospitals.

On their arrival at the Mater Hospital, a nurse told Christine to try Dr Steeven's Hospital; many of the serious cases had been brought there to the National Burns Centre. Here they finally heard the news they were waiting for: one Keegan girl had been admitted. With a rush of relief, John and Christine ran through a packed ward. Christine was thinking: "Thank God we've found one of them; the others must be in another hospital."

Antoinette had just opened her eyes when she saw her parents rushing straight past her bed. She tried to get their attention but was unable to talk. Finally, Christine glanced around and saw her practically unrecognisable daughter. "She looked like a coal woman," recalls Christine. "I couldn't believe it when I saw her. Her face was completely black and there were tubes coming out of everywhere. I only knew it was her by her bright teeth. The last time I had seen her she was leaving the house the night before, looking beautiful."

In her state of shock, Antoinette was still frightened that her parents would be angry that she had not looked after her sisters. John and Christine wept as they tried to soothe their badly injured daughter. Antoinette tearfully asked about Mary and Martina and her parents gently assured her that her sisters were both safe in the Mater Hospital with minor injuries. "It broke my heart to tell her those lies but I couldn't risk setting her back," explains Christine.

In fact, Antoinette was in a particularly fragile condition, hanging perilously between life and death. She was unaware that she had received the last rites on a number of occasions during the course of the night. The hospital chaplain had thought she was losing her battle for life.

In the car on the way home, both parents tried to remain strong for one another. They stopped driving and got out to walk towards the Stardust in the faint hope that their other daughters were somehow wandering around, dazed. When they reached the burnt-out building and took in the extent of the devastation, the cold realisation dawned on Christine that her two girls might not be in any of the hospitals. "We were putting it off for as long as possible," she admits. "Up until that point we assumed they had escaped. I wanted to believe they were still alive. We wanted to look around an empty field rather than accept that anything else might have happened to them." John and Christine returned home to tell their other children that they had located Antoinette, but the good news was overshadowed by the fact that they still had no word of Mary or Martina.

Across the city, Garda stations were besieged with hundreds of panic-stricken relatives. At the centre of the emotional storm was Coolock Garda Station, less than a mile from the Stardust. This was the Keegans' next stop. Mothers, fathers, brothers and sisters crammed into the small room at the enquiries desk, all demanding answers. Husbands tried to comfort their wives, many inconsolable and in floods of tears. The station was a hive of activity as every available Garda was brought on duty to help cope with the emergency.

A young officer at the front desk had the first lists of those known to be injured. His phone rang relentlessly. There were agonising moments of uncertainty as he ran through his incomplete list, checking the requested names. The Garda told the Keegans to call a special number in Dublin Castle. "When we rang we were told to go to the morgue and that's when I almost died," says Christine. "I got a sudden rash all over my arms and I started scratching and scratching. My nerves were going and that was the first sign I had developed psoriasis."

As dawn stretched out over Dublin, numerous families were directed to the morgue in Store Street. Many had arrived after failing to find their children, brothers or sisters in any of the hospitals. For some, the hope that those missing had safely escaped the fire gave way to the possibility that they might be lying injured in a hospital. For others, however, the City Morgue would be the final port of call in their heartbreaking search for loved ones.

The scene at the morgue was one of indescribable grief. In trance-like shock, parent after parent arrived. One father cried as he asked his wife what their daughter had been wearing. Paralysed by fear, the mother was unable to leave the car. "A white blouse, wine coloured trousers and a long black coat," she quietly replied to her husband. The man left his wife to join the ranks of distressed parents but returned soon after, choked with tears. The authorities could not cope with the growing crowd and an appeal was made to those gathered outside to leave and come back at 10 a.m.

* * * *

Albert Buckley had been one of the first people to arrive at the morgue that bleak February morning. He had failed to locate his brother at any of the hospitals. To his growing frustration, Jimmy's name was not on any of the casualty lists. Reluctantly, Albert headed to the mortuary.

At the morgue Albert met his good friend, John Burke, a detective attached to the fingerprint department of the Garda Forensics Division. Albert had known the older Garda since he was a child. John had played football and hurling for the Craobh Chiarain GAA Club in Donnycarney and Albert had sat outside his house waiting for a lift to the game or training sessions. While John played, Albert would watch over the team's gear. The two became close friends and John brought Albert everywhere with him, even to the local pub after a game, where he would fill him with crisps and lemonade. John was also a good friend of Albert's missing brother.

As they greeted each other in the car park outside the City Morgue, Albert broke the news to him that Jimmy was unaccounted for. "As soon as I got to the morgue I realised how bad the situation was," recalls Albert. "The place was in a mess. They were caught by surprise by the amount of bodies coming in and I don't think they realised fully what had happened. I asked John to keep an eye out for Jimmy. As a professional, John didn't display any visible emotion. He was obviously worried, but he had a job to do and there were other families arriving all the time, demanding his assistance."

Meanwhile, the mammoth task of identifying the dead would shock even experienced coroners. Three of the country's leading consultant pathologists, including the State Pathologist, Dr John Harbison, arrived later in the morning. Six grim-faced Garda forensic experts arrived to conduct examinations. Each of the bodies lying in the morgue was eventually subjected to a full post-mortem examination conducted by a team of five pathologists working under the direction of the City Coroner, Dr P.J. Bofin. The forty bodies were divided into categories, depending on the extent of their injuries. The largest group comprised those who had been burnt almost beyond recognition. Some could only be identified by the jewellery they were wearing.

The City Coroner appealed through the media for parents of missing children to contact the gardaí and give as many details as they could before coming to the morgue. "We are looking for as much information as possible," Dr Bofin told reporters. "Even if people can remember what clothing their children were wearing, it would be of tremendous help."

The Coroner's Court was turned into a reception area where the stunned and distressed relatives could be interviewed. A proper system was established for handling the ever-increasing number of calls and queries in the wake of the disaster. Blood and urine samples were taken from each body and a microscopic examination of tissues was carried out in some cases. As the preliminary examination of the dead got underway, Dr Bofin admitted it would be several days before positive identification of all the bodies was completed. At least ninety per cent of the victims were so badly burnt that they were almost beyond identification. Dr Bofin had dealt with the aftermath of the North Strand bombings in 1942, when German aircraft accidentally attacked Dublin, and now felt that the results of the Stardust disaster were far worse.

By 11 a.m. on Saturday morning only one body had been positively identified by a father who recognised the remains of his daughter. A further fourteen corpses had been identified but would require more detailed examination. The remaining bodies were in such bad condition that it would take many painstaking hours of scrutiny, including research of dental records, before their identities could be determined.

* * * *

The Keegans arrived at the morgue shortly after 11 a.m. As soon as they got out of the car, they met Christine's cousin, who was working as a hearse driver. He put his arms around John and Christine and said he had seen Mary and Martina inside and they hadn't a mark on them. From the look of horror on their faces, he suddenly realised that the Keegans hadn't known their girls had died. John and Christine ran to a Garda and demanded to see their daughters.

"Everyone was crying," recalls Christine of the scene at the morgue. "There was a door through which people were guided after identifying their child. Every time it opened there was a wail; a terrible heartbreaking screech. People were not just crying, they were screaming. It's particularly sad when you see a man cry and there were men there sobbing like babies. Two nuns were moving slowly among the parents, telling them their children were now angels in heaven. But I didn't want that. I told them I didn't want angels in heaven – I wanted my two daughters here with me."

People were handed small plastic bags containing jewellery taken from the dead. As families recognised a ring or necklace belonging to their loved one, they would let out a piercing scream. Christine was handed a small bag with a necklace that looked like one worn by Mary, but the mauve hearts had been burnt away by the fire and she wasn't sure if it was her daughter's. The police asked if anyone at home would recognise it, so Christine suggested they speak to Lorraine.

A squad car was dispatched to collect Lorraine from the house. A family friend arrived with the gardaí and told the frightened teenager that her parents wanted her urgently. Lorraine asked if they had found Mary and Martina, but the officers would only say that they needed her to identify a necklace. "I couldn't understand what was going on," Lorraine remembers. "I assumed that if they had the jewellery, then they must have found Mary and Martina. But they insisted that they hadn't. They weren't going to tell me they found the necklace and rings on their bodies. I asked if Mary and Martina were dead but they wouldn't answer me. But when I got to the morgue and I saw my mam and dad crying, I knew they were dead. My mam handed me a plastic bag and inside was Mary's necklace. It was black and burnt, but it was hers. I suddenly felt like I couldn't breathe and I almost collapsed. I think a ban-Garda took me away."

Christine heard Lorraine confirming that the necklace was Mary's. Her next memory was waking up on the ground, looking up at a motorcycle cop's thick leather leggings. She was hauled to her feet and escorted outside where an ambulance was waiting to take her to hospital to be sedated. She refused to go, screaming that she would not leave without her children.

* * * *

As Jimmy Buckley's body had not yet been identified, Albert decided to go back to his family home on Clanree Road in Donnycarney to check if there was any word of his brother. In the house, the family was reeling in shock. Albert's older brother, Pat, was minding Jimmy's daughter, Julie-Ann, whose first birthday her parents had gone out to celebrate on the night of the Stardust fire. Jimmy's wife, Christine, was inconsolable. She demanded to go to her own mother's house with the child. The brothers sat and had tea while they listened to news reports of the tragedy on the radio. They phoned Albert's mother in Birr and told her that Jimmy was missing.

"It was like a famine had broken out," Albert remembers. "We all sat around and asked ourselves what were we going to do now. We just didn't know what to do. There was more drinking of tea and sitting around. Later [Taoiseach] Charles Haughey arrived and spoke with my mother who had come up from the country. He was a great man and was very popular on the north side of Dublin at that time. We had a lot of time for Charlie. He couldn't do enough for us. He was very good to us and he always bought the Craobh Chiarain GAA teams new socks and jerseys every year. He knew my family and he knew almost everyone in Donnycarney.

"But we were still hoping against hope that Jimmy would turn up at one of the hospitals, even though we had checked them all. We just waited. We consoled ourselves with the belief that Jimmy was a strong person. It gave us a glimmer of hope that he was alive. The fact that survivors told me he had been helping other people out suggested he was all right. Also, as all the hospitals were on call that night, there was the possibility that while we searched one, he had turned up at another. It was the longest night and day of my life but we did our best to find him. But it was starting to cross my mind that if he was dead, at least he would know we did all we could. At the end of the day, it was a lost cause. It was heartbreaking to think that the last time I had seen him was when he told me to go back onto the dance floor."

Just after 12.30 p.m. the following day, Albert Buckley's family got the dreaded call from the morgue. "I was expecting that call, although I didn't tell the rest of them what I was thinking," he says. "I kept it to myself. I remember a policeman called to the house. He asked us to come to the morgue because they needed us to identify or confirm what the forensics people had found. The morgue was like a market on Moore Street where people queued for vegetables. A family was brought in one at a time and dealt with in a court-like manner. Everyone was crying. It was packed with families and gardaí, all quietly grieving over the devastation. Some of the younger people were loud and aggressive, venting their frustration, which was understandable. There are loads of ways of letting out your frustrations and I suppose for those young people at that time, all they could do was let out a roar. The police presented us with a wedding ring which had the same serial number as Christine's and that was enough for a positive identification. There were tears. I felt numb as I looked around. We wanted to see Jimmy but [detective] John Burke told us to remember him the way he was. The only thing we had to prove he was gone was his wedding ring. But I trusted John and I believed what he said."

* * * *

With the casualty toll now standing at forty-four, the part-time administrator of the Mater Hospital, the future Taoiseach, Bertie Ahern, warned that the real danger for many of the injured would be the shock that followed the fire. "It will be several days before we know how many are going to pull through," Ahern admitted. This was borne out by the fact that four more victims would die in hospital from their injuries. Despite valiant attempts by medical staff to save them, the flames had claimed them four days, five days, eleven days and twenty-five days, respectively, after the tragedy.

Subsequent medical examinations established that thirty-four victims were charred in varying degrees, with a loss of portions of limbs in many cases. Only sixteen of the immediate forty-four victims were found to be in the less burned category. Of the forty-four victims who died immediately in the fire, all but one was observed to have soot or carbon in their air passages. This indicated heavy inhalation of smoke. The exception was shown by analysts to have inhaled a combination of smoke and fumes.

None of the victims, including the sixteen whose bodies were not severely charred, escaped without burns on some parts of their bodies. Three fully-clothed corpses were superficially burned on their hands, face or neck. Only in the case of three of the bodies was there evidence of injury accompanied by bleeding, indicating an injury sustained while the person was still alive. One bore a bruise behind the right ear, another on the forehead, and a third had a bruise on the deep muscles on the left chest wall, although this was not accompanied by any rib fractures. A fourth body had some minor bruising on one shin.

In his evidence to the tribunal of inquiry into the Stardust fire held some months later, Dr Harbison considered all of these particular injuries as quite minor. He added that superficial injuries to the charred bodies could not be ruled out. However, all the skull cases, many skull vaults, all the spines and pelves and virtually all the ribcages were preserved and none of these showed any signs of pre-death injuries. Dr Harbison stated that he and the other pathologists agreed that it was reasonable to conclude from the findings that no major crush injuries had occurred. He thought that crush asphyxia could not be excluded in the more severely burned, since there was heat-blackening of the chest organs in some. He reported finding evidence of asphyxia in one of the post-mortem examinations but this was in a minimally burned victim with no evidence of crushing.

In toxicological analyses of specimens from the deceased undertaken by forensic science laboratories, blood alcohol levels were studied carefully. Three of the dead had blood alcohol levels greater than two hundred milligrams per cent. Dr Harbison said that while this level of alcohol might have made them somewhat unsteady on their feet, they would nonetheless have been able to walk. Although none of the deceased had levels of alcohol in their blood which would have incapacitated them, Dr Harbison did suggest that, in the case of those with relatively higher levels, the manner in which they reacted to the fire might have been affected.

Carbon monoxide played a particular role in causing the deaths of many of the victims. When carbon monoxide enters the blood stream, a type of intoxication effect occurs. Medical experts are divided about what percentage of carbon monoxide in the blood stream will cause death. Some believe that a forty per cent saturation of the blood will kill, whereas others quote a saturation figure of over fifty per cent. However, it is generally agreed that levels of carbon monoxide saturation greater than twenty per cent will affect an individual's ability to behave rationally.

Dr Harbison divided the victims into three groups: those with levels of carbon monoxide in the forty per cent and upwards bracket, which he regarded as potentially lethal; those with levels of carbon monoxide of less than twenty per cent, which could have been derived from smoking cigarettes or high exposure to petrol exhaust fumes in the street; and a third intermediate group with significantly raised levels of carbon monoxide. Samples taken from the bodies of the victims revealed that thirty-six of the forty-four analysed had blood saturation levels of more than twenty per cent.

In Dr Harbison's opinion, an accurate cause of death could only be stated in the four victims who subsequently died in hospital. These consisted of three cases of bronchopneumonia, two with lung abscesses and one with irreversible brain and heart muscle damage as a result of shock sustained in the fire. Examination of lung tissue under the microscope from three of the four cases showed a change in the lining membrane of their air passages, suggestive of severe irritation. Dr Harbison concluded that the other forty-four victims died directly from shock due to extensive burns or from inhalation of smoke and fumes.

Over two hundred people received treatment in hospital for injuries sustained in the Stardust fire. Evidence as to the nature of the injuries suffered by those admitted to the city's hospitals was given to the tribunal of inquiry by surgeon Brendan Prendiville of Dr Steeven's Hospital.

Dr Prendiville noted that a total of eighty-six persons were treated as outpatients, having suffered small areas of superficial burning or distress from their experiences in the Stardust. Many were released after initial examination. For the remaining 126 admitted as in-patients, the range of injuries varied from shock, distress and relatively moderate superficial burns to minor respiratory complications. Thirteen patients were regarded as having significant respiratory complications and nine required intensive therapy. Many who were eventually discharged required subsequent admission for further surgery. The patients who survived respiratory complications had settled down satisfactorily, although Dr Prendiville warned they could become more susceptible to respiratory diseases in the future. In fact, two people were subsequently re-admitted to hospital after developing pneumonia as a result of the Stardust fire.

Eleven patients suffered appalling burns with the full depth of skin destroyed over a significant area. These areas were resurfaced by grafting operations. All of those who required grafting would have significant scarring and permanent disfigurement. They would require continuing treatment, including extensive surgery. Dr Prendiville had no doubt that some would be permanently disabled from doing work which required power and dexterity in their hands.

* * * *

Three days after the fire, Jimmy Fitzpatrick finally regained consciousness in the intensive care unit of the Mater Hospital. A nurse was gently bathing his eyes as the light returned to his vision. His parents stared at the figure in the bed, hardly able to believe it was their son. His blonde hair was burned away, exposing his swollen, destroyed face. Tears flowed down their faces when they finally recognised their son's bright blue eyes. "It was my eyes that gave it away," says Jimmy. "The nurse said I had the most beautiful eyes she had ever seen and when my parents saw them, they knew it was me." As he came around, Jimmy could not have known that he was destined to make medical history by eventually recovering from his horrendous injuries. He would also be the last Stardust survivor to leave hospital – a full five months after the fire.

Six

A Nation Grieves

*"No words can adequately express my sense of shock
and anguish at this appalling disaster."*

– Taoiseach Charles J. Haughey, February 14, 1981.

Many parents first learned of the Stardust tragedy on Saturday morning, when they awoke to find their children's beds empty. A number of residents living near the Stardust first heard or saw the fire from their homes. In most cases, what first attracted their attention was a crackling or banging noise, similar to shots being fired from a gun. By the time the first units of the emergency services reached the Stardust at approximately 1.50 a.m. – less than ten minutes after the fire was discovered – the entire ballroom was already a raging inferno. The lights in hundreds of houses in the area were turned on as people became aware of the disaster.

Alan Buffini, a post-graduate music student, was listening to tapes in his bedroom in No. 8 Maryfield Drive, Artane, in the early hours of the morning. As the music he was listening to was for an examination piece, he was carefully monitoring the time. He glanced at his bedroom clock and noticed it was 1.38 a.m. As he took off his headphones, he heard a loud, crackling noise and he went out to the back garden to investigate. Glancing around the garden, he saw his neighbour, Anthony Pasquetti, standing on his garage roof, looking towards the Stardust.

Pasquetti had left his girlfriend's house in Coolock ten minutes earlier. He arrived home and was about to put his car in the garage when he heard shouting and screaming. He thought it was coming from a lane at the back of his house but, as the screams intensified, he ran into his back garden to find out what the commotion was. Just yards away he could see people fleeing from a fire escape,

probably Exit 1, located at the back of the Stardust. The crackling
became louder and he could see thick, black smoke pouring from
the doomed building. Pasquetti ran upstairs to his parents' room
and told them there was a fire in the Stardust. As he glanced out of
their window, he could see a huge, orange glow seeping from under
the disco's roof. In the seconds it took for him to get back downstairs
and out to his garage, flames had broken through the roof and were
soaring ten to twelve feet high into the night-time sky.

Others had first heard the appalling news being announced by
Ronan Collins, then an early morning DJ on RTÉ Radio 2. Taoiseach
Charles Haughey gave his first reaction to the tragedy on a radio
news bulletin at 7.30 a.m. That night's "Late Late Show" television
programme was immediately cancelled and the GAA called off the
Railway Cup games as a mark of respect for the dead. This day
would be forever etched in the minds of Irish people – it was Ireland's
very own JFK moment; people would always remember where they
were and what they were doing when they first heard about the
Stardust fire.

Political reaction to the disaster was swift. The Stardust was
located in the heart of Haughey's constituency and he knew many of
the victims personally. Fianna Fáil's main Ard Fheis address, which
was to take place on St Valentine's Day, was immediately cancelled.
Haughey, fighting back tears, declared that the following Tuesday
would be a national day of mourning and announced plans for an
immediate public inquiry into the fire. He said the disaster would
give rise to calls for tighter security at dance halls.

The Taoiseach attended the scene of the disaster and also visited
the injured throughout the city's major hospitals. He was unable to
bring himself to go to the morgue. Among the first survivors to receive
a visit from Haughey was one of his own employees, 19-year-old
Walter Byrne, a stable boy at the Taoiseach's Abbeville mansion in
Kinsealy. "The whole thing has been particularly harrowing for me,"
an ashen-faced Haughey told reporters. "It happened in the middle
of my own parish, as it were. No words can adequately express my
sense of shock and anguish at this appalling disaster. I extend my
heartfelt sympathies to the families and friends of all the victims,
many of whom I knew personally as friends and neighbours. I can
only pray that God may give every consolation to all those who

have been so tragically bereaved."

After witnessing the chaotic scenes at the City Morgue, the Minister for Health and Social Welfare, Dr Michael Woods, promised there would be a full-scale Government investigation into the causes of the fire. Dr Woods told journalists he was horrified by what he had seen at the morgue. "I have talked to some people who had dealt with the Dublin bombings and they told me that this scene is much worse because of the effect of burning," Dr Woods said.

That morning an impromptu Cabinet meeting was held at the RDS (where the Ard Fheis was underway) and preliminary reports of the disaster were presented to the Government. The Minister for the Environment, Ray Burke, made arrangements to meet with fire chiefs later in the day. The leader of opposition party Fine Gael, Dr Garret FitzGerald, called for a "vigorous investigation" into the cause of the tragedy. "I am appalled by the magnitude of the disaster that has struck our city," he said. "On behalf of all those I represent, I offer our deepest sympathy to the relatives, many of whom must have spent agonising hours of uncertainty waiting to hear if their family had been struck by the holocaust. The cause of the fire and the question of how such a tragedy can be prevented in future must be vigorously investigated."

Messages of sympathy flooded in that day and for the rest of the week. The British Prime Minister, Margaret Thatcher, sent a personal message to the Taoiseach expressing her sympathy to the relatives of the fire victims on behalf of the U.K. Government. One of the first of many messages of sympathy from Northern Ireland – two of the victims were Belfast natives – came from the Reverend Ian Paisley, who sent a telegram to President Patrick Hillery. "Northern Ireland is appalled and shocked at the fire tragedy in Dublin," Rev. Paisley wrote. "Please convey our sympathies to all the sorrowing ones. Our prayers are with the bereaved that God may comfort them." Belfast's Lord Mayor, Alderman John Carson, also sent a telegram. "The sympathy of Belfast goes out to those who have lost their loved ones," it read. "It's a terrible blow, it's a great shock to us all and it's a terrible tragedy."

Queen Elizabeth contacted the Irish President. "I heard with great sadness the news of the tragedy in Dublin last night," she was reported to have said. "I send my very deep sympathy to you, to the families of those who died and to the injured."

The Archbishop of Dublin, Dr Dermot Ryan, said in a statement: "I am deeply shocked at the appalling tragedy and extend my sympathy to all the families who have suffered bereavement. I invite the people of the diocese to join with me in praying that God may console those who mourn their dead." Cardinal Tomas Ó Fiaich sent a telegram to Archbishop Ryan to express his sympathy. Pope John Paul II, who had made an exhilarating visit to Ireland just seventeen months earlier, also sent him a message. "I am deeply saddened by the news of the deaths and suffering of so many young people in the fire disaster in Dublin and I am at one with the parents and families in their grief. I would ask you to give assurance of my fervent prayers that God may give comfort and serenity to the sorrow-stricken, healing to the injured and eternal happiness to the dead."

The sponsors of the disco-dancing competition at the Stardust that night, K-Tel, issued a statement of sympathy to the bereaved families and injured for what they described as "an enormous tragedy".

That day's *The Evening Press* reported that a forty-year-old Beaumont mother had died of shock on learning that her three children had survived the blaze. Mrs Mary Coyne's son was recovering in Jervis Street, suffering from smoke on the lungs, and her two daughters had arrived safely home. She had collapsed and died on the street after hearing the good news. More parents would die in the years following the tragedy, with many families attributing their deaths to the unbearable stress and heartache of the Stardust.

Newspaper reports in the wake of the disaster made for harrowing and often disturbing reading. For every tale of bravery and selfless heroism, there were heartrending stories of grief and gruesome descriptions of injuries. One of the first newspapermen on the scene was photographer Myles Byrne, who was working for *The Evening Press* on the night of the tragedy. He had been in the newspaper office printing photographs when news of the fire at the Stardust came in. "As the taxi got closer to Artane we met a lot of ambulances rushing into town with their sirens blaring," he told *The Evening Press*. "We realised it must be something serious. But the scene at the Stardust when we reached it is almost indescribable. It was just panic and uncontrollable hysteria. There were hundreds of people rushing about, shouting, calling for friends, brothers and sisters. Some of them were blackened, some had burns, several had cuts on their hands and faces, and nearly all were spluttering, coughing from the smoke and crying."

The Evening Herald's front page headline on February 14 was "Cabaret Holocaust". The opening paragraph of the report read: "Dublin mourned its dead children today. A tangled mass of charred wreckage stood as their funeral pyre."

There was the poignant tale of 21-month-old Lisa Lawlor, who was orphaned by the Stardust fire. Her parents, Francis and Maureen Lawlor (both 25), from Finglas, were killed in the blaze. "A baby girl is still waiting for her mummy and daddy to return from the tragic disco in the Stardust on Friday night," reported *The Evening Press*. "What she does not know is that they will not be returning home to cuddle her again. For it has been proved that the baby's parents are still among the … bodies in the temporary morgue at Store Street Garda Station."

Stories of bravery abounded. One of the first firemen to arrive on the scene from Kilbarrack Fire Station described the scene that greeted him to a reporter: "There was pandemonium. Hundreds of people were running around the place and it nearly came to digging matches with the crowd outside. We found it very hard to get in and when we did we saw the bodies lying around the two side doors and inside. It was awful. They were everywhere and I think most of the people who were burnt were those who went back into the club to try and save their friends or members of their family. We rescued about twenty-five or thirty people from the toilets, where a lot of them ran. I'd say the place was destroyed in about ten to twenty minutes."

The gardaí and firemen who attended the scene were praised by all newspapers. "The coolness and efficiency of all the gardaí and firemen was remarkable," *The Evening Press* wrote. "Despite all the difficulties they endured, they never seemed to think of themselves for a moment but did everything they could to save the people still inside and to comfort those outside."

Survivors told of being dramatically rescued by firemen as they huddled together, terrified, in the toilets. "We were dead only for the firemen and I want everyone to know that," survivor Tom Stacy, himself a hero on the night, told reporters. A photograph of Tom emerging from the complex carrying a young woman in his arms would appear in newspapers around the world. Tom was one of many survivors who found themselves trapped in the toilets at the front of the complex, their escape through the windows impeded by steel sheeting. A fireman shouted to Tom and the girl he'd found in the toilets to stay where they were; someone would come and get them. Eventually, a fireman with a torch came into the toilet and gave them both an oxygen mask before leading them to safety. "I think the people who left the toilet died and myself and the girl survived because we stayed and did what they told us to do," Tom told a journalist.

Also hailed as a hero by newspapers was Fr Heber McMahon, who had helped rescuers remove bodies from the Stardust while administering the last rites. The priest, however, recalls an element of unwanted media intrusion during the rescue efforts. Fr McMahon was familiar with the Stardust, having performed there just one week earlier as part of the All-Priests Show. He claims that a number of exits were locked during the show, something that causes him great distress to this day. "The place was packed," he recalls. "Half-way through the show I got a call to see somebody back at my house. I decided to leave to make the appointment and run back to the Stardust in time for the show's finale because my house was only five minutes down the road. I remember going to several exits but I couldn't get out because they were locked. Even though I was a third level graduate with a strong sense of social awareness, it just struck me as inconvenient that the doors should be locked in this manner. It just goes to show you that in those pre-Stardust days, it was acceptable to lock fire exit doors rather than pay out the expense of hiring people to mind them.

"It crosses my mind on occasions that had I done something that previous week and kicked up a shindig about the locked doors, it might have made a difference. In my heart of hearts, I don't think it would have, but nonetheless it's something I have to live with for the rest of my life. I have to admit, it comes back to haunt me on a regular basis."

Another media hero of the blaze was Whitehall local Sean Flood, who was credited with saving seven people on the night. His parents told newspaper reporters how their 18-year-old son selflessly dragged others out of the inferno before collapsing from his own injuries. After a two-day battle for his life in the intensive care unit of St Vincent's Hospital, he was considered out of danger by doctors.

There had been arrests on the night of the fire and three men were charged with obstructing gardaí in the execution of their duties. A number of weeks after the fire, the State agreed to drop the charges against Ronald Prouse, Ronald Brown and Christopher Ryan, all from Coolock. Garda James McGowan, of Store Street Station, had told an earlier court hearing that the obstruction was serious but there were no injuries involved. He said he had asked the men to keep the entrances clear to allow ambulances to move in and out. Two of the young men had refused and became very aggressive, he told the court. However, all the men involved claimed that they were simply trying to get back inside the Stardust to rescue friends and loved ones. In fact, it emerged that Ronald Prouse, a signalman with the Army, had rescued one girl on the night by pushing her out of a window.

The DJs at the Stardust also featured in the newspaper reports that weekend. Colm Ó Briain, the 21-year-old assistant DJ on the night, told reporters that he had just spun a record when he noticed smoke coming from one end of the ballroom. "At first, people didn't panic," he said, "but when they saw the smoke spreading right across the ceiling, they began to shout and then scream, looking for a way out. I told them to be calm and not to panic. People were rushing up to me asking: 'Please tell me how to get out.' There was smoke all around us. I could hardly see myself and I was being pushed and pulled in all directions by frantic kids. I found my way into a ladies' toilet and locked myself in. Then I found I could breathe a little. I tried to get out through the ceiling but I couldn't. I came out of the toilet because the smoke was so thick. I had to feel my way along by the walls. It all happened so fast. People were even trying to break into the toilets."

As Ó Briain made his way to the toilets he found fellow DJ Dave Browne in a collapsed state close to the door and had to drag him out. The main DJ that night, Danny Hughes, had left the stage at 1.40 a.m. and was in the Silver Swan bar when he heard that there was a small fire. "At first I thought that it was only a fire in a wastepaper basket, but then people were rushing out of the place," he told *The Evening Press*.

* * * *

By Monday, February 16, when the initial shock of the Stardust disaster had lessened somewhat, grief had turned to anger. Survivors and victims asked two questions: how and why? There were scenes of unrelenting grief in housing estates throughout Coolock and Artane, which had suffered the highest number of casualties in the Stardust. In fact, at least fifty-four of the dead and injured came from within a one-mile radius north of the complex. Journalist Gerry McMorrow summed up the local mood perfectly in *The Evening Press*: "The people of Coolock, numbed by Saturday's disco disaster, yesterday slowly came to grips with the full scale of the horror which has cast its shadow over the whole life of the community. In the sprawling suburban housing area yesterday, youngsters were missing from school and from jobs in stores and factories. Coolock took on the character of a west of Ireland fishing village in the aftermath of a sea disaster."

With each passing day that week, newspapers released more and more names of the dead as they were identified. By Monday, just twenty-four victims had been named. *The Irish Times* reported that up to ninety detectives had been drafted in to investigate the cause of the disaster. A Garda spokesman said that although the possibility of arson would be considered, they were keeping "an open mind".

The media was also beginning to examine eyewitnesses' claims that a number of exits at the Stardust were either chained or blocked. An investigation by *The Irish Times* journalists revealed that people were unable to open at least three of the six exit doors from the Stardust when the fire broke out. Reporters found that doorframes were undamaged though the insides of the doors were burnt, suggesting that the doors remained closed during the fire. Their conclusion was backed by a forensic expert who visited the scene in the aftermath of the disaster.

Even before the smoke had settled over the nightclub, the blame game was already underway. The most prevalent rumour – fuelled, in part, by Eamon Butterly – was that the fire had been started maliciously. Curiously, the fire seemed to have originated in a cordoned-off area of the club where nobody was supposed to be. There was also much unsubstantiated talk of named individuals who were alleged to have started the fire.

Dublin Corporation was first out of the traps in denying responsibility for the tragedy. Corporation officials blamed the high loss of life on "pure panic". A spokesperson for the Corporation told *The Evening Press* that their initial investigation had disclosed nothing to indicate that there was inadequacy of escape. This was an incredible statement, given the fact that the Stardust owners had been warned by Dublin Corporation in the past about fire exits being either chained or obstructed.

By Monday, Patrick Butterly was nailing his colours to the mast. He openly blamed arsonists – and Dublin Corporation – for the blaze. Speaking to reporters for the first time since the fire, Butterly insisted that the Stardust was completely fireproof and met the regulations prescribed by Dublin Corporation. "The Corporation laid down the specifications for the Stardust," several newspapers quoted him saying. "The ones to blame are Dublin Corporation. They are the ones to talk to."

Eamon Butterly was convinced that the fire was started maliciously. He was also satisfied that all exit doors were open at the time of the fire. Dublin Corporation's public relations officer, the late Noel Carroll, countered that "if people were starting to look for a scapegoat at this stage, it was inappropriate to say the least".

Eamon Butterly displayed astonishing insensitivity later in the week. As the funerals of the Stardust victims were taking place, he was quoted in newspapers saying that he saw no reason why the complex should not be re-opened. "I see no reason why we should not re-open the premises if we are allowed to do so," he said. "But if I were building it again I would build it in concrete which does not burn." Butterly conceded that the decision would have to be deferred until gardaí said he could go back onto the premises. "But since the Lantern Rooms and the Silver Swan bar are still there, I can't see any reason why I wouldn't go back into business if I'm allowed," he added.

On the question of reopening the Stardust itself, Butterly said he would have to await the outcome of the tribunal of inquiry into the fire. He would also have to assess the recommendations of the Minister for the Environment, Dublin Corporation, and fire chiefs. Butterly's comments appeared on the front page of *The Evening Herald* beside a photograph of three coffins containing the remains of three victims from the one family: Marcella, William and George McDermott.

On Tuesday, the national day of mourning, the Church of Our Lady of Mercy in Artane was packed to capacity. Thousands of people gathered to pay tribute to the dead and injured at a special requiem Mass. Dignitaries in attendance included Taoiseach Charles Haughey, President Patrick Hillery, Fergus O'Brien, who was then the Lord Mayor of Dublin, Fine Gael leader Garret FitzGerald, and Labour Party leader Frank Cluskey. Speaking at the Mass, Archbishop Ryan insisted that the victims did not die in vain. "If the Stardust tragedy causes us to reflect seriously and purposefully on the great mysteries of life, suffering and of death, then the victims will not have died in vain," Dr Ryan said.

By Tuesday, February 17, a total of thirty-one victims had been positively identified. Throughout the parishes of north Dublin, the remains of the young began arriving at churches amid scenes of grief and anguish. As some of the victims had still not been identified, a number of funerals weren't held until the following week. Some churches held multiple funerals on the same day, such was the concentration of the dead in certain communities. The first funeral held was that of 21-year-old waiter Brian Hobbs, whose remains were taken from the Church of the Holy Child in Whitehall to St Fintan's Cemetery, Sutton, on Tuesday. The unrestrained grief displayed at Brian's funeral was mirrored in churches throughout the city for the next two weeks.

Wednesday saw the death of the fire's forty-fifth victim, Carol Bisset, an 18-year-old girl from Ringsend, who died in hospital from her injuries. Newspapers reported that Carol came within feet of escaping the blaze but lost her grip on the hand of a friend as panic erupted. She died from severe burn injuries in the Mater Hospital just before 8 a.m.

The Keegan family laid their two beautiful daughters, Martina, 16, and Mary, 19, to rest on Wednesday after a funeral Mass at the

Church of St Joseph the Worker in Bonnybrook, Coolock. Meanwhile, their sister, Antoinette, remained seriously ill in Dr Steeven's Hospital. At the time her sisters were buried at Balgriffin Cemetery, Antoinette had still not been told that Mary and Martina had died in the fire. Her family and doctors were afraid that the shock would kill her, given her precarious condition. The Keegan sisters' funeral was attended by many of their former classmates from nearby Coláiste Dhulaigh. Students from the school's choir sang hymns at the Mass, while others formed a guard of honour outside the church. David McKane, a close school pal of the popular sisters, wore a badge on his lapel that read: "Why?"

Many victims were buried in St Fintan's Cemetery in Sutton. Some mourners missed the burials due to two-mile-long traffic tailbacks caused by the thousands of Dubliners who descended on the scenic Howth peninsula to pay their last respects. As gardaí struggled to sort out the traffic jams, some motorists abandoned their cars and walked over a mile to the cemetery.

Over on the south side of the city at Mount Jerome Cemetery, near Harold's Cross, John Melia, the bereaved boyfriend of Jacqueline Croker, was overcome with grief at her graveside and had to be assisted by the victim's mother.

The funeral on Thursday of 17-year-old Marcella McDermott and her two older brothers, William, 20, and George, 19, was described by one newspaper as "perhaps the saddest of them all". At St Monica's Church in Edenmore, firemen from all over the country formed a guard of honour; the victims' father, James, had been attached to Tara Street Fire Station.

By Saturday, one week after the tragedy, seven victims remained unnamed, adding to the anguish and pain of their loved ones. Plans were arranged for a joint funeral that Monday in Donnycarney, which was presided over by the Archbishop of Dublin. Five unidentified bodies were later buried separately in St Fintan's Cemetery. Two more victims had been identified shortly before they were laid to rest. A total of forty-seven injured were still in hospital, five seriously ill.

There was cold comfort for the victims and their families at the end of that week as Dublin Corporation announced plans for fire checks to be carried out in clubs throughout the city. A ten-man team of inspectors was set up to carry out spot checks on hotels, dance halls and discos. Over 250 "places of public resort" would fall under their remit. Earlier in the week, the Minister for the Environment, Ray Burke, had instructed every fire authority in the State to re-examine public amenity buildings. Any building not conforming to fire safety regulations was to be immediately closed by Government order. A Dublin Corporation spokesman said: "We are initiating an accelerated programme of inspection of places of public resort in accordance with the directive of the Minister. Starting this evening, a team of ten inspectors will carry out spot checks on city establishments that come within the terms of the Minister's directive."

If anything, the Stardust had brought the country's antiquated fire safety standards under scrutiny. It was generally agreed that a complete overhaul of existing legislation would be needed if further tragedies were to be averted in the future. It emerged that the law under which the fire services operated had not been amended since 1940, despite huge changes in Irish society over the previous four decades. The law, for example, did not adequately address the fact that new plastic products, such as polystyrene, could have hazardous consequences in the event of a fire.

An investigation by *The Irish Times* revealed that most of the recommendations in a major report on the fire service in 1975 had yet to be implemented. These included the establishment of a comprehensive system of fire safety inspections. The newspaper also claimed that far too few personnel in the fire service or local authorities were fully qualified to carry out thorough fire safety inspections of buildings. Furthermore, very few dance halls or discos were equipped with sprinkler systems. These issues would later be addressed by the tribunal of inquiry into the Stardust disaster.

As the nation grieved, funds began to pour into a special Stardust Disaster Fund set up by Ultan Courtney, a CIE bus conductor and part-time social worker. By the time the fund was officially launched by the Lord Mayor of Dublin, Councillor Fergus O'Brien, the public response was described as one of "overwhelming generosity". The aim of the fund was to help victims' families with burial expenses and medical fees. When the fund was officially wound up in 1983, over £430,000 had been raised. Little did its organisers realise how valuable the initiative would prove to the victims and their families. It would take almost five years before any of them would receive compensation for the deaths of their loved ones.

As the last of the dead – for now – were buried, media focus shifted back to the Butterlys, who had been having a busy week. As Eamon Butterly talked up the prospects of reopening what remained of the complex, Dublin Corporation received three malicious damages claims for up to four million pounds. According to *The Irish Times*, the number of claims was indicative of "the multiplicity of companies involved in the ownership of the premises". The first claim had been lodged just three days after the fire by Silver Swan Ltd, trading as Stardust Cabaret. At two million pounds, it was the largest single compensation demand ever made against a local authority. By Thursday, a separate claim for a million pounds had been made against Dublin Corporation by Scott's Foods Ltd. Before the end of the week, yet another claim for one million was made by Butterly Enterprises Ltd, RW Scott (Ireland) Ltd and Scott's Foods Ltd.

In a preliminary notice of application for their claim, Scott's Foods stated that their premises was valued at two million pounds and had been "wantonly and maliciously damaged by fire". They intended to apply to the Circuit Court on March 2 for a million pounds in compensation. The Silver Swan Ltd claim related to the Stardust section of the complex. It also emerged that the owners of the Stardust held public liability insurance for only £250,000.

At a finance committee meeting that week, Dublin City councillors expressed concern about the Silver Swan Ltd claim for two million (they had yet to learn of the further claims from Butterly-controlled companies). The City and County Manager, Frank Feely, stressed that the claims could not be met unless it was first proved in court that the fire had been started maliciously. The Stardust claims would have to remain in abeyance until after the public inquiry into the disaster.

In essence, the quest for justice for the victims of the Stardust commenced with a vigil outside the burnt-out shell of the complex by Vincent Hogan. Vincent's 25-year-old brother, Eugene, had died in the tragedy and a second brother, Bernard, was badly burned and recovering in hospital. As he began his 24-hour "vigil for justice" outside the Stardust, Vincent told reporters that he did not want the matter "swept under the carpet". Vincent said that the disaster would have to be kept in the public eye until justice was achieved for the victims. He called for others affected by the tragedy to join his vigil until the matter was settled.

The long quest for justice was about to begin.

Seven

The Public Probe

"Too many people know too much to allow a Watergate-type evasion of the facts to succeed."

– Brian McMahon, former chairman
of the Chief Fire Officers' Association.

The Stardust complex was still smouldering as Taoiseach Charles Haughey promised the nation a full investigation into the fire. True to his word, on February 15, 1981, the Government announced that a public probe would be held into the disaster under the provisions of the Tribunals of Inquiry (Evidence) Acts, 1921 and 1979. A High Court judge, Ronan Keane, was appointed to preside over the tribunal. Mr Justice Keane – who went on to become Chief Justice – had been a High Court judge since 1979 and was highly respected within the legal profession.

In some ways, Haughey was in a no-win situation when he established the tribunal of inquiry. If the Butterlys were found responsible, Haughey would have been criticised for allowing them to operate the Stardust complex in the first place; if the Butterlys were exonerated, this would have been attributed to Haughey's influence in setting up the tribunal, which had restricted terms of reference.

Within political circles, a storm over the tribunal's terms of reference was brewing. Senator Mary Robinson, who would later be elected President of Ireland, criticised the fact that the tribunal would have no power to examine the alleged failure of the Department of the Environment to implement several recommendations from reports on fire prevention made by experts over the years. Neither did it have the authority, she noted, to call witnesses from the Department who might be asked why the 1976 building regulations were never "carried out". She said the public were entitled to know what responsibility the Department might have had for the disaster. According to Senator Robinson, there was widespread alarm and concern about allegations that the Department had shelved several reports drawn up by experts on fire prevention. "We are not facing up to our duty by trying to bypass where much of the responsibility lies," she warned.

Three assessors were appointed to the tribunal: Professor David Rasbash, Department of Fire Safety, Edinburgh University; Mr Gunnar Haurum, Chief Inspector of Fire Services, Denmark; and Mr Pierce Pigott, head of the Construction Division of An Foras Forbartha (the Development Authority).

An independent forensic expert, who was to give evidence before the inquiry, pledged that there would be no State cover-up into the blaze. Brian McMahon, former chairman of the Chief Fire Officers' Association, was quoted in newspapers saying: "I intend pinpointing incidents of inefficiency in the Department of the Environment's fire regulations – and naming names. Too many people know too much to allow a Watergate-type evasion of the facts to succeed. Too much has been swept under the carpet in the Department and I intend putting the whole story before the tribunal."

McMahon was also highly critical of the fact that Ireland's "Mr Fire" – Captain John Connolly, the sole technical adviser to the Minister for the Environment on fire matters – had been kept off the tribunal's panel. "In Britain, Denmark or France, their chief inspector of fire services would be an automatic choice for such a tribunal," McMahon said. "It can only be seen in the context of the Government attempting to hide something."

An order appointing the tribunal was made on February 20, 1981, by the Minister for the Environment, Ray Burke. He believed the inquiry would cover any potential questions raised and would satisfy the concerns of the general public. "We have a duty to the victims of this disastrous fire and to their relatives, and indeed to all our people, to do everything in our power to establish the causes and circumstances of the fire," Burke told the Dáil. "We must seek out as fully as possible the lessons to be learned from this terrible event so as to prevent, as far as is humanly possible, such a disaster occurring again."

The tribunal would inquire into:

- the immediate and other causes of – and the circumstances leading to – the fire at the Stardust;

- the circumstances of and leading to the loss of life and personal injury at the Stardust;

- the measures and their adequacy, taken on and before February 14, 1981, to prevent, detect and to minimise and otherwise to deal with fire at the Stardust;

- the means and systems of emergency escape from the Stardust – and their adequacy;

- the measures (including the application of the Draft Building Regulations published on November 29, 1976) – and their adequacy – taken on and before February 14, 1981, at the Stardust to prevent and to minimise and otherwise deal with any other circumstances that may have contributed to the loss of life and personal injury; and

- the adequacy of the legislation, statutory regulations and bye-laws relevant to fire prevention and safety, so far as material to the granting of planning and bye-law permission for, and the conduct, running, supervision, official inspection and control of the Stardust; the adequacy of the application, observance and enforcement of such legislation, statutory regulations and bye-laws in relation to the club.

The tribunal would also have the power to make recommendations in respect of fire safety standards and procedures.

The first public sitting of the tribunal was held on March 2, 1981, just over two weeks after the Stardust tragedy which, by that stage, had claimed forty-seven lives. All sittings were held in the premises of the Incorporated Law Society at Blackhall Place in Dublin, with the exception of one preliminary session in the Four Courts. At the first sitting, the tribunal considered applications for legal representation and dealt with matters of procedure. The hearing of oral evidence began on April 6 and the tribunal ran until November 26 that year. In total, the tribunal sat for 122 days, hearing evidence from 363 witnesses, 160 of whom had been at the Stardust on the night of the blaze. Over three and a half million words were given in evidence.

The State agreed to pay the legal costs of the victims and their families. The main team of counsel representing the relatives was headed by Paddy MacEntee, SC. Solicitors engaged by relatives and victims included Liam Lysaght and former Dublin footballer Tony Hanahoe. Both solicitors would later represent the majority of victims and families in their protracted legal battle for compensation.

Some families and victims couldn't face the trauma of attending the tribunal, particularly as many were still suffering from horrific injuries. For others, however, attending the inquiry's hearings became a near-obsessive ritual. In the belief that the tribunal would establish the entire truth of why the Stardust disaster occurred, the families sat through tedious sessions of legal arguments and about technical or scientific details, much of which was highly confusing. Some attended just to sit in the same room as Eamon Butterly, whom they had come to blame for the deaths of their loved ones because of his alleged policy of keeping the doors locked.

Jimmy Fitzpatrick was one such victim. He was extremely badly burned in the Stardust and his survival by doctors was described as "a miracle of medical science". He spent five months in hospital, longer than any other victim of the fire. He attended the tribunal of inquiry twice, "just to show Butterly the devastation".

Christine Keegan remembers sitting directly behind Eamon Butterly at the inquiry on one occasion. Throughout the hearing, she kept poking him in the back and whispering accusations in his ear. The next day, the families and relatives were moved away from Eamon Butterly to the opposite side of the room, where they would remain for the rest of the sittings. "I was now seated facing Butterly and was able to look him straight in the eye every day," recalls Christine.

Much of the evidence given was harrowing and gruesome. Many families left the tribunal each day in tears. According to Christine, it was "the lies" being told each day that caused her the most anguish. Indeed, these lies would be exposed when Justice Keane finally published his 633-page report on the Stardust disaster in June 1982.

At first glance, the report contained mixed fortunes for the victims and their families. Its findings didn't bode well for Eamon Butterly, who was singled out for damning criticism by Justice Keane for the policy of keeping exits chained or locked. The report also made solemn reading for Dublin Corporation and the Department of the Environment, who had to take part of the blame for the disaster. However, most crucially, the report concluded that the fire was "probably" started deliberately.

Evidence of standard and non-standard tests carried out was given by six expert bodies or individuals commissioned by An Garda Síochána, the tribunal and the owners of the Stardust. The exhaustive technical and scientific details of all the tests were outlined in the tribunal's report. Also examined were the possible causes of the fire, which ranged from a careless smoker, or an electrical fault, to a deliberate attempt to ignite seating in the west alcove. But, despite all the professional technical testimony, Justice Keane conceded: "The cause of the fire is not known and may never be known. There is no evidence of an accidental origin and equally no evidence that the fire was started deliberately."

Before reaching its conclusion, the tribunal examined six hypotheses of an accidental or deliberate origin. Of the possibilities considered, the tribunal was satisfied that the lowest degree of probability was attached to a fire caused by an accidental smoker. Other theories based on a smouldering bag of rubbish, coat or other object were not supported by the evidence, the report found. With the possible exception of the bag of rubbish, this theory provided no satisfactory evidence for the rapid spread of fire from seat to seat, nor could it be explained by either a fault in the immersion heater or an accidental fire in the roof space.

This left the tribunal with two possibilities: a fire started deliberately in either the roof space or the west alcove. It found that it most likely originated in the west alcove, which accorded with the evidence of eyewitnesses who did not recall seeing the ceiling on fire during the early stages of the disaster.

Even the technical witnesses were divided on the cause of the blaze. Three experts – including Mr Michael Norton of the Forensic Science Laboratory at the Department of Justice – believed the fire was more probably caused deliberately. Two others, however, were inclined not to rule out the possibility of a fire caused by some electrical fault. Of the various methods that might have been employed by the arsonist or arsonists, the most likely was either the slashing of a number of seats with a pen-knife or other sharp object, followed by their ignition using a match or cigarette lighter. The lighting of newspapers on or under a seat was another possibility.

The tribunal also found that the motive, the number of persons involved, their sex and age, the degree of premeditation and the precise time at which the fire was started "must remain matters for conjecture". A number of theories in this regard had been put forward during the hearing.

Garda evidence had established that at some time prior to the fire on the night of February 13, 1981, four youths had succeeded in getting onto the roof of the complex by climbing the drainpipes. The four in question, Harry Wade, John Finnegan, John Hartnett and Desmond Byrne, had made an unsuccessful attempt to force open Exit 6 from the outside to get into the Stardust. However, they were unable to achieve their aim due to the presence of a lock and chain on the ballroom side of the door. While they were on the roof, Harry Wade unsuccessfully tried to open a glass skylight by lifting the metal flashing. John Finnegan attempted to crack one of the pieces of asbestos but was unable to do so. They then became aware of the presence of a Garda car and lay down in the valley between the apexes to hide. Moving towards the west side of the building when the coast was clear, they jumped down to the area in the vicinity of the fire escapes.

When the youths knocked over some metal beer kegs, the noise was heard by members of the bar staff in the Silver Swan pub, who rushed outside. The four made their escape at approximately 11.45 p.m. and gardaí were satisfied that they did not return to the Stardust that night. Their investigation into the fire ruled out the involvement of the four young men. If anything, their actions had simply established that it was possible to get onto the roof of the Stardust with little difficulty.

Other evidence established that a number of members of staff went into the alcove where the fire was thought to have started during the course of the night. None of the staff concerned, who were there on their breaks, saw or heard anything that aroused their suspicions.

Possible friction between doormen and individuals who had been ejected from the premises was also explored. The tribunal found that there was, from time to time, some disorder in the Stardust on disco nights. There were also frequent attempts by individuals to get in without paying. When detected, they were ejected from the premises without much ceremony by the doormen. This undoubtedly led to animosity between some of the patrons and the doormen, according to the tribunal's report.

There was also evidence to suggest that gangs of youths from the Artane and Donnycarney areas – known as "The Dragon Gang", "The Animal Gang" and "The Soap Gang" – were in the habit of frequenting the premises. The tribunal emphasised, however, that troublemakers constituted only a small minority of those attending the Stardust on disco nights.

While there had been at least one serious assault on a doorman and frequent threats by individual patrons or groups to cause trouble at the Stardust, the evidence of a motive for a deliberate act of arson on the premises remained "tenuous", according to the report. The owners of the Stardust had their own theory. They suggested that the fire might have been started in the west alcove with the aim of diverting the doormen's attention while a robbery of cash, spirits or cigarettes from other parts of the premises was carried out. However, the tribunal found there was no evidence to support this theory.

The fact that the majority of the staff and patrons were engrossed in the disco-dancing competition immediately before the fire started may have been nothing more than a coincidence, the report noted. However, a sinister explanation was "more probable". The section of the report dealing with the cause of the fire concluded: "It may be, and this again must remain no more than conjecture, that the object of the arsonists was to do no more than cause a fire in the alcove itself, for whatever motives; and that, in carrying out this reckless criminal enterprise, they had not intended to cause any injury or death, still less on the appalling scale that, in fact, resulted."

The tribunal's conclusion on the "probable" cause of the fire was a piece of good news for Eamon Butterly, who would go on to settle his claim against Dublin Corporation for malicious damages. But there was little else of comfort for him in Justice Keane's report.

During the course of the Garda investigation into the fire, there were direct conflicts of evidence between management and staff of the Stardust and survivors in relation to the status and condition of exit doors. There were eight possible points of exit from the Stardust, six of which were specifically intended to be a means of escape in an emergency: Exit 1 consisted of two doors connected by a passage, the outer door opening onto a steel fire escape descending to a concreted area; Exit 2 was the main entrance to the complex; Exit 3, on the south side, consisted of two doors connected by a passage, the outer door opening on to a flight of five steps down to the concreted area; and Exits 4, 5 and 6 on the east side opened directly onto the concreted area. Each fire exit consisted of double emergency doors with panic bars attached. Two other possible routes of escape could be accessed from the Stardust through either the Lantern Rooms or the kitchen.

While many survivors reported that a number of the doors were either blocked or chained during the fire, Eamon Butterly would claim all exits were unlocked earlier in the evening. However, there appeared to be little substance to his claim, particularly after a number of conflicting statements were made to investigating gardaí by his own doormen. Serious questions arose in relation to evidence given by a number of doormen and Eamon Butterly on the issue of the unlocking – or not – of fire exits on the night of the fire.

Statements made by security staff about the fire exits came under scrutiny after one of the doormen, Michael Kavanagh, admitted lying in his original statement to gardaí and on the television programme "Today Tonight". Aged just 20 at the time, Kavanagh, from Donnycarney, had been a part-time doorman at the Stardust since May 1980. He suffered great personal tragedy on the night of the fire: his girlfriend, Paula Byrne, was killed.

In his statement to gardaí on Monday, February 16, Kavanagh said he had unlocked each of the emergency exists at 9 p.m. on the night of the fire. He repeated this claim on RTÉ television that evening. However, the following Thursday, on February 19, Kavanagh made a further statement to gardaí in which he admitted that his earlier claim about unlocking the doors was untrue. In evidence to the tribunal, Kavanagh explained that he told lies to the gardaí and on television because he was in a state of grief and shock following the death of his girlfriend. He was also angered by criticism in his neighbourhood of the conduct of the doormen during the fire and by what he considered to be bogus claims of heroism by certain patrons. He said that fellow doormen, P.J. Murphy and Leo Doyle, had called to his house and asked his mother to tell him to go back to the gardaí and make a new statement.

The tribunal was satisfied, beyond doubt, that Kavanagh's original claim of opening the exits was untrue. It took into account the fact that the statement was made when Kavanagh was in a state of "acute and understandable emotional distress" following the death of his girlfriend. "The fact remains that he told a brazen falsehood to the gardaí and, through the medium of television, to the public at large, on a matter which he knew to be of the utmost gravity," Justice Keane's report noted. "In these circumstances, his sworn evidence to the tribunal as to his actions on the night in question is to be treated with great caution."

The tribunal's attention then switched to head doorman Thomas Kennan, Eamon Butterly's uncle. A brother-in-law of Patrick Butterly, Kennan had worked part-time at the Stardust for three years and had been head doorman for twelve months. His full-time job was as a maintenance engineer with *The Irish Times*. He was answerable solely to Eamon Butterly. Including Kennan, there were nine doormen on duty on the night of February 13, 1981. Kennan's role on the night would be crucial in establishing whether or not all exits were unlocked at the time of the fire.

On Friday, February 20, the day after Kavanagh admitted lying, Kennan made a second statement to gardaí. He claimed that he was the one who had unlocked the fire exits. However, on the day of the fire, February 14, Kennan's statement to gardaí had made no reference to any unlocking of exit doors during the course of the evening. Neither did he refer to his alleged role in unlocking exits in his statement to the Butterlys' solicitors. Kennan didn't go to the Garda station of his own volition to make his second statement. Gardaí had called to his Beaumont home at 7.30 a.m. and requested that he accompany them to the station to assist with their enquiries.

Thomas Kennan was unable to give any satisfactory explanation to the tribunal as to why he chose to withhold this crucial information about the unlocking of the doors until nearly a week after the fire. The tribunal accepted that his failure to mention it in his first statement on the Saturday may have been due in part to the form of questions put to him by gardaí, coupled with the fact that he was still somewhat shaken by the experience. However, the tribunal was satisfied that Kennan was well aware Kavanagh was falsely asserting to the world at large that he had opened the fire exits. The tribunal said there could only be two explanations for Kennan's failure to go to the gardaí at that stage: the first was that the version of the unlocking of the doors given by him under oath before the tribunal was untrue; the second was that his version was true in whole or in part, but withheld by Kennan from gardaí in the hope that they – and the public – would remain under the impression that the doors had been opened at 9 p.m. on Friday, February 13.

The report stated: "Irrespective of which of these explanations is the correct one, the Tribunal is satisfied that Mr Kennan's motive in misleading the gardaí, whether by telling falsehoods or remaining silent when he had a clear duty to speak out, was his fear as to the consequences for himself and his nephew, Mr Eamon Butterly, if it transpired that the emergency exits were not merely chained and locked until midnight on the night of the fire, but on other disco nights as well. In these circumstances, the Tribunal has also treated this witness's sworn evidence with great reserve."

Three other doormen – Leo Doyle, P.J. Murphy and Frank Downes – also made statements to the gardaí on the Saturday of the fire. None of them had made any reference to an incident in the foyer that was brought up later on. Doyle and Murphy alleged that Kennan threw the keys to Downes and told him that the exits were open. The doormen in question did not make any attempt to get in touch with gardaí on the matter. It was only when they were each invited to make further statements on the following Friday that they all gave a version of the incident. Downes, in the course of his first statement, said: "Prior to the disco starting, one of the door staff opened all exits leading from the Stardust Club." However, he qualified this assertion in his second statement: "When I said in my original statement that a doorman had unlocked the doors, I assumed that it would have been done because it was normal practice."

Downes' failure to tell the gardaí of the throwing of keys to him until a week after the fire was criticised by Justice Keane. The 34-year-old doorman from Drimnagh was unable to give the tribunal a satisfactory explanation as to why, on February 14, he had informed gardaí that one of the doormen had opened all the exits when, in fact, he did not know this to be the case. The tribunal was also compelled to treat his evidence with great reserve.

P.J. Murphy and Leo Doyle also came under fire. The tribunal was satisfied that at the time they both went to Kavanagh's house and left a message for him to go back to the gardaí, they were not only aware that he had claimed to have opened the doors, but knew Kennan was also asserting at this stage that he had unlocked the exits. Furthermore, they both claimed in evidence that keys had been thrown to Downes by Kennan. The tribunal ruled that they had a clear duty in these circumstances to inform the gardaí as soon as possible of this information. Their evidence, too, was treated carefully by Justice Keane.

The same applied to doormen Phelim Kinahan and Gabriel O'Neill. In his first statement to gardaí on February 14, Kinahan did not say that he was aware of the practice of keeping the doors locked for a portion of the night, nor did he tell of his tour of inspection of the doors, yet he had told a newspaper reporter on the same day that all the fire regulations were adhered to at the Stardust. In his statement on February 24, O'Neill told gardaí that he had opened Exit 5 without any difficulty and a fellow doorman, Michael Griffin, had opened Exit 4. In another part of the statement, he retracted this and gave a version of events which corresponded with the evidence given by him later under oath to the tribunal. "Mr O'Neill's initial attempt to mislead the gardaí cannot be in any way due to the form of questions put to him, nor was it due to his being physically or emotionally distressed in the immediate aftermath of the fire," the tribunal report found.

Now the focus shifted to Eamon Butterly. On February 14, 1981, Butterly made a statement in the presence of his solicitor that concluded: "I would like to add that in accordance with normal procedures, I asked Tom Kennan, the head doorman, if all the fire exits were unlocked and he answered me that they were and he had men stationed at each exit in accordance with standard procedure. I personally saw that ten [*sic*: this was an error in transcription and should have read "two"] of the exits were open and Tom Kennan then went over to the other exits himself and came back to me and said everything was okay. This occurred between 11 p.m. and 11.30 p.m."

However, there were some conspicuous omissions from Eamon Butterly's statement to gardaí. He failed to mention, for instance, that in accordance with the procedure in operation for at least four weeks prior to the fire, Exits 1, 5 and 6 were, to his knowledge, locked and chained until at least midnight. Nor did he tell gardaí that the statement which he alleged Kennan to have made was, to his knowledge, untrue: there was no point in the evening at which men were stationed at each of the emergency exits. "The tribunal is satisfied that Mr Butterly must have known that his failure to disclose his full knowledge as to the state of the exits that night could only have been seriously misleading," the report stated.

The tribunal also found that Butterly was aware, following the "Today Tonight" broadcast, that Kavanagh was giving an untrue version of events as to the unlocking of the exit doors. On March 8 he had been furnished with a written questionnaire containing 127 questions by Detective Inspector Ronayne. A number of the questions related to the locking of the exit doors, which the gardaí wished to have answered in order to assist them with their investigation into the fire. Butterly decided to take legal advice in relation to the questions and they remained unanswered for over eight months.

"The tribunal is satisfied that Mr Butterly was under a clear duty to tell the gardaí all he knew in relation to the locking of the exit doors on the night of the fire and, in particular, to tell them at the earliest possible opportunity that Mr Kavanagh's version was wholly untrue," Justice Keane said. "In these circumstances, the tribunal has been compelled to treat Mr Eamon Butterly's evidence with great reserve."

On the key issue of the fire exits, Butterly and a number of his doormen had been discredited by the tribunal. The conduct of these witnesses (Kavanagh, Kennan, Doyle, Murphy, Downes, O'Neill, Kinahan and Butterly) was described by the report as "deplorable and indefensible". A number of families of the deceased suggested that some of these witnesses had been bribed with a view to withholding information from, or actively misleading, the gardaí. They implied that this was being done either directly by, or at the instigation of, Eamon Butterly. This suggestion was never put to Butterly while he was in the witness box and, in the opinion of the tribunal, there was no substance to the allegation. The tribunal also ruled out a suggestion by next-of-kin that the failure by certain doormen to assist the gardaí was part of an organised conspiracy to suppress the truth about the exit doors.

Nevertheless, the tribunal formed the opinion that it was unsafe to arrive at any conclusion as to the locking or unlocking of the exit doors based solely – or even principally – on the evidence of Butterly and the doormen named above. This was due to: the lack of credibility of the principal witness; the discrepancies between the different versions of events given by the witnesses; and the fact that no member of staff appeared to have been responsible for seeing that the exit doors were unlocked at midnight, or thereabouts, on disco nights.

Fortunately, Justice Keane noted, a volume of eyewitness evidence did not suffer from the same imperfections. This, coupled with the physical condition of the doors as found by gardaí after the fire, enabled the tribunal to reach a definite conclusion as to the condition of each exit. The report found that, immediately before the fire, Exit 2 was locked and had been locked since sometime between midnight and 12.30 a.m. Exit 3 was locked with a chain and padlock and had been locked since the public were admitted to the premises at 10 p.m. The remaining exit doors were unlocked before the fire, but in each case the lock and chain had been draped across the bars so as to give the impression that the doors were, in fact, locked. Exit 5 was seriously obstructed by two plastic skips. At Exit 4 there was some degree of obstruction, mainly caused by loose seats. At Exit 3 the free passage of patrons out of the building was impeded by a white van at the foot of the steps.

Other factors affecting the evacuation of the premises – which at just over eight hundred patrons was only half full on the night of the tragedy – included: the failure of the lights; the absence of any evacuation procedures or any organisation to deal with an emergency of this nature; the lack of knowledge of the staff as to the location of the fire extinguishers; the absence of hose reels; and the ineffectual nature of the attempts at extinguishing the fire.

"The tribunal is satisfied that if the appropriate precautions to ensure an efficient evacuation had existed on the night of the fire, the injuries sustained would almost certainly have been reduced," the report stated. "It cannot be said, however, that even with such precautions, all the deaths which actually resulted would have been avoided."

Justice Keane laid the blame for keeping exits locked squarely with Eamon Butterly. "The tribunal is satisfied that the policy of keeping the exit doors chained and locked until at least midnight led to one exit being actually locked and chained while the fire was in progress; and that this policy was pursued by Mr Butterly with a reckless disregard for the safety of people in the premises," the report said. "Mr Butterly's legitimate objective of preventing unauthorised persons from gaining access to the Stardust could have been readily achieved by the stationing of doormen at each of the exits, but he deliberately elected to pursue a policy which was more economical in the use of doormen and was manifestly dangerous."

The tribunal also examined why the fire had spread so quickly. It noted that, although a significant saving of injuries and lives would probably have been achieved by a prompt and efficient evacuation of the complex, the rapid and disastrous spread of flame and smoke had certainly contributed to the carnage. The fire, when first seen, appeared to be confined to one seat in the back row of the alcove closest to the main bar. Within a period of no more than two minutes from the first observation, the flames had spread to at least two or three more seats and changed in appearance from a small and controllable fire to a raging inferno accompanied by intense heat. By the time four minutes had elapsed the flames had reached the ceiling, portions of which collapsed, and thick black smoke appeared in the west alcove. Approximately ninety seconds later, the fire had spread to the greater part of the west alcove and black smoke filled the entire ballroom and began to penetrate the main foyer at Exit 2 and the corridor of Exit 3. The fire then broke through the roof in the form of flames, sparks and smoke.

Following a number of scientific tests and experts' evidence, the tribunal came to the conclusion that the rapid spread of the fire throughout the Stardust was due to a combination of factors: (1) the presence of a tier of seats containing quantities of combustible material abutting a wall lined with combustible carpet tiles; (2) the presence of a low ceiling; and (3) the presence of a large area of combustible seating to which the fire could, and did, eventually spread. The tribunal said that the tables and carpet on the floor probably played a secondary role in the spreading of flames. The combustion of the furnishings in the alcove produced quantities of carbon monoxide sufficient to cause or contribute to many of the deaths, the report found. The combustion of the PVC covering of the seats produced quantities of hydrogen chloride sufficient to cause high levels of irritancy. The combustion of the polyurethane foam produced quantities of hydrogen cyanide, but it was unlikely, in the opinion of the tribunal, that the quantities were sufficient to contribute substantially to the total lethal effects of the combustion gases.

A full chapter of the tribunal report examined areas of specific responsibility for the disaster. This looked at the role of the Stardust owners and their advisers, Dublin Corporation and the Department of the Environment. The report found that the low level of expertise availed of by the Butterlys when converting the building from a factory to an entertainment complex contributed specifically to the scale of the disaster in two respects: the use of carpet tiles as wall linings; and inadequate consideration given to the suitability of Exit 2 and the extent to which it failed to comply with the requirements of the Draft Building Regulations. Undesirable practices in relation to the main exit of the Stardust included the locking of the door's two side-leave shutters and the wedging of the centre leaves in the well of the doormat. Other breaches of regulations included the use of loose floor seating; the unsatisfactory location of Exits 1 and 3; the use of timber partitions to enclose the Store Room and Lamp Room; and inadequate ventilation in some of the toilets.

Throughout the investigation, Eamon Butterly insisted that his responsibility in relation to fire safety had been discharged once he had satisfied Dublin Corporation's requirements. This was also the attitude of Patrick Butterly. In the view of the tribunal, this was a wholly unacceptable approach for persons who were converting a building into a place of public resort and who intended to attract audiences in excess of a thousand people. "When the building was opened to the public, the owners were under a high degree of responsibility to ensure that the premises were properly and efficiently managed so as to ensure fire safety," the report stated. "This they manifestly failed to do."

Apart from the Butterlys' breaches of the building bye-laws and fire safety regulations, they were also criticised for the lack of evacuation procedures and for not training staff in the use of extinguishers. Had proper fire drills and evacuation procedures been in operation at the Stardust, serious mistakes and omissions would have been avoided and the number of deaths and injuries reduced, the tribunal found. "Both Mr Patrick Butterly and Mr Eamon Butterly must share the responsibility for these matters," said Justice Keane.

"Mr Eamon Butterly, however, bears a special responsibility for the practice of keeping the emergency exits secured with chains and padlocks until midnight at the earliest, a recklessly dangerous practice which regularly endangered the lives of over one thousand people and, in the event, led to one exit being locked and chained on the night, and possibly contributing to avoidable injuries and death. While all the doormen who knew of the practice must share some degree of responsibility for the consequences which ensued, a special responsibility is attached to Mr Thomas Kennan, who, as the head doorman, was directly responsible for implementing the policy. Mr Leo Doyle, as his deputy, also must bear some of the responsibility for carrying the policy into effect."

Incredibly, Patrick Butterly would later write in his memoirs: "The only good the tribunal did us was to prove that it was malicious damage and that we were not responsible for the deaths of the people there."

Dublin Corporation was also held partly responsible for the disaster in the tribunal report and would later dispute its findings. The tribunal found that the Fire Prevention Department was grossly understaffed when the Butterlys' applications for planning permission and bye-law approval were referred to them. It remained so throughout the period preceding the fire and at the time of the tribunal's public hearings, the report stated. Also, it added, the staff there did not have the specialist qualifications required for the proper assessment of an application such as this. The tribunal was satisfied that this deficiency resulted in an inadequate assessment of the drawings and specifications furnished.

An adequate assessment, it said, would have resulted in the applicant being asked to provide wall linings which complied with the Draft Building Regulations. The Butterlys would also have been ordered to redesign Exit 2. A proper assessment would also have considered the proximity of the suspended ceiling to the banked seating in the west alcove.

Dublin Corporation was castigated by Justice Keane for never

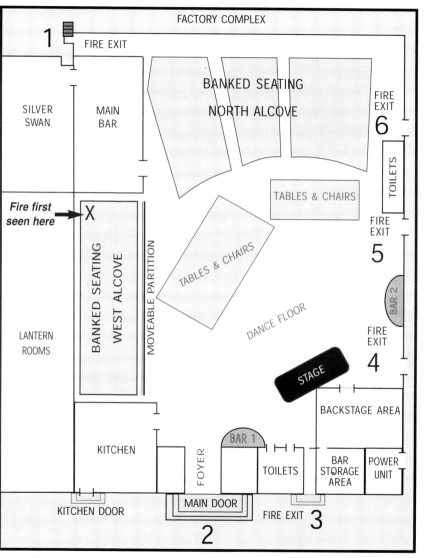

The layout of the Stardust, showing all the exits and where the fire was first seen.

The hoarding at the front of the Stardust, advertises events for the weekend of the tragedy.
Maxwell Picture Agency

Patrick and Eamon Butterly outside the Stardust, shortly after it opened.
Maxwell Picture Agency

The chaotic scene as young people are rescued from the fire.
Myles Byrne, *Irish Press*

LEFT: Firemen entering the burnt-out Stardust the morning after the fire.
Maxwell Picture Agency

RIGHT: Garda and a fireman at the main door the day after the fire.
Maxwell Picture Agency

BELOW: Emergency services removing a body from the Stardust.
Maxwell Picture Agency

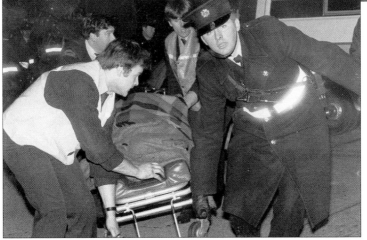

After the fire: an aerial view of the Stardust
Irish Independent

The burnt-out interior.
Irish Independent

Coffins containing the remains of Francis Lawlor and seven unidentified victims at the Church of Our Lady of Consolation, Donnycarney.

Maxwell Picture Agency

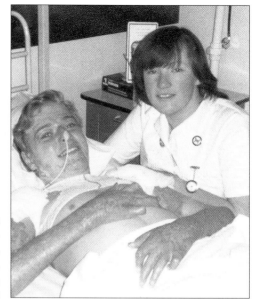

RIGHT: Jimmy Fitzpatrick recovering in hospital after the fire.

BELOW: Michael Woods T.D. visits Antoinette Keegan in hospital.

Courtesy of the Fitzpatrick and Keegan families

Brendan O'Meara

David Flood

David Morton

Eugene Hogan

Francis Lawlor

George McDermott

Jacqueline Croker

Jimmy Buckley

John Stout

Liam Dunne

Marcella McDermott

Maureen Lawlor

Michael French

Michael Griffiths

Paula Lewis

William McDermott

Robert Kelly

Sandra Lawless

Michael Farrell and
Thelma Frazer

Mary Kenny and Mary Keegan

All photographs courtesy of the victims' families

LEFT: ; Eamon Butterly leaving the Dublin Circuit Court on June 13, 1983, after winning his case against Dublin Corporation for malicious damages.
Irish Independent

RIGHT: Fireman Paul Shannon, now retired
Darren Kinsella

BELOW: The Stardust memorial at Beaumont Hospital
Darren Kinsella

THEY SHALL NEVER GROW OLD
AS WE THAT ARE LEFT GROW OLD
AGE SHALL NOT WEARY THEM
NOR THE YEARS CONDEMN
AT THE GOING DOWN OF THE SUN
AND IN THE MORNING
WE SHALL REMEMBER THEM

ABOVE: The Stardust Victims' Committee arriving at the High Court on August 9, 1985, for the contempt case brought against singer Christy Moore by the Butterlys. *From left*: William Mulvey, Christine Keegan, John Keegan, Larry Stout, Noel Osborne.
Irish Independent

LEFT: Protestors march along O'Connell Street, Dublin, in May 1985, demanding compensation for the victims of the Stardust.
Irish Independent

Charles Haughey turns the first sod
for the Stardust Memorial Park, May 30, 1991.
Lensmen

Christy Moore and Christine Keegan lay a wreath
at the opening of the Stardust Memorial Park, September 18, 1993.
Courtesy of the Keegan family

The Stardust Memorial Park fountain.
Courtesy of the Keegan family

ABOVE: Lisa Lawlor, who was orphaned by the Stardust fire, at the graves of her parents, Francis and Maureen.
Darren Kinsella

RIGHT: Albert Buckley, who lost his brother Jimmy in the fire, holding a picture of Jimmy's daughter, Julie-Ann.
Darren Kinsella

The site of the Stardust today.
Darren Kinsella

carrying out a fire inspection of the Stardust. "The fact that there was no inspection whatever of this building by any member of the Fire Brigade, either in the Fire Prevention Department or fire-fighting service, from the day it opened until the fire, was one of the most disquieting facts to emerge at the inquiry," he said. The report noted that the only regular inspections of places of public resort carried out at this time were by Martin Donohoe, whose primary function was to ascertain the existence of electrical faults. This meant that certain crucial features of the converted Stardust building went unnoticed, such as the use of carpet tiles on the walls. In addition, an adequate inspection of the premises by qualified staff, particularly members of Dublin Fire Brigade, would have revealed the total absence of any fire drill or evacuation procedures. The report stressed that no blame should be attached to Mr Donohoe, who had raised the issue of locked fire exits at the Stardust with his superiors even though it was an area outside his responsibility.

The tribunal took the view, however, that some blame should be allotted to Mr Dermot King, the senior building surveyor with Dublin Corporation. The report said that it was difficult to understand why an official of his experience should have failed to investigate the presence of floor tiles on the walls of the Stardust. It also questioned why no prosecutions against the Butterlys were ever initiated following breaches of the bye-laws in relation to the locking and obstruction of exits. In the tribunal's opinion, the "grave inadequacies" of both the fire-fighting service and the Fire Prevention Department were primarily the responsibility of Dublin Corporation.

The Department of the Environment was also held accountable by the tribunal. The report found that the absence of a modern code of building regulations having the force of law seriously increased the workload on the already understaffed Fire Prevention Department. It was of vital importance, it said, that steps should be taken by the Department to bring into force either a complete code of building regulations or a partial code dealing with fire safety. The delay of almost twenty years in introducing such regulations was described as "wholly unacceptable". Despite being made aware of the critical state of morale in the Dublin Fire Service by the city manager in 1978, the Department had failed to treat the introduction of the regulations as an urgent matter.

Crucially, the terms of reference of the tribunal precluded Justice Keane from conducting a general investigation into the operation of the fire services in the State or even in the Dublin area. The evidence to the tribunal was therefore limited to the manner in which the staffing problems of Dublin Fire Brigade were dealt with by the Department of the Environment in the years immediately preceding the fire. In the view of Justice Keane, the crisis in the Dublin fire service had ceased to be a local problem and had become what he called "a national scandal". The report pointed out that the catchment area of the Dublin Fire Brigade represented over one quarter of the population of the entire country. During the period of the most rapid expansion in the history of the area, the staff of the Fire Prevention Department actually declined and comprised only four officers and one typist. "Once the local authority had shown that it was not capable of dealing with a crisis of this magnitude, it became the responsibility of Central Government, and specifically the Department of the Environment, to deal with it as a matter of urgency," the report stated.

The Department of the Environment was also slammed for the absence of training in the Fire Brigade, which had implications for morale and efficiency. The Working Party on the Fire Service had brought this problem to the attention of the Minister in 1975 and had recommended the establishment of a National Fire Service Training Centre. There was no evidence that any steps had been taken by the Department to implement this recommendation in the almost six-year period between the presentation of this report and the Stardust fire. The tribunal concluded that it should have been apparent to the Minister for the Environment that the limited role assigned to him under the Fire Brigades Act 1940 was not adequate in modern conditions. It was clear that amending legislation was urgently required to ensure more effective supervision by the Government of the discharge of fire safety duties by local authorities.

The Garda investigation into the disaster was praised by Justice Keane. Conducted under the supervision of Detective John Courtney, a total of 1,649 statements had been taken by gardaí. The tribunal said that the detective work was carried out in an exhaustive manner and with meticulous attention to detail, much to the credit of the officers involved. However, the report highlighted serious shortcomings in the forensic investigation by the gardaí and the Department of Justice. Its main criticism was that it was not carried out by a senior Garda officer and the senior scientists in the Forensic Science Laboratory at the Department of Justice. In some instances, the report noted, samples of material which could have been "crucial" were not taken and important tests were not carried out.

Under its terms of reference, the tribunal had the power to make recommendations in relation to fire safety. Justice Keane found there were deficiencies in the approach to fire safety in Ireland. This was in spite of the fact that, in the wake of the Stardust tragedy, the Fire Services Act 1981 had replaced the antiquated Fire Brigades Act 1940. Although the new legislation had addressed many of the defects in the system, Justice Keane said it was clear that the country urgently needed a modern fire safety code, embodied in appropriate legislation and regulations, and implemented by effective fire safety organisations.

The report recommended the establishment of appropriate courses in fire safety engineering in third level institutions. A radical overhaul of draft building regulations incorporating fire safety measures was also called for. The tribunal said that no place of assembly should be opened to the public unless a fire certificate had been obtained. It called on the Government to have a more active role in the State's fire service. A key recommendation was the establishment of a National Training Centre for fire personnel, which would have the dual role of improving fire-fighting skills and boosting morale in the emergency services.

The consequences of the neglect of fire safety by the Government, local authorities and public at large could not be doubted, according to the tribunal's recommendations, which concluded: "It is clear that their continuing neglect in Ireland has now contributed to a disaster on an appalling scale which will cast a shadow across one Dublin community for years, and perhaps generations, to come."

As the tribunal ended its public hearings on November 26, 1981, the only clear winners were members of the legal profession. In fact, so lucrative was the tribunal for several Senior Counsel that it was nicknamed "Goldust" in the corridors of the Law Library. In legal fees alone, the Stardust inquiry was costing the taxpayer £5,000 a day and would eventually run to £1.75 million – a huge figure at the time. The amount of money earned by Senior Counsel and solicitors from the tribunal was substantially more than some victims of the fire or the families of the deceased would receive in compensation five years later. In spite of this, as far as the victims were concerned, the massive legal fees incurred would be money well spent if the tribunal came close to establishing the truth about the circumstances surrounding the Stardust fire. After the sittings closed, it would be another eight months before the tribunal's assessment of the truth would be published.

Eight

Was This Justice?

*"It's a great shock to learn that nobody is accountable
or responsible for the deaths of these children."*

– statement by Stardust relatives, August 1982.

On Friday, July 9, 1982, one week after the publication of the
tribunal of inquiry's report, a committee representing the
Stardust victims called a press conference. The mood was solemn in
the ATGWU hall on Malborough Street, as members of the media
waited for the first official reaction to Justice Keane's findings from
the people to whom it mattered most.

In a statement issued to journalists, the committee thanked the
judge and his assessors for their thorough investigation into the
tragedy. In particular, Justice Keane was praised for presenting the
report in a manner that could be easily read and understood. The
victims hoped it would create a new fire safety awareness in
Ireland. "We are highly conscious of the fact that a fire of a similar
magnitude could have – and may still – hit another Irish community
and it is with this possibility in mind that we have approached the
task of judging the Stardust Tribunal Report," the press conference
was told.

As the process of condemnation got underway, the staff and
management of the Stardust were first in the line of fire. The lack of
positive action by the doormen when the fire first broke out and the
inability of staff to deal with such an emergency were criticised by
the committee. "We condemn them [the named doormen criticised
in the tribunal report] for accepting the instructions and upholding
the practice of locking and chaining, and also the practice of wrapping
of chains on exit doors," their statement said. "We feel they were
morally bound by any standard to challenge this practice but failed

to do so. Also, their failure to co-operate with the gardaí leaves the quality of their evidence suspect."

The Stardust families were deeply unhappy at the premature leaking of details of the tribunal report to sections of the media, particularly as, in their view, many newspapers had given the impression that Justice Keane had reached a positive finding on the malicious origin of the fire. "We wish to make it clear that we have no quarrel with the legal probability of arson arrived at by Mr Justice Keane," the victims' statement stressed. "Indeed, if it in any way leads to fresh evidence of the possibility of a deliberate starting of the fire, we welcome it. But we do emphasise, in the interests of the communities living in the area, that no positive finding of arson was arrived at and no such evidence to date has materialised."

The families were also critical of aspects of the Garda investigation into the fire. They questioned the apparent reluctance of gardaí to prosecute the Butterlys for breaches of the licensing laws, particularly in relation to underage drinking. There's little doubt that underage drinking was widespread on the night of the fire. Garda records show that of the 841 patrons attending the doomed disco, 274 were under the age of 18. A number of teenagers who survived the blaze later admitted in their statements to gardaí that they had obtained alcohol on the night. One 16-year-old youth said he had no interest in the disco-dancing competition and simply spent the night drinking. He had consumed about six or seven pints of Smithwicks, bought for him by two older friends.

Despite the fact that thirty per cent of patrons attending the Stardust on the night of the fire were under the age of 18, a licence had since been granted for the Butterlys' Silver Swan bar. The families asked why gardaí did not present evidence of underage drinking in the Circuit Court at the original renewal hearing the previous November. Such evidence was clearly at their disposal, as the Garda report on the disaster contained clear admissions of underage drinking.

The families also blamed money-saving measures taken by the owners of the club for contributing to the scale of the tragedy. They pointed to the fact that although Eamon Butterly refused to tolerate gatecrashers at the Stardust, he was not willing to hire extra security staff to man the exits. The families claimed that Eamon Butterly's policy of locking exit doors was designed to reduce staffing levels and save on wage costs. Their statement pointed out that if he had simply employed an extra three men to supervise the exit doors on the night of the blaze, the cost in wages would have been around £50: approximately £1 per life lost.

Then there was the issue of the toilets. When Butterly had discovered that alcohol was being passed in through the toilet windows at the front of the complex, he took immediate action to deal with the problem. Just two weeks before the fire, sheets of mild steel were ordered, cut to size to fit the windows, and welded in place. On the night of the fire, when screaming punters tried to escape through these windows as the blaze edged ever closer to them, they were met with an impenetrable wall of steel. Efforts by the emergency services to remove the steel sheets from the windows failed.

For all their grievances with the tribunal's findings, the Stardust relatives and victims welcomed Justice Keane's damning indictment of Eamon Butterly. Referring to specific remarks in the report about Butterly's "recklessly dangerous practice" of keeping exit doors chained or locked, the committee sent a letter to the Director of Public Prosecutions, Eamon Barnes, calling for the owners of the Stardust to be prosecuted. They claimed that "reckless negligence leading to death" was the basis for a charge of manslaughter under Irish law. They also believed that the wording of Justice Keane's remarks had been constructed in such a way as to suggest that proceedings be brought against the Butterlys.

The Stardust victims felt that, on this level at least, there was cause for optimism. However, their hopes came crashing down on Saturday, August 28, when the D.P.P. decided there were "insufficient grounds" to take criminal proceedings against the owners of the Stardust alleging negligence resulting in manslaughter. His decision was immediately relayed to the gardaí and the Stardust committee's legal representatives. According to legal sources at the time, charges of this nature would have been difficult to sustain in the circumstances. It would have had to be possible to prove, beyond doubt, that some action by those responsible for the premises could be linked directly to at least one death. Secondly, the law did not clearly define who was responsible for a premises in such a situation – was it the owners, those who managed it, or the workers who ran it?

The reaction to Mr Barnes' decision from the Stardust relatives was one of disbelief. A statement issued by the committee said: "Nothing has been done and nothing has been learned. It's a great shock to learn that nobody is accountable or responsible for the deaths of these children." The victims condemned the D.P.P.'s decision as "contradictory and dismissive" of the tribunal's findings.

Dr Michael Woods, who was a member of Government at the time, recalls that there was no option but to accept Mr Barnes' decision. "We would never question the D.P.P. – that's why you have an independent D.P.P. to make those decisions," says Woods today. "I can fully understand how people would feel about it but the D.P.P. has to see whether there is actually a criminal case to be met."

* * * *

In reaching his decision, the D.P.P. not only had the findings of the tribunal at his disposal, but also a comprehensive Garda report into the Stardust disaster. This confidential report, never released to the public but leaked to this book's authors, raises a number of interesting issues in relation to the Garda investigation.

To the credit of the gardaí, their report to the D.P.P. offered an exhaustive breakdown of possible causes of the fire. Every conceivable conspiracy theory was investigated, with gardaí paying particular attention to remarks made to the media by surviving patrons. Rumours of a malicious origin were rife, partly fuelled by the presence of the four teenagers on the roof of the complex just hours before the fire. However, investigating gardaí were satisfied that the youths' only purpose was to try and gain free admission to the Stardust. As had been earlier outlined to the tribunal, gardaí accepted that the youths concerned had left the Stardust at least one-and-a-half hours before the fire.

A theory that the fire had been started by local gangs was also explored in detail. In the course of the Garda investigation, it came to light that a group of youths from the Edenmore area, known as the "Dragon Gang", had attended the disco on the night of the fire. Although there were about forty-three members of the gang, mostly aged about 17 and 18, it was established that only sixteen of them had attended the Stardust on February 13, 1981. One member of the gang, Robert Kelly, had perished in the fire.

The rumour circulating at Belton's pub on Collins Avenue was that the Dragon Gang had started the fire. This unfounded theory was thought to have originated from the fact that one member of the gang, Patrick Morgan, had received a present of a cigarette lighter from his sister for Christmas. He later told gardaí that he had the lighter with him on the night of the fire and used it quite frequently for cigarettes. The members of the gang had been sitting at a table beside the passageway which separated them from the tables immediately outside the screened-off area in the west alcove. All sixteen members of the gang were thoroughly interrogated by gardaí and gave detailed statements. No information was elicited to throw suspicion on any member of the gang of involvement in causing the fire.

During the questioning of members of the Dragon Gang, the existence of another group of youths from the Harmonstown area, known as the "Soap Gang", came to the attention of gardaí. Apparently there was some degree of rivalry between the Dragon Gang and the Soap Gang, and the scene had been set for a major confrontation at the Stardust disco on the night of February 13. Gardaí established that members of the Harmonstown gang did attend that night, but the expected fracas did not materialise. In fact, it was learned that members of both gangs settled their differences peacefully and parted on amicable terms.

Ten months after the Stardust tragedy, an incident involving two members of the Dragon Gang at the Shieling Hotel in Raheny was investigated by gardaí. On November 11, 1981, members of the gang were refused admission to a disco in the hotel. They went around to the rear of the hotel and threw bricks and stones through the windows. Two members of the gang were identified by doormen as having caused the damage and were charged by gardaí. At the same time, two exit doors of the hotel were set alight from the outside. Gardaí were never able to establish who set fire to the doors and no charges were ever preferred against any member of the Dragon Gang for the potentially serious arson attempt. However, in view of the incident, the two members of the gang charged with breaking the windows were questioned in relation to the Stardust fire. Nothing emerged to connect either youth with the blaze. In fact, one of the teenagers was working aboard the "Connaught" car ferry on the night of the disaster.

In the days immediately following the Stardust fire, as the community tried desperately to come to terms with the tragedy, many survivors and their relatives sought hate figures on whom to pin the blame. There were many slanderous accusations: a number of individuals were named as having started the fire, some of whom were still recovering from their injuries in hospital. Gardaí nevertheless had to follow up what they called "loose talk" about every named individual, however spurious the claim. A number of victims were interviewed by gardaí in their hospital beds. In the end, there was nothing to connect any of them with the probable causes of the fire.

Some of the stories spun to gardaí were simply untrue but, in the blur of grief, had become accepted as fact on the streets of Coolock. One woman claimed that, as she fled from the Stardust, she saw a youth on the stage and heard him shout: "Let them all burn!" Gardaí initially gave credence to this story, as it was corroborated by the woman's sister. However, both women later admitted that this information was untruthful.

In the Garda report to the D.P.P. on the Stardust tragedy, it is clear that no evidence of the fire being started maliciously was ever uncovered during the course of the investigation. Local police informers, who had proved reliable in the past, were contacted by gardaí on numerous occasions but were unable to come up with any useful information into the cause of the fire.

Put simply, gardaí never believed the fire was started maliciously and had been taken by surprise by the tribunal's findings. Commenting on the tribunal report, a Garda spokesman said their inquiries would only be reactivated if new evidence could be produced to strengthen the arson theory. Senior gardaí pointed to the fact that practically all of the patrons attending the disco on the night lost relatives or friends in the fire. "In the course of our investigation it has been stated a number of times to our members that if anyone was in possession of any item of information which would be of assistance to the gardaí concerning the Stardust fire disaster, it would most willingly be passed on to them," the Garda report stated. "Nothing has come to notice which would indicate how the fire started."

However, a number of intriguing statements were made to gardaí which seem to point to an accidental fire at the Stardust. Despite their undisputed relevance to the investigation, they are not mentioned in the tribunal report. Some of these statements claim that patrons experienced excessive heat in the west alcove area of the Stardust in the wecks before February 13, 1981.

In early December 1980, James Murphy noticed a strong smell of rubber burning in the Stardust. This had been noticed on a few occasions previously by Declan Burnett, although he could not define the "unusual" smell. He believed the smell could have come from the air vent over the main bar. Doorman Phelim Kinahan remembered James Murphy telling him about the smell, which he described as "very bad". When he turned off the heaters, the smell dissipated. He reported the matter to Eamon Butterly. The next day, Butterly complained that he had to buy a new motor for the heater which had cost him "a fortune". Waitresses at the Stardust had also noticed the burning rubber smell. Some were satisfied that it came from a vent in the ceiling. In her statement to gardaí, Michelle Murray said she often heard the young fellows who washed the glasses asking the barmen if they could smell something burning.

A sighting of smoke was made by Declan Burnett just before Christmas, 1980. He recalled seeing a light smoke or mist of some kind on the balcony, which was curtained off. He was told by a superior to look under the seats in case there was a cigarette or something smouldering.

Approximately three weeks before the fire, smoke was also observed by staff near the main bar, which directly adjoined the west alcove. Although the exact date is unknown, those interviewed agreed it was a Sunday night. Jack Walsh, assistant manager of the Stardust, observed smoke on the left side of the main bar, which he said was reflected in a large spotlight. He reported the matter to the bar manager, Brian Peel, who immediately investigated the matter. According also to Peel, the smoke was showing up in the light of the spotlight. He went to the sound room and removed a couple of panels from the ceiling. He put his head through to have a look but could find nothing wrong. Peel formed the opinion that the smoke was simply dust.

Doorman Michael Kavanagh told gardaí that, three or four weeks before the fire, he took up duty at the Stardust between 9 p.m. and 9.30 p.m. He noticed several of the staff searching around the complex with torches; they appeared to him to be very concerned. He saw what he thought was smoke all around the general area of the main bar. It was faint and there was no smell. He said the commotion over the smoke was almost over by the time he arrived.

A waitress, Patricia Gallagher, also saw smoke coming from the direction of the light control room about three weeks before the tragedy. She described it as "thick smoke, like a light mist". She recalled that "the people in charge got very concerned about it". Around the same period, staff member Pauline McConalogue also saw what looked like cigarette smoke beside the lighting room. Again, there was no smell from it.

Another employee, Patrick Lennon, told gardaí that on a Sunday night about a month before the disaster he saw what he thought was smoke coming from the front of the light control room. He got a lamp and went up on the catwalk in the main bar to examine the ceiling. He found nothing wrong but, just to be certain, went outside to check. Again, everything seemed fine. When the spotlight and the fan were turned off, Lennon told gardaí that he could hardly see any smoke. He came to the conclusion that what he thought was smoke was in fact dust caused by the fans.

Barman Gerard Guilfoyle also recalled the incident. He said that after a full check, staff decided it was simply dust. He added, however, that in his two years working in the Stardust he had never seen dust like that before.

One Sunday night, around four weeks before the fire, waitress Elaine Stapleton was working in the Lantern Rooms and went into the Stardust for her break at 9.45 p.m. She saw smoke coming from the top of the main bar and going in a line across the ballroom towards the stage. She was satisfied it was not cigarette smoke, dust or fog.

Barman Larry Neville was also working on a Sunday night in late January 1981. He noticed something like smoke collecting on the beam of the spotlight and thought it was unusual. He went to the Silver Swan bar where he had been working and after about five minutes was approached by Gerard Guilfoyle, who wanted to show him something in the Stardust. On entering the ballroom, Guilfoyle asked him: "Does that look like smoke to you?"

Patrick Joseph McGrath, a maintenance man, was informed of the smoke incident by the assistant manager of the Stardust about three weeks prior to the fire. Jack Walsh told him smoke had been seen the previous night at the back of the club and was thought to have originated from the heating duct. McGrath replied that this was impossible, as the heat in that section of the club had been out of order for some time.

Numerous other members of staff reported seeing smoke around the same period. In each case, no-one could smell anything. Gardaí also heard claims of excessive heat originating in the west alcove area of the Stardust just weeks before the tragic blaze.

On Sunday, January 25, 1981, Joseph Coughlan was enjoying a lads' night out at the Stardust disco. He and his friends were sitting in the west alcove area, where the fire is thought to have started three weeks later. During the course of the night they could feel heavy heat around them. In fact, it was so hot that their drinks became warm. One of the group, Peter McGovern, said he was unable to finish his drink because of the heat. Another friend, Paul Kealy, didn't take much notice of the heat but also recalled that their drinks became warm. Gardaí made extensive enquiries to locate other patrons who were seated in that section of the Stardust on the same night but failed to find them. However, eight other patrons made similar claims of excessive heat levels in the west alcove area on unspecified dates prior to the fire. They all agreed that the night in question was a Friday.

Almost exactly one month before the tragedy, on January 15, 1981, two major British bands of that time, The Beat and The Specials, played a sold-out concert at the Stardust. It was the height of what was known as the "Ska" music craze and the double bill was one of the most eagerly anticipated gigs ever held at the Stardust. Fiona Doherty attended the concert that night with two friends, sisters Susan and Mary McCluskey. Doherty told gardaí that when the first group started playing she heard a crackling noise above her and saw sparks in the ceiling, which she likened to the effect of sparks from bumper cars in an amusement centre. Sparks were also seen on the ceiling by Susan McCluskey, which she described as purple flashes.

Eamon McCann, who promoted that concert, later told gardaí that the public address system used that night was large by Irish standards. It was brought to the Stardust by the bands performing. The lighting system, he said, consisted of two "Geni" towers on each side of the stage. As far as he could remember, there were twenty 1,000-watt lights hanging from each tower. These would have reflected off the bands' instruments, he believed. McCann also claimed it would not have been possible to hear a crackling noise during the performance.

Just hours before the Stardust fire, at approximately 10.10 p.m., the neon strip-light on the adjoining Silver Swan bar was observed by Stephen Byrne to be dimming. He was on his way into the bar with John Fagan. Both men were electricians by trade. When Byrne saw the neon light fading, he formed the opinion that this was the result of a short in the circuit. He believed it could cause a fire and later told gardaí he was familiar with neon lighting.

Gardaí also took a statement from a member of staff, Marian Mulvanney, who reported a smell of some sort of oil in the ladies' toilets of the Lantern Rooms, just over ten minutes before the fire was first discovered in the Stardust. She mentioned this to Patricia Murray and Patricia Gaynor, who were with her in the toilets at the time. Both women remembered the incident, but neither one had noticed any smell. After investigating Mulvanney's claim, gardaí were satisfied that there was nothing to connect the incident with the fire. Because the window in the ladies' toilet in the Lantern Rooms faced out on to a car park, gardaí believed it was possible that Mulvanney had simply got a smell of leaked oil from a car or lorry. Despite the fact that gardaí had discounted the incident as irrelevant, Mulvanney would later repeat her claim in evidence when the Butterlys' case against Dublin Corporation for malicious damages was heard in court.

Then there was the evidence of taxi driver Robert O'Callaghan, whose version of events lent a puzzling twist to the investigation. According to the tribunal report, O'Callaghan said he picked up a fare at the Adelphi Cinema on Abbey Street at approximately 1.20 a.m. on the night of the fire. He brought the passenger to an area of Beaumont Road, near the Stardust. As he was waiting for the man to get money from his house to pay him, he looked at the clock in the taxi and saw it was 1.30 a.m. He then drove towards the Stardust with a view to picking up a fare. As he came to the junction with Skelly's Lane, he saw flames above the Stardust building "about the size of a house". At this stage, he was approximately a hundred yards from the complex. He drove to the concreted area and parked his car on the west side of the building, outside the Lantern Rooms.

O'Callaghan said he could see disco lights and hear music. He then went towards the front of the building in the direction of the main entrance and saw people he described as elderly or middle-aged coming out the door with drinks in their hands. He told them there was a fire and they replied that they knew this. One of the patrons said he should get his taxi out of the way, so O'Callaghan reversed it. Although he remembered seeing at least one girl coming out screaming, he said she appeared to be more "over-excited" than anything else. He did not recall seeing any panic-stricken crowds in the area. Some girls asked Callaghan if he was a taxi man and he accordingly took them to their destinations and left the scene.

O'Callaghan's evidence raises a number of questions. He reported seeing flames shooting from the roof of the Stardust shortly after 1.30 a.m., yet the first sightings of the fire in the west alcove area of the Stardust were not until at least 1.40 a.m. On his arrival at the complex, the disco was apparently still underway, as he could see lights and hear music, yet his sighting of flames shooting from the roof would have indicated that, by then, the fire was at an advanced stage.

The Garda report to the D.P.P. was compiled in advance of the findings of the forensic experts brought in to investigate the cause of the fire. However, even the experts were divided on this issue, as outlined in the tribunal report. While far from offering conclusive evidence into the cause of the fire, many statements made to gardaí certainly give rise to reasonable suspicion that it could have started accidentally. Clearly, there were problems associated with either the heating system or the lighting room. The tribunal report made a brief reference to Stardust staff noticing smoke three or four weeks before the fire but concluded: "They were satisfied that what they had seen was not smoke and was probably dust." This is at variance with at least one statement given to gardaí by a member of staff who believed that what she saw was not fog, dust or cigarette smoke. Nor does the tribunal report deal with the allegations of excessive heat experienced in the west alcove area just weeks before the fire.

For the owners of the Stardust, the finding of the tribunal that the fire was "probably malicious" was most welcome. It exonerated them of much of the blame for the tragedy and paved the way for a successful malicious damages claim against Dublin Corporation.

However, the report submitted to the D.P.P. by gardaí opens the possibility that the cause of the Stardust fire might not have been malicious, but a result of faulty wiring or a defective heating system.

* * * *

There are references to the Garda investigation in the hundreds of pages of the final tribunal report, but no mention of many of the eyewitness accounts described above. Could the tribunal have considered them to be irrelevant? Did the tribunal have access to all of the statements that were given to the Director of Public Prosecutions? If such evidence was in fact made available to the tribunal during its sittings, why was it excluded from the final report?

Nine

A Father's Revenge

"This man really wouldn't hurt a fly but the bitterness was growing in him as each day went past."

– Christine Keegan on her husband's plot to shoot the owner of the Stardust.

Eamon Butterly probably never realised how close he came to death as an indirect result of the Stardust tragedy. Only for the intervention of one woman, Butterly would have been shot and killed by a grief-stricken father bent on revenge.

In the immediate aftermath of the tragedy there had been a lot of emotive talk about retribution. Almost inevitably, the talk in houses throughout Coolock and Artane turned to the roles of Eamon and Patrick Butterly in the disaster. By the middle of the following year, not only had the Butterlys escaped criminal proceedings for keeping fire exits chained, but their Silver Swan pub was open for business again.

There were numerous conversations among some of the victims' families in low, threatening tones regarding the form of punishment that should be visited upon the manager and owner of the Stardust. Christine Keegan remembers many people promising that "Butterly would pay". She paid no notice to what she felt was just angry, dangerous talk. But Eamon Butterly came perilously close to being shot by one parent who laid the blame for the deaths of his two teenage daughters firmly at his feet – Christine Keegan's husband, John.

On October 23, 1983, two-and-a-half years after his daughters had been laid to rest, John Keegan sat down beside his wife Christine in their Coolock home and slumped into the chair. John was restless, repeatedly getting up and sitting back down. He told Christine he was going to the toilet, but a few minutes later she heard the car door closing outside the front of the house and listened as her husband drove away. Momentarily surprised, Christine asked one of her young daughters where her daddy had gone. Then, in a beat, she guessed that her tormented husband had gone to visit his two daughters in their graves in Balgriffin Cemetery. They had been buried just in front of their best friend, Mary Kenny.

It was not unusual for John to drive up to the cemetery late at night to say prayers over the graves. He often convinced Christine to come with him. They would park the car in such a way that the headlights illuminated the rows of headstones. The couple would make their way to the graves and sit for hours, sobbing into each other's arms. John told Christine that this was the right place for him to be; that his daughters' spirits were here and he could feel them. Christine went to the graveyard every chance she got, but it frightened her to go in the dark. This, however, would be very different from other nights.

By 2 a.m. John was still not home and Christine sat up waiting, beginning to get very worried. At last the telephone rang; when the caller identified himself as the sergeant on duty in Coolock Garda Station, Christine braced herself for the worst. With mixed emotions of relief and fear, Christine was informed that the police had her husband. They jokingly reassured her that he was being well looked after in the "bridal suite" cell in the station. Christine burst into tears and asked if John had been involved in an accident. The Garda informed her that John was all right. He was not injured but had been arrested for assault. He would be locked in the cell until the gardaí got a report back from the hospital on the condition of his victim: Eamon Butterly.

John Keegan had left the family home that night with a length of heavy steel chain in the boot of his car. He normally used it to lock the gates at the entrance to the driveway of the family home. This time, as he carefully unravelled it from the gate, something snapped in his head and he placed the chain gently in the boot. He told Christine later that he had every intention to "kill Butterly". He was bitter that the Director of Public Prosecutions had decided that there was not enough evidence to proceed with a case alleging manslaughter against the owners of the Stardust. Even though the compensation cases by the victims and families were yet to be heard in court, John Keegan was convinced that he would never get justice for the loss of his two daughters. As far as he was concerned, the system had failed him. He had decided to take matters into his own hands, regardless of the consequences.

Arriving at the Butterlys' business park on the site of the Stardust, he calmly walked into the yard and took the length of chain from the boot of his car. The first casualty of John's simmering rage was one of the Butterlys' vans. With slow, deliberate swings of the chain, John smashed the windscreen and then the rear window. He moved to the side of the vehicle and took his anger out on the bodywork and then on windows of the building. The noise attracted the attention of one of the security guards on the premises, who confronted John.

"Don't worry, it's not you I'm after," John told the doorman.

At that moment Eamon Butterly stepped out from the doorway of the office and urged John to put the chain down. John responded by throwing the heavy chain back over his shoulder and bringing it down across the top of Butterly's head. The force of the blow opened his victim's skull and blood splashed over both Eamon and John's shirts. In shock, Butterly stood on the same spot, feeling the blood pour down over his face. He appealed to his attacker to come inside the Silver Swan for a drink, but John quietly told him to call the gardaí.

Drained after the first rush of adrenaline, John calmly put down the chain and waited for the police to arrive. After his arrest, John was quizzed about his reasons for carrying out the attack. He kept repeating: "This is the man who killed my children." He later told Christine that he was well looked after by the gardaí in Coolock, who knew the Keegan family well and were sympathetic to their grief. After being held in the "bridal suite" for a number of hours, the hospital notified the gardaí that Butterly was not seriously injured and the prisoner was released. John was dropped at the entrance of his housing estate to save his family the embarrassment of having the neighbours witness him arriving home in the back of a squad car.

Despite his arrest and detention, John Keegan was unrepentant. When he came through the door, still in his stained shirt, he expressed disappointment that he had not killed Butterly. As soon as she got over the initial shock of seeing her husband in that bloodied state, Christine began to feel heartbroken at John's regret that he had not ended a life.

"Two wrongs don't make a right," she kept telling her husband. But he refused to listen. Over the course of the next few months, Christine noticed a change in her husband. The normally unassuming John Keegan had become a bitter and angry man fixated on retribution. He was consumed by rage.

"The life was being sucked out of him," she recalls. "This man really wouldn't hurt a fly but the bitterness was growing in him as each day went past. He thought he was getting the anger out of him and for that brief moment when he hit Butterly over the head, he got some of that poison out of his system. But the anger and the hurt was slowly killing him."

A few months after John's arrest, Christine was to experience another incident that confirmed in her mind how far John was prepared to go to exact his own revenge on the owner of the Stardust disco. An avid pool player, John Keegan had installed his own table at the back of his house in Greencastle Crescent. He loved a friendly game over the green baize table with members of his family and often challenged his son's friends for a few quid. He would sometimes talk Christine into joining him and the lads for a game in the shed at the bottom of the garden and would instruct her where to hit the ball to make a shot. Christine quickly learned that his advice wasn't always honest and sometimes the cue ball would veer off in the opposite direction to where she wanted it to go, leaving John with the advantage.

He saved his best thought-out strategies for the competition in his local pub, Campion's, where he could hold his own against the "sharks" who hovered over the tables. One Sunday morning Christine joined John when he went to Campion's in search of a game. Christine enjoyed the respite of getting out of the house for a few hours. She was sitting near the pool table when a man she had never seen before leaned over to John and asked him how he was. John replied that he was grand and the stranger whispered he was "looking after that" for him. Christine never gave a second thought to what the man was talking about. John glanced at his wife before telling the man he would "believe it when he saw it". Christine later asked John who the man in the pub was, but he would not answer her, saying only that he had some business to take care of.

The following Sunday, John was getting ready to go back to Campion's for a game and he convinced Christine to join him once again, although on this particular day she was in no mood for the pub. The couple played pool for about two hours and then moved out of the lounge and into a quiet corner of the bar. Christine left to go to the ladies' room and, when she came back, John was still sitting on his own. As Christine sat down, he told her that he had something to show her and slid a heavy object into her hand. When Christine glanced down, she saw the dark steel of a heavy handgun. Calmly, she asked where he had got it from, but John just sat staring at her, not saying a word. She enquired if it was it loaded; he nodded that it was and pointed to the five bullets in the chamber.

Christine knew instantly that John was going to kill Eamon Butterly. She took her husband's hand and, looking intently at his face, told him very quietly that if he left the pub with the gun, he would not be returning home to a family. She threatened that if he went outside, he would never see his wife or his children again. She told him that he would have to face God and his two daughters in heaven and live forever with the consequences of what he was about to do. John left the pub without Christine, but when he returned home, he no longer had the gun with him. Christine never discovered the identity of the man who had given John the gun but later learned from her husband that he was from north county Dublin and had a grudge against the Butterlys.

Although he had been talked out of his private plot to shoot Eamon Butterly, John Keegan still had to face the rap for the assault incident. On November 21, 1983, he appeared in the Dublin District Court charged with assaulting Butterly and causing him actual bodily harm. He pleaded guilty to causing £1,457 worth of damage to the windows at Scott's Foods Ltd, beside the Silver Swan pub, but pleaded not guilty to assaulting Eamon Butterly. He told the court that he had been having trouble at home since the fire and went out at about midnight to "cool off" and drive around for a while.

"I was drawn like a magnet to the Stardust complex," he told the court. "Normally I would go to the graveyard, but I didn't stop that night." He admitted that he had taken a chain out of his car and had broken some of Butterly's windows. He claimed that Eamon Butterly had come from the pub and had hit him. He agreed he had called the Stardust owner "a murderer" but asserted that he had struck him only after Butterly had hit him and warned he would have Keegan killed.

In his evidence, Eamon Butterly said that some time between 12.30 a.m. and 1 a.m. he had heard the sound of breaking glass and had gone out to see what was going on. He encountered John Keegan. "He told me I was a murderer and I told him that this would have to stop," said Butterly.

Handing down a one-year suspended sentence to John Keegan, Judge Connellan said: "Mr Butterly did not go out to kill this man's two daughters. We are all very sorry for this man [John Keegan] and we all regret what has happened. But that does not give him the right to assault Mr Butterly or break this man's windows." The judge said he would suspend Keegan's sentence on condition that the window-breaking would not occur again. He agreed to a State application that Keegan enter into a bond to keep the peace for two years.

There were emotional scenes as Christine Keegan was removed from the court while Judge Connellan gave his ruling. She had misheard the judge and thought her husband had just received a jail sentence. On the question of compensation for the damage to his property by John Keegan, Butterly was informed that this would be a matter for his insurance company.

Shortly after the court case, John, Christine and Antoinette Keegan were having a quiet drink in Campion's pub when a man approached and started taking photographs of them. He was quickly overpowered by the three Keegans who, by their own admission today, "gave him a hiding to remember". As John smashed the man's camera to pieces, Christine poked him sharply in the eye with her sovereign ring. Clearly shaken by the ordeal, the mystery man – who allegedly told the Keegans he was taking photographs on behalf of the Butterlys – left the pub, only to return shortly with the gardaí. After a quick conversation with the owner of the pub, the police left without approaching the Keegans. The family heard nothing more about the incident.

Eamon Butterly would be regularly subjected to taunts and harassment at the hands of certain Stardust victims and relatives. Antoinette Keegan admits today that she used to go to the Coachman's Inn, near Dublin Airport, on the nights when Butterly was known to drink there. She would scour the car park for his Mercedes and then vandalise it, smashing the lights and mirrors.

There are conflicting reports within the ranks of the Stardust families about a second attempt to murder Eamon Butterly. One version claims that the father of a seriously injured victim put a shotgun in a golf bag and made his way to the Silver Swan pub by bus. He waited at the entrance to the right of the complex for Eamon Butterly to leave the premises. Butterly came out of the Silver Swan and got into his car but left via the left entrance, unwittingly foiling the attempt on his life. This story is today dismissed as "pub talk" by the Keegans but another member of the Stardust Victims' Committee, William Mulvey, insists that it happened. The truth probably lies somewhere in the middle.

Ten

Business As Usual

*"I don't want this place opened again. In my opinion,
the Stardust is a crematorium."*

– Margaret Griffiths, whose son Michael died in the blaze,
Dublin Circuit Court, May 5, 1982.

Patrick Butterly died a wealthy man. After he passed away in
January 2000, it emerged that he had left an estate worth over
six million pounds. The Stardust was just one of his many business
interests. Despite suffering the setback of the fire in 1981, the
Butterlys' business talents ensured a lucrative future for the
enterprising family.

The Butterlys didn't waste any time in picking up the pieces
following the fire. One week after the tragedy, the various companies
behind the Stardust lodged malicious damages claims for up to four
million pounds with Dublin Corporation. That same week, Eamon
Butterly also talked to the media about the possibility of re-opening
the premises. Relatives of the victims were understandably appalled
at the prospect of an entertainment complex or public house opening
again on the site of the tragedy.

On September 30, 1981, just eight months after the fire, the
Butterlys gave notice in the press of their application for a liquor
licence in respect of the Silver Swan bar and the Lantern Rooms.
An ordinary publican's seven-day on-licence for the sale of
intoxicating liquor for consumption upon the premises was being
sought. Earlier that week, these two sections of the Stardust complex
– which had been largely unaffected by the fire – reopened for lunches
and dinners, although no alcohol was served. There were angry scenes
as members of the relatives' committee picketed outside the pub.

One woman, whose daughter died in the tragedy, said it turned her stomach to think of people eating there. John Keegan, who had lost two daughters, said the Stardust complex should be regarded as "sacred ground" and never be allowed to reopen to the public. Peter Hobbs, whose brother Brian perished at the Stardust, said the committee would oppose any part of the complex being opened again for entertainment purposes. "It is our hope that the Silver Swan, the Lantern Rooms and the Stardust will revert back to being a jam factory or a warehouse," he told *The Irish Times*. "This may seem subjective but we have gone around Coolock and because of the magnitude of the tragedy, found that this feeling extended into far more homes than just those where lives were lost. There was little support for a bar or restaurant or anything like that ever opening there again."

Two months later, on November 24, 1981, the Butterlys were granted their licence for the Silver Swan, provoking angry outbursts in the Dublin District Court. The courtroom was packed, mostly with relatives of the dead, as Judge Gerard Buchanan announced his decision to grant the licence. As the judge was summing up, one woman shouted: "We know the verdict – injustice. Forty-eight children died in vain." Judge Buchanan ordered the woman's removal from the court.

Three TDs – Michael Woods, George Birmingham and Noel Browne – had turned up in court to object to the Butterlys' application. However, they were not allowed to give evidence. Judge Buchanan explained that politicians could not testify unless they were resident in the civil parish of Artane, where the premises were located, or unless they gave evidence of personal experience in relation to the complex. He rejected a plea on behalf of counsel for the objectors, Séamus Ó Tuathail, that TDs should be allowed to give evidence of the atmosphere in the area regarding the licence application. The judge apologised to the public representatives who had turned up in court and thanked them for taking an interest in the case. Michael Woods today describes the licence application as "insensitive and inappropriate", particularly as it came so soon after the tragedy. "The personal and human devastation that came from such a traumatic disaster really was too deep," Dr Woods says.

The main objections to the licence application were based on claims of underage drinking at the Stardust. Six witnesses gave evidence stating that they had been served alcohol at the complex, even though they were under the minimum legal age. Objecting also on other grounds, five witnesses were called to give evidence of noise and disturbance outside the premises in the past. There were claims of fighting, teenage drunkenness and cars being revved-up late at night. One local resident said he had considered moving house because of late-night noise and disturbances associated with the entertainment complex.

Delivering his ruling, Judge Buchanan rejected Garda claims that the premises were not suitable for a restaurant. He accepted the fact that Silver Swan Ltd had not had a licence for the bar for three years, which he felt was a "technical breach" of the licensing law. He pointed out that the failure of the company to make returns to the Companies Office for the past six years did not have a bearing on the granting of the licence. The Judge said that the complaints about underage drinking were most serious allegations and had caused him deep trouble. However, he took into account testimony that young people were prepared to lie about their age and said there was an obvious difficulty in enforcing the age limit. He could not accept that underage drinking had been condoned by the management of the Stardust.

The Judge also noted that complaints about noise had mainly been attributed to the Stardust disco. Eamon Butterly had given an undertaking that there would be no more discos or late-night exemption certificates sought. Judge Buchanan granted the publican's licence and adjourned the application for a restaurant certificate to the following month to allow for the removal of the public bar from the Lantern Rooms, as it was only seeking a restaurant certificate. Judge Buchanan stressed that, to some extent, the applicants were being granted the licence on a trial basis for a year and objections could be made to the renewal of the licence the following September.

In March 1982 the Dublin District Court rejected an application by Eamon Butterly for dancing, singing and music licences in the remaining parts of the Stardust complex. Butterly appealed to the Circuit Court but the decision was upheld by Judge Frank Martin, who commented that, at this point in time, the application seemed to him to be of "an extraordinarily insensitive nature". This time, the court heard evidence from ten teenagers who claimed to have been served alcohol in various parts of the complex when they were under the permitted age. Two mothers of Stardust victims made impassioned pleas for the licences to be refused. Margaret Griffiths, who lost a son, told the court: "I don't want this place opened again. In my opinion, the Stardust is a crematorium."

A local TD, George Bermingham, was one of a number of politicians in court to oppose the application for the licences. "There is a deep feeling in the area that it is unseemly and inappropriate that the place of the disaster should become the scene of singing and dancing," he said.

The Government issued a statement denying an evening newspaper report that the Taoiseach, Charles Haughey, had no objection to the licences. The report was "untrue and misleading", it said, as the Taoiseach had made known his objection to these licences on numerous occasions. The Government also pointed out that the Taoiseach and the Minister for Health and Social Welfare, Dr Michael Woods, along with Dáil deputies Vincent Brady and Ned Brennan, had been represented by counsel and a solicitor at the initial hearing for the licences at Dublin District Court. They had taken an active part in supporting the relatives' objections, the statement added.

Judge Martin told the court that he had not had any difficulty making up his mind after the three-hour hearing. The evidence of underage drinking was coercive, he said, and it would be perverse on the part of the court that such was not the case. Identifying underage drinkers was a very difficult matter for a licensee – but that was his problem, the Judge found. He upheld the earlier District Court decision to refuse the licences.

A spokesperson for the Stardust Relatives' Committee expressed satisfaction at the outcome of the appeal hearing. He advised the Butterlys to forget about opening the premises as an entertainment venue and revert it to industrial use. Eamon Butterly told newspaper reporters that the question of obtaining licences for music, dancing and singing in the future would be a matter for his solicitors. He confirmed that portions of the premises would be reopened as a bar and a restaurant, for which licences had already been obtained. "If I find five or six months after the opening that things are not going as well as I expected, I would have to make a change of plan," he was quoted as saying in *The Irish Times*. "If it's not going to be viable, it won't be staying there."

A change of plan wasn't far away. Within months the Butterlys let it be known that they were getting out of the licensing trade. According to media reports, mounting political pressure and ongoing protests outside the Silver Swan by members of the relatives' committee had placed intolerable pressure on the Butterly business. It emerged that the lease on the Silver Swan bar and Lantern Rooms had been sold to a Dublin businessman, William Kenny, just two days before the Butterlys were due to apply in court for the renewal of their liquor licence. As expected, numerous objections to the licence had been lodged by the Stardust families. This, apparently, was the last straw for the Butterlys, who decided to get out of the pub trade altogether.

Despite news of the sale, the Stardust Relatives' Committee insisted that they still wanted the premises closed. They had been assured by Charles Haughey that the upcoming licence renewal would be met with considerable opposition from the gardaí. "The complex will always be a reminder of that terrible tragedy," said a spokesman for the relatives. "The Butterlys should have left a year ago but they stubbornly persisted. At least now we feel our objections have not been in vain."

However, the sale of the Silver Swan and Lantern Rooms would be described in court as "a subterfuge". At the licence hearing in Dublin District Court on September 29, 1982, it emerged that the sale price was a token ten thousand pounds and the same staff would be retained by the new owner, Mr Kenny, to run the premises. Kenny told the court that he became aware that the directors of Silver Swan Ltd were anxious to dispose of their interests in the pub. He admitted he was friendly with the Butterlys on a social basis. He said he had obtained a caretaker's agreement which gave him exclusive use of the premises. He intended to take possession of the pub as soon as a licence was granted. Although the sale price of £10,000 was described by Kenny as "a bargain", he pointed out that the deal also involved a very heavy rent amounting to a thousand pounds a week. Kenny told the court he would get his money back from Patrick Butterly if the licence was not granted.

The President of the Dublin District Court, Justice Thomas

Donnelly, granted an interim transfer of the licence, but on November 9, 1982, the same judge refused to confirm the transfer of the licence to Kenny. He said the applicant was "not a fit character" to hold a licence and decided that Kenny had lent his name to a transaction which was not bona fide. It also emerged that Kenny, along with his wife and child, had taken a holiday with Patrick Butterly abroad shortly before the sale of the pub. Kenny said they had not discussed the deal while on vacation. Objectors to the licence transfer had pointed out that Kenny had no previous experience of bar management – he ran an aluminium windows and doors installation business. Since purchasing the Silver Swan, Kenny's problems at the pub were compounded by a picket on the premises following the sacking of two staff. In court, Kenny insisted that the transaction to buy the pub "had not been set up for the convenience of someone else". He said he was involved for his own and his family's benefit.

Kenny was refused the licence transfer by Justice Donnelly on the grounds of his lack of previous experience in the bar trade; his lack of investigation into the business he was buying; the mere continuance of existing staff; and the highly informal agreement to take over the premises. "I am convinced that this was not a bona fide sale," Justice Donnelly commented. "This is of interest to me only in so far as it refers to the character of Mr Kenny. If Mr Kenny is prepared to lend his name to a transaction for the purpose of preserving a licence for the premises, this holds to his character. Then, in my view, Mr Kenny is not a fit person to hold a liquor licence."

The aborted sale of the Stardust complex was to be the least of Eamon Butterly's worries. On September 13, 1982, a journalist working for *The Irish Press*, Tim Hastings, claimed that two exit doors had been chained and locked in the Lantern Rooms the previous night. Hastings had been contacted by members of the public who allegedly saw chains wrapped around two exit doors in an area of the premises now used for snooker. After receiving the call, Hastings visited the Silver Swan, accompanied by a photographer. Butterly insisted that the doors had been left locked and chained by a man who "did not carry out his duties". He said, when contacted on the telephone by the journalist, he was "shocked" to learn that the doors were locked. "I am shattered and very upset by the whole thing," Butterly was quoted saying in *The Evening Press*. "The person involved simply had not carried out my instructions."

Coming just eighteen months after the Stardust disaster, the alleged incident disturbed the authorities. Dublin Corporation officials immediately carried out an inspection of the premises while the Minister for the Environment, Ray Burke, called on gardaí to investigate the allegations. Burke said that any prosecution under section 18 of the Fire Services Act 1981 – introduced after the Stardust tragedy – would be a matter for the Director of Public Prosecutions. The maximum penalty for breaches of the Act on conviction was a £10,000 fine or two years in prison.

A case by the State was eventually brought against Eamon Butterly and a barman, John Dignam, who had been on duty the day the alleged offence took place. The case was heard in Dublin Circuit Criminal Court before Judge Thomas Neylon in April 1984. On the second day of the trial, Inspector John Geary of Coolock Garda Station gave evidence of Dignam's statement. Dignam said that he and another man were the charge hands, which meant they had the keys to the premises. Butterly had told him to keep the premises clean and to refer any problems to him. Butterly had also insisted to him that there were not to be chains on the doors at any time when the public were on the premises. In his statement, Dignam said he would usually take the chains off the exit door in the Silver Swan when opening the premises. He would then go to the Lantern Rooms and remove the chains there. He would put the two padlocks on the shutter and leave the chains in the storeroom and at the entrance to the Lantern Rooms. There was no procedure for the "holy hour" from Monday to Saturday, as there was always a barman on the premises. On Sundays, he said, one barman would leave early, at around 2 p.m., while another would clean up and put the chains on the exit doors before leaving, usually around an hour later.

Dignam said that on Sunday, September 12, 1982, he had left the pub at 2.20 p.m. and returned at about 4 p.m. There was one customer standing outside. He went to lift the shutters but found that somebody had already done so. When he saw there was no chain on the main Silver Swan exit, he took it for granted that another barman had stayed on the premises during holy hour and so had not locked the place up. Dignam said he did not go into the Lantern Rooms at all.

Judge Neylon directed the jury to find Eamon Butterly and John Dignam not guilty of the charge because the State had not produced *prima facie* evidence of *mens rea* (the guilty mind), as required by law. The Judge found there had been a misunderstanding between two members of staff as to whether the doors had been unlocked and that there had not been any criminal intent. The ruling was met with dismay by the Stardust relatives, who believed that a guilty verdict would have forced Butterly out of the licensing trade for good. In fact, gardaí had lodged an objection to the upcoming renewal of the liquor licence for the Silver Swan on the grounds that "Butterly was not a fit character to hold a licence". They alleged that he had allowed exit doors to be locked while members of the public were on the premises in September 1982.

When the renewal case was heard in June 1984, Eamon Butterly admitted the doors had been locked but said he was not responsible. He claimed that one barman had been sacked for failing to follow instructions to keep exit doors unlocked. It was pointed out in court that Butterly had already been acquitted of this offence. District Court Judge Connellan granted the application for a licence, despite objections from Charles Haughey – now leader of the Opposition – and TDs Liam Fitzgerald, Michael Woods and Vincent Brady.

* * * *

The Stardust disaster had the potential to cripple the Butterlys' business empire. The complex was only insured for a quarter of a million pounds and hundreds of compensation claims against the Butterlys by the injured and relatives of the dead were expected. But the Butterlys always claimed that they, too, were victims. Within hours of the disaster, Eamon Butterly had openly speculated that the fire had been started deliberately. Spurred on by the tribunal of inquiry's finding that the fire was "probably" started maliciously, the Butterlys' battle with Dublin Corporation finally commenced in Dublin Circuit Court on June 10, 1983.

The two malicious damages claims amounted to a massive three million pounds, the largest ever brought against Dublin Corporation. The principals in the case were Scott's Foods Ltd, owners of the Stardust, and Silver Swan Ltd, who had leased the entertainment complex. Scott's Foods Ltd was seeking two million for loss of the building, while Silver Swan Ltd claimed one million for loss of interior furnishings and fittings. The case was heard in a crowded courtroom before Judge Sean O'Hanrahan.

Senior Counsel for the applicants, Dermot Gleeson, said the fire had been started deliberately. The suggestion that it might have been caused by a piece of burning paper or by an accidentally dropped cigarette butt would be refuted by forensic experts, he told the court. Mr Gleeson said it had also been suggested that an electrical fault could have caused the fire but there was no evidence to substantiate this. The fire, he asserted, had been started by somebody in the west alcove of the dance hall, screened off from the main floor, who had ripped out the interior of a seat or seats and set the material ablaze.

Phelim Kinahan, floor manager of the Stardust, was the first witness to give evidence. He said he had initially seen flames on seats at the rear of the west alcove. Two doormen were attempting to extinguish the fire and others were helping patrons towards the exits, he told the court. The lights of the ballroom had been dimmed for a disco-dancing competition but he immediately went to the switchroom and turned them on fully. The ballroom was filling with black smoke. Then there was a bang and all the lights went out, he recalled. Mr Kinahan told counsel for Dublin Corporation that there had been three false alarms to the Fire Brigade relating to the Stardust in the six-month period before the fire.

Evidence was also given by Anthony Tennyson, an electrical engineer retained by the Butterlys. He said he had inspected the building on two occasions in the week following the fire and twice more in March 1981. He had found the electrical system generally to be of good quality. The distribution boards in various locations around the building were of a better quality than that required by the regulations, he said. He explained that the exit signs over the emergency doors, which were kept permanently lit, were powered by two separate systems – one fed from the public electricity supply and the other from a back-up, battery-operated system. Tennyson had formed the impression that if two faults developed in the primary system simultaneously, they could, in some circumstances, knock out the whole system. However, he did not believe that this design fault could have been the cause of the fire.

Tennyson also pointed out that the only electrical installation in the alcove where the fire started was a socket on a wall behind the back row of seats. This had been badly damaged in the fire but it had been determined in tests carried out by the State Forensic Laboratory that the wires were firmly attached to their terminals. Because of this, he did not believe that the socket could have been a cause of the fire. Tennyson noted that caps which had been attached to the immersion unit in the water-heating system were missing. He said it was possible that any exposed electrical wiring which came into contact with inflammable material could cause a fire – but this had not happened in the case of the Stardust. He also found that the other electrical systems in the building were of low voltage and could not have caused the fire. In his four investigations of the burnt-out building, he had discovered no electrical faults in any of the systems which could have started the blaze.

Michael Norton of the Department of Justice had been one of six forensic experts called to give evidence before the tribunal of inquiry. Mr Norton had come to the conclusion that the fire was "probably" started maliciously. In the Butterlys' case for damages, Norton gave evidence on behalf of the State Forensic Laboratory. He said he had carried out a series of tests of the inflammability of the materials used to stuff and cover the seating in the Stardust. These tests had shown that a discarded match or cigarette lighter could not have started a fire on the seat covering. But when the covering was ripped and the stuffing exposed, it had proved possible to ignite it by holding a naked flame to it for about one minute. "Given that there is no other explanation, it appears that someone ripped one of the seats and set fire to it," Norton told the court.

Other members of staff also gave evidence on behalf of the Butterlys. Patrick McGrath, a maintenance man at the Stardust, said there was nothing stored in the roof space above the false ceiling of the west alcove. He claimed that on at least two occasions people had broken in through the roof. One such break-in occurred about a month before the fire. Another employee, Marian Mulvaney, said she had smelled what she thought was paraffin in the toilets of the Lantern Rooms at about 1 a.m., less than an hour before the fire began. Mulvaney had originally made this claim in her first statement to gardaí shortly after the fire. However, they had ruled it out of their investigation and believed the smell was probably leaked oil from a truck or car parked outside.

Although the case was expected to last for about a week, Judge O'Hanrahan made his ruling after the second day of evidence. That morning, an English forensic scientist, Dr Robert Watt, had told the court that tests carried out by him indicated that the Stardust fire had been started deliberately. His evidence was of a similar nature to that of Michael Norton, particularly in relation to tests carried out on the seats. He ruled out the possibility of an electrical fault or disco lights causing the blaze and completely discounted a cigarette packet and partly burnt match found near where the fire started in the west alcove. He said the fire had spread so rapidly "because the heat generated would be considerably greater than that from several power stations".

Counsel for Dublin Corporation submitted that it was possible the seat might have been split open by some person and the fire accidentally started by someone else. This could have been caused by a cigarette end or lighted match accidentally dropped through the slit on the seat. Counsel for the local authority claimed it was also possible that someone had then spilled alcohol on the seat, and that might have acted as an accelerant. However, counsel for the Butterlys argued that this theory was not borne out by the evidence and was not within the balance of probability.

Judge O'Hanrahan said he was satisfied that the fire was started maliciously. He adjourned the assessment of the damages to be awarded to the Butterlys' companies until the following month. The matter would first have to be assessed by surveyors acting on behalf of the firms involved and Dublin Corporation. Building industry sources predicted that the actual size of the award would be considerably less than the three million claimed by the Butterlys and was more likely to be in the region of one million pounds.

The verdict, nevertheless, was a major victory for the Butterlys. The Judge had gone one crucial step further than the tribunal by finding that the fire was actually started maliciously. There was now a legal basis to the Butterlys' claims for compensation because of malicious damages. Speaking immediately after the ruling, Eamon Butterly said: "The court finding that the fire was deliberate was final proof of what I have maintained all along."

Families of the Stardust victims reacted to the verdict with fury. Speaking on radio, Peter Hobbs, the acting chairman of the Stardust Relatives' Committee, expressed surprise that the court had firmly identified arson as the cause of the blaze, as no new evidence had materialised since the tribunal of inquiry. He said that, in light of the ruling, he would be expecting gardaí and the D.P.P. to make further efforts to identify the arsonist and bring him or her to trial.

John Keegan was angry and upset at the verdict. "I lost two daughters and a third one is still suffering," he told *The Irish Independent*. "They could not establish that the fire was malicious before, and now he [Eamon Butterly] has had a malicious injuries claim awarded to him. This country will be the laughing stock of the world if that claim goes through our legal system."

Lucy Croker, who lost her daughter Jacqueline in the fire, summed up the feelings of many victims when she told a newspaper: "I just don't know how that happened in the courts. I miss my daughter terribly and so do my husband and two other children. We're getting treated like dirt since the fire. He's [Butterly is] in and out of the courts getting things sorted out and we're left aside. I still haven't had my daughter's rings returned – they're in some police station. And we haven't heard from the courts yet about when our claim will go through. We're being treated like dirt."

Media coverage was largely critical of the ruling, with many newspapers pointing to the fact that taxpayers – Stardust victims included – would end up footing the bill for the fire. The sense of injustice was further compounded by the fact that not a single penny in compensation had yet been paid to the relatives of the dead or those injured in the Stardust. That weekend's *Sunday Independent* reported that the Stardust Relatives' Committee had decided to disband following the verdict: "After two years and four months they are bitter and disillusioned, resigned to the fact that Mr Eamon Butterly will walk away with more than £1 million in compensation which they, as taxpayers, will end up paying."

The Butterlys would receive just over half of that amount. After a hearing at Dublin Circuit Court on July 8, 1983, the Judge held that the figure should be in the region of £600,000. Later that month, a settlement figure of £581,496 was announced in court. Approving the decree, Judge Sean O'Hanrahan commented that all those involved in the negotiations had shown common sense in avoiding a protracted legal battle in the courts to decide damages. The sum awarded would later be subjected to a legal challenge from the Butterlys' insurance company, which sought to recoup what had already been paid out since the fire.

There were further malicious damages claims against Dublin Corporation relating to the Stardust. On October 13, 1984, Cadbury (Ireland) Ltd was awarded £177,789 after a fire in a warehouse attached to the Stardust complex destroyed machinery stored there by the chocolate company. The incident took place in the early hours of April 16, 1981, just two months after the tragedy. An attack in revenge for the forty-eight deaths at the Stardust was thought to have been the motive.

In another claim for damages against Dublin Corporation in November 1984, disc jockey Danny Hughes, who lost equipment in the Stardust fire, was awarded £11,200 in compensation after originally seeking more than £25,000.

* * * *

Although frustrated by the Butterlys' seemingly endless run of court victories, it was the continuing trade at the Silver Swan bar and Lantern Rooms that incensed the Stardust relatives most. Year after year they would object to the application for the pub's liquor licence, only to see a judge renew it. By 1985, the dissatisfied relatives had reorganised themselves as the Stardust Victims' Committee and their campaign strategy took on a more militant form. While primarily set up to battle for compensation for the victims, the Committee was determined to make life as difficult as possible for Eamon Butterly, as long as he continued to operate a pub on what they considered to be solemn ground.

Victims and relatives regularly picketed the Silver Swan after it reopened for business in 1981. At one stage, the Butterlys succeeded in obtaining a court injunction to have the pickets of his premises lifted. While the protests were generally peaceful, the atmosphere sometimes threatened to turn ugly and gardaí always kept a watchful eye on proceedings. A public appearance at the Lantern Rooms by world snooker champion Dennis Taylor would result in scenes of violence on October 12, 1985.

Taylor was to play an exhibition match in a section of the complex now used for snooker. The night before his Lantern Rooms appearance, as he officially opened a new snooker room in Coolock, Taylor was handed a letter of protest by John Keegan, chairman of the Stardust Victims' Committee. Keegan appealed to the champ's "good nature" and urged him not to help promote Eamon Butterly's venue. The exhibition match was initially cancelled by Taylor's manager, Barry Hearn, who was contacted in London about the unfolding controversy. However, Eamon Butterly arranged an urgent meeting with Taylor and his Irish agent, Eugene Crozier, in Jurys Hotel. Up to the last minute there was doubt as to whether Taylor would keep his Lantern Rooms engagement. After eleventh hour talks with Eamon Butterly, who was accompanied by his solicitor, Taylor left the hotel and made his way across the city to Artane, where he was eagerly awaited by 250 snooker fans.

As Taylor wowed patrons with his snooker skills inside the Lantern Rooms, members of the Victims' Committee demanded admission to the private exhibition. When they were refused entry, a mêlée ensued involving Eamon Butterly and various doormen. Gardaí on duty at the scene were unable to contain the protesters and reinforcements were called. Victims alleged that Butterly was extremely abusive towards them. It was also claimed that gardaí drew their batons as they tried to remove the protestors from the hallway of the venue. The picket resumed outside the gates of the complex with some relatives lying down on the road to block traffic. At the end of the exhibition match, Dennis Taylor had to be smuggled out of the Lantern Rooms in what proved to be a public relations nightmare for the star. The Stardust Victims' Committee had failed to stop the event but claimed a moral victory over Eamon Butterly when the following day's newspapers all reported the embarrassing incident.

* * * *

The Stardust Victims' Committee objected to numerous planning applications relating to Fairdale Industrial Estate, the site of the

Stardust. In 1985 permission was granted for an outdoor Sunday market at the front of the complex, much to the dismay of the victims. Later that year they failed stop the development of a Maxol petrol station at the entrance to the estate, despite appealing to An Bord Pleanála against Dublin Corporation's decision to grant permission. Ostensibly, the Committee's objections to both developments were based on concerns about increased traffic levels in the area and issues of fire safety. In truth, however, they simply regarded any commercial development at the Stardust as inappropriate. The Committee made it clear that it would only support the provision of a youth training centre for local unemployed people on the site. There was some joy for the Committee when the outdoor market in the Stardust car park was closed by Dublin Corporation over concerns about traffic. This decision was upheld by the planning board on appeal in February 1986. The petrol station development went ahead, however, and was operated at the time of writing by Colm Butterly.

The biggest battle was yet to come. In May 1988 an application in the name of a company called Amadale Construction Ltd was lodged in respect of the Stardust site. It proposed the development of a major entertainment complex comprising snooker rooms, a restaurant, gymnasium, bar and bowling alley. The Stardust Victims' Committee described the application as "sick" and immediately set about mobilising the support of local politicians to oppose the plan. The identity of the applicants was shrouded in mystery. Dublin Corporation was unable to obtain details of the directors of Amadale Construction from either the Companies Office or the architects who submitted the application. Eamon Butterly, while pledging to facilitate Amadale's plan, denied to *The Star* newspaper that he had any part in the proposed complex outside of owning the land.

Through the media, Stardust relatives made it clear to the mysterious developers that they were in for a long fight. Christine Keegan told *The Star* defiantly: "Whoever wants to build where my daughters have died will have to lay blocks on my head first. The people involved obviously didn't lose a loved one in the fire."

There was a real fear among Victims' Committee members that the application would receive planning permission, as the Stardust site was zoned "D1" under the 1980 City Development Plan, providing for mixed uses. Dublin Corporation acknowledged that the Amadale Construction application would not constitute a material contravention of the Plan.

Local politicians were unanimous in their opposition to the application, including Senator Sean Haughey, a local Fianna Fáil councillor for the area at that time. Fine Gael TD Michael Joe Cosgrave was outraged on learning of the planning application. "I am totally against the site being used for entertainment purposes," he said. "It would cause a lot of grief in the area and bring back many bad memories." Pat McCartan, then a Workers' Party TD, also opposed the plan. "I've always been concerned about the development of this property and feel that an entertainment complex of any description should not be put here. These people have been tortured enough."

Outlining their objections to the application, the Stardust Victims' Committee said in a statement: "This venue was the scene of a major disaster resulting in the deaths of 48 children in February, 1981. The parents of those who died, those who were injured, and the residents in the immediate and surrounding areas strongly object to the development of this complex. The parents of the deceased deem this ground sacred and feel it would be sacrilege for any sort of entertainment in the place where their loved ones died. The premises would be better suited to the needs of the people of the area through the development of a training workshop."

At a meeting of Dublin City Council's planning committee in June 1988, the Amadale Construction application was branded "obscene" and unanimously rejected. Former Lord Mayor of Dublin Councillor Michael O'Halloran said: "These plans bring back tragic, unhappy memories to a community. Relatives have a right to their grief and feelings."

Predictably, Amadale Construction lodged an appeal to the decision with An Bord Pleanála on July 25, 1988. A major showdown between the faceless developers and the Stardust relatives was anticipated when the planning board announced that an oral hearing on the application would be held on October 11, 1988. The Stardust Victims' Committee campaign against the development was stepped up to include the collection of over five thousand signatures by local people opposed to the plan. Politicians were contacted and reminded of their promised support in the run-up to the appeal.

Then, just weeks before the oral hearing, Amadale Construction abruptly withdrew the controversial application. It was understood that it had been shelved temporarily to allow the developers time to take into account the relatives' objections. Although a fresh, revised application was expected to be submitted to Dublin Corporation, the plan never surfaced again.

The real reason for the application's withdrawal is apparent today. Company records in the possession of the authors show that the three listed directors of Amadale Construction Limited were, in fact, Patrick, Colm and Eamon Butterly. The records reveal that the business was incorporated on March 24, 1988, shortly before the planning application for the leisure and entertainment complex was lodged with Dublin Corporation. Why had Eamon Butterly denied having a part in the proposed complex when he was a director of Amadale Construction? Did the Butterlys withdraw the plan for fear that they would be exposed as the applicants during the oral hearing process? Did they believe they could act as directors of a new complex without the victims knowing? Whatever the reason, it now appears that the Butterlys' role in this planning saga was, at best, less than open.

Due to the persistence of the Stardust Victims' Committee, the Butterlys had to restrict their licensing business to the Silver Swan pub, now renamed Skelly's Lounge. Since 1990 the licence for the pub has been held in the name of John Ramsbottom of Bergami Enterprises, yet today the Butterly name is proudly emblazoned across the business park on the site of the tragic disco. A Maxol service station is located at the entrance of the complex.

There was evidence in the Companies Office of Eamon Butterly's involvement in another pub, one outside Dublin. He was listed as the owner of the Riverview Bar in Roundstone, County Galway until early in 2001. When visited by the authors, however, the pub appeared to have been closed for some time. It is understood that this pub has since been sold; the new owners are expecting to renovate it. While a number of the Butterlys' other businesses have been dissolved, such as Amadale Construction Ltd, companies still registered as trading include Butterly Business Park Ltd, Patrick Butterly and Sons Ltd, and Scott's Foods Processing Ltd.

This was a considerable legacy left by Patrick Butterly, despite the Stardust tragedy; a far cry from his days selling turf from a pony cart.

Eleven

The Battle for Compensation

"It's not just a question of money; it's just that someone will have to be held responsible for what happened."

– John Keegan, September 1985.

On May 1, 1985, a new committee was formed to represent the interests of the Stardust victims and their families. At the meeting, in the Camelot Hotel in Coolock, there was an atmosphere of quiet desperation. More than four years had passed since that dreadful night of February 14, 1981. The intervening years had failed to numb the sorrow and hardship experienced by those left behind. For many, financial difficulties exacerbated the pain. Some victims hadn't worked since the fire, while numerous families had lost their principal breadwinners.

The Lord Mayor's Disaster Fund, which raised over £400,000 through voluntary donations, went some way towards helping the affected families. Initially, the money paid for funeral expenses and headstones. In the absence of compensation, it soon became a financial lifeline for many victims who would never work again. Taxi fares, for example, would often be paid from the fund to victims who needed to attend hospital on a regular basis. Some families, however, would later criticise the manner in which money from the fund was allocated. They felt that they were too stringently assessed when applying for expenses. "It was like we were being means tested," says Antoinette Keegan, one of the most seriously injured victims of the fire.

Every claim processed by the Lord Mayor's Disaster Fund was dealt with on an individual basis and the amounts allocated were not disclosed. While most of the disbursements were small, designed to help Stardust victims with miscellaneous, out-of-pocket expenses, there were payments of over ten thousand pounds in a few extreme cases. A number of special payments went to seriously burned victims who needed central heating installed to keep their homes at an even temperature.

The fund, however, was dogged by controversy as the Stardust Relatives' Committee fought an uphill battle to have representation on its board of trustees. According to *The Irish Times* journalist Maurice Walsh, the fund became an object of wonderment and its workings the subject of suspicion. "Rumours circulated as to the amount individual families received," he wrote in 1985. "Among some neighbours, the arrival of a new car or any signs of prosperity were put down to what they had got out of the Stardust fund."

The Stardust Relatives' Committee had disbanded in 1983 after the awarding of malicious damages to the Butterlys. Already disillusioned by their failure to have the Silver Swan pub and Lantern Rooms closed, the £581,496 payout to the Butterly companies was the final insult for Committee members. The Stardust families and victims retreated from the public eye to fight their private compensation cases individually.

By mid-1985 it was clear that they were getting nowhere fast. Despite the fact that 245 writs had been issued by Stardust victims, not a single case had been heard in court. There were other issues of concern, too. One solicitor representing the majority of Stardust cases had sought a payment of a thousand pounds from each client to cover his expenses. Then there was the question of medical cards. In the immediate aftermath of the tragedy, medical cards had been issued unconditionally to the injured by the Government. Since then, some of those fortunate enough to be able to return to work swiftly had their cards withdrawn by the health board. This was despite the fact that many were still attending doctors as a result of injuries sustained in the fire.

Against this backdrop, the Stardust Victims' Committee was formed. During their inaugural meeting, it was accepted that the only way of speeding up the compensation claims would be to highlight publicly the ongoing plight of the Stardust victims as a national scandal. A no-holds-barred approach would be needed to expose the weaknesses of a legal system which had led to such unacceptable delays in hearing compensation claims. The victims resolved to make the Stardust compensation battle a major political issue for the Government of the day, a Fine Gael and Labour coalition under Taoiseach Garret FitzGerald.

John Keegan, who was elected chairperson of the new committee, spoke of the families' frustration at being caught in a legal morass. "We were told two years ago it would take two years to get the cases before the courts," he said. "Now we are told it will take another eighteen months. There are fears among the relatives and survivors that the claims are being stalled until the jury system is abolished and the compensation can be reduced. We have been on to politicians and the Law Society to try and find out what is causing the delay but we are being met with a brick wall."

The reasons for the legal paralysis in bringing the victims' cases to court were numerous and complex. The writs issued on behalf of the Stardust victims involved forty-two different solicitors. The majority of cases were taken by Liam Lysaght & Company and Tony Hanahoe of Michael Hanahoe & Company. As Liam Lysaght and Tony Hanahoe had represented the majority of the Stardust victims during the tribunal of inquiry into the fire in 1981, it was felt they were best placed to handle the compensation cases. Lysaght had first come to the attention of the Stardust families shortly after the fire. He had attended their public meetings in the Black Sheep pub in Coolock and offered his legal advice for free.

There were six main defendants – the State, Dublin Corporation, Eamon Butterly, Patrick Butterly, Silver Swan Ltd and Scott's Foods Ltd – each denying liability. The victims had been forced to attach Dublin Corporation and the State to their actions after it emerged that the Stardust was only insured for £250,000. It was clear that, unless liability could be proven against the State or Dublin Corporation, the Butterlys' insurance cover would scarcely be enough to compensate even one of the most seriously injured victims.

To fully appreciate the reasons for the delay in bringing the compensation cases to court, it is important to understand the nature of such litigation. In a typical High Court case, there are several stages of pleadings. The plaintiff, in this case a Stardust victim, first issues a writ or plenary summons. This states the plaintiff's intention to proceed with a case against named defendants. The plaintiff then issues what is called a "statement-of-claim". This document is usually prepared by a barrister and lists specific details of the plaintiff's claim. The defendant then has to issue a defence in response to this statement-of-claim. Only once a defence has been received can the plaintiff serve a notice of trial; the case then joins a queue for a High Court hearing. If there is a delay in a defence being received, the plaintiff can go to court and force it to be issued.

In the Stardust cases, there were various delays in lodging statements-of-claim and receiving defences. Furthermore, there were problems "discovering" documents, mainly from the State and Dublin Corporation. There was also an apparent reluctance by some solicitors to be the first into court with their claims. For the Stardust victims and their solicitors, the stakes were high. Considerable money would be needed to pursue the actions. Apart from the usual legal expenses incurred, such as barristers' fees, various experts would have to be flown in from abroad if there was to be a realistic chance of winning any of the cases.

The cost implications of bringing the Stardust cases to court were highlighted in February 1985 when solicitor Liam Lysaght sent ninety of his clients a letter seeking a thousand pounds from each of them to cover his expenses. Lysaght had even arranged a bank loan, which he would guarantee, for each client. The loan and the interest would be repayable at the conclusion of a case and be deducted from any damages award. Eighty of his clients availed of the loan offer but the solicitor's demand for money was met with shock and surprise by some of the victims.

Liam Lysaght denied he had "taken a liberty" in organising bank loans on behalf of his clients. He pointed out that he and his firm had already paid out sixty thousand pounds in expenses in relation to the Stardust cases. He said that each case would have to be proved individually, despite the evidence already heard at the tribunal of inquiry. His expenses involved Garda and medical reports, as well as barristers' fees. Although it is not unusual for a solicitor to seek barristers' fees from clients in advance of a court case, the incident sullied relations between Lysaght and many of the victims. After his daughter, Antoinette, received the thousand-pound request, John Keegan formally complained to the Incorporated Law Society. However, the Society responded that Mr Lysaght was justified in asking for the loan. "Basically, he can no longer expend those sums of money from his own funds since to do so would rapidly place him in debt," wrote Chris Mahon, the Law Society's director of professional services. "Certainly, as matters currently stand, Mr Lysaght could not fund the case without some form of contribution from you as the client."

Initially, there had been talk of all the victims' solicitors combining their efforts to bring one test case before the courts. This could have established the key issue of liability and served as a basis for settlement in the other cases. This proposal, however, reportedly met with much hostility at Stardust Committee meetings.

Liam Lysaght told *The Irish Times* that he intended to take each of his 117 Stardust cases separately to court. "The first case may become a test case but I hold the view that all individual cases are different," he said. "They were injured or died in different parts of the premises."

Genuine, legal reasons for the delays aside, the smaller practices made no secret of the fact that they wanted bigger firms like Hanahoe's or Lysaght's to make the running first. "You wouldn't want to be the first to bite the cherry," one solicitor was quoted as saying.

There were good reasons for solicitors to be hesitant about their clients being first into court. As there were a number of defendants involved, it was possible that claims would only succeed against some of them. This invited the prospect of costs being awarded in a defendant's favour at the expense of the plaintiff. There was a real fear that some Stardust victims could end up losing money – even if they were awarded compensation. In the event of an award or verdict being appealed, a further two or three-year delay could be expected.

Speaking at a Stardust Victims' Committee meeting, the Lord Mayor of Dublin, Michael O'Halloran, launched a scathing attack on the "inefficiency" of the legal profession and criticised the delays in bringing the cases to court. "Something has to be done," he said. "The legal profession must have a commitment to the people who suffer, over and above the receipt of fees." When the Lord Mayor's remarks were reported in newspapers, they were treated by the Incorporated Law Society as an official complaint. The society wrote to the solicitors concerned and asked them to respond to O'Halloran's comments. The Lord Mayor was subsequently told by the Law

Society that they would need specific details of an individual complaint if they were to bring the matter further. Their spokesman said it was not realistic for the Lord Mayor to call for a probe. He said that the law, together with the basic requirements of the courts system, were responsible for the delays.

Dublin Corporation was also partly to blame for the legal logjam. The local authority was strenuously defending each action and had rejected many findings of the tribunal of the inquiry in relation to its role in the disaster. In fact, an internal Dublin Corporation report on the tragedy refused to accept that there were serious deficiencies in the fire service and planning department, as outlined by the tribunal. The Corporation also rejected Justice Keane's claim that inspections of the Stardust had been "grossly inadequate". Dublin Corporation intended to argue that it was immune from prosecution in a personal injuries claim by reason of section 5(2) of the Fire Brigade Act 1940. This provision of the Act exonerates the Corporation's necessity to accept liability. Commenting on the Stardust cases, a Dublin Corporation spokesman said: "As a legal entity we have to fulfil our duties. We cannot settle on a human basis; we must settle on a legal basis."

One aspect of the State's defence alleged contributory negligence on the part of the plaintiff. This would have related to those who sustained their injuries while they attempted to rescue others from the burning disco. In effect, it was being argued that they were partially responsible for their own injuries.

Many of Liam Lysaght's cases had been delayed by his attempts to "discover" documents from Dublin Corporation and the State. On August 28, 1985, Dublin Corporation was given three months to produce documents relevant to a damages action being pursued by Stardust victim Jimmy Fitzpatrick. The Corporation had appealed against an order for discovery granted the previous month by the Master of the High Court. The order related to documents concerning planning permission granted in 1977 for the Stardust complex, as well as Fire Brigade and Department of the Environment reports. Mr Justice Murphy said that a series of cases rested on the documentation sought and all plaintiffs and defendants were entitled to have their cases heard without delay. This was a case of very special consideration, he said.

* * * *

The Stardust Victims' Committee organised a number of high-profile meetings and protests to highlight their frustrations, undeterred by the fact that the tribunal of inquiry and its subsequent report had already soaked up much of the public interest in their plight. When a fire on May 11, 1985, at Valley Parade football ground in Bradford, England, claimed fifty-two lives and injured almost five times that number, media interest in the Stardust fire was rekindled back home. As the public inquiry into the blaze got underway in Britain, the Stardust Victims' Committee sent a message of condolence to the British Prime Minister, Margaret Thatcher.

With fire safety issues back in the news, the Stardust Victims' Committee took their campaign to the streets of Dublin, with over a hundred protesters blocking rush-hour traffic on O'Connell Bridge. They then marched on to Dáil Éireann. Spokesman Sean Reinhardt explained that the protest was not just about compensation. "The fact is that, four years after the event, people's suffering and agony is being prolonged by legal wrangles," he said. "In 1981 politicians couldn't promise or demand enough for us. After four years of waiting, we think that those affected by the horror of the Stardust fire have every reason to feel aggrieved and angry."

Charles Haughey, as leader of the Opposition, pledged his full support to the Victims' Committee in their call for a special court to be set up to deal with their claims. At a meeting in Coolock, Haughey declared that the delay in compensating the victims and families was "an absolute scandal". On June 6, 1985, Haughey raised the issue in the Dáil, as over fifty Stardust relatives and victims crowded into the public gallery. During a debate with the Minister for Justice, Michael Noonan, Haughey said it was horrifying that not a single penny had been paid out to the victims or the families of those who died. He appealed to Noonan to look at the possibility of making money available from the Civil Legal Aid Fund so that the victims could pursue their cases. Another possibility, Haughey said, would be to allow them to take their cases before the Criminal Injuries Tribunal, since it had already been established that the fire was malicious. If this was found not to be feasible, Haughey said the Minister should look at the possibility of setting aside a High Court judge to deal specifically with the Stardust cases. If special legislation was needed, Haughey suggested that it could be passed in a single day. "This House can confound its critics by showing that it is responsive to the needs of people," Haughey said. "We can act quickly and expeditiously to get this matter settled; to remove this horrible feeling of injustice and neglect; and take this load off their backs."

Noonan, in his reply to Haughey, said he had tremendous sympathy for the Stardust victims. Matters raised by Haughey, he stressed, were complex and touched on fundamental areas of constitutional law, notably the separation of the executive and the judiciary. However, he vowed to have the issue examined as a matter of urgency. The Minister suggested that, as one case was progressing more quickly than the others, this might be regarded as a test case to expedite matters. Noonan accepted that the people involved felt very aggrieved and he agreed that some method would have to be devised to deal with the matter. If all other systems failed, the Dáil itself would have to accept responsibility for seeing that justice was done. Noonan made it clear that, although he would have the matter examined, it did not imply any commitment on his part.

Michael Noonan's words rang hollow with the Stardust relatives who screamed abuse at him from the public gallery. "You don't care about us – you never have," one woman shouted. "Your words won't make our children come back. They all died in vain." The Stardust families were ejected from the gallery by Dáil ushers. They had made their point in a most public fashion and the outburst was reported in the following day's newspapers.

Some weeks later, John Keegan wrote to the Minister for Justice asking if his examination of the issues raised by Charles Haughey had been concluded. Minister Noonan's private secretary sent the following reply a month later: "I am to say that the Minister has since given further consideration to the matter and he is satisfied that, as the matter is before the courts and therefore *sub judice* [in the course of trial]; and also, as the State has been joined as a defendant in some Stardust cases, it would not be proper for him to make any further comment, other to say that the question of how any particular case might be expedited would be a matter for the High Court, the parties in the case and their legal advisers."

A letter received from the President of the High Court, Mr Justice Liam Hamilton, also brought little joy to the relatives. "So far as I am aware, no application has yet been made to the court on behalf of any of the parties in these cases to have a date fixed for hearing," Hamilton wrote. "A number of cases have appeared in the list but have been adjourned at the request of the parties because they were not in a position to proceed with them. Unless and until any of these cases are ready for hearing and an application is made to the court for a date of trial, there is nothing I can do to expedite the hearing of these cases."

The Stardust Victims' Committee decided that the only way forward was to embarrass the Government into taking action. A plan was hatched to send a delegation to picket the European Parliament or the next EEC summit meeting. Highlighting the Stardust case in Europe would prove costly, so a number of fundraising events were organised by the Committee.

It was around this time that the Committee was reacquainted with Veronica Guerin, the crime reporter who would be brutally murdered in 1996. Guerin first came to the attention of the Stardust relatives shortly after the fire and had been seen taking notes at many of their meetings in local pubs or hotels. It was widely suspected that she was unofficially attending these meetings as Charles Haughey's eyes and ears. Guerin was a devout Fianna Fáil supporter and worshipped Haughey, even naming her son, Cathal, after him. A former colleague and friend of Guerin's clearly remembers her telling him that she had to go to a Stardust meeting for "Charlie".

In August 1985 Guerin was running her own public relations company. Learning of the Stardust relatives' bid to bring their case to Europe, she put together a fundraising proposal. Guerin decided that a céilí and cabaret should be held that October in the Mansion House and claimed that The Furey Brothers, Paddy Reilly, U2's Larry Mullen, Christy Moore and Mary Black had all verbally agreed to perform. An auction was also to take place on the night, with items ranging from autographed U2 albums to continental holidays. Worthy as Guerin's proposal was, legal complications resulted in the cancellation of the function. With over £3,000 already raised through ticket sales, Guerin was informed by her solicitor that the high-profile concert and other planned fundraising activities should not proceed until the issue of liability in the Stardust cases was settled.

* * * *

Meanwhile, frantic efforts were being made at Government level to end the deadlock. For the Fine Gael/Labour Government, the Stardust compensation fiasco was a public relations and political nightmare. The Opposition were having a field day with the Government's failure to act on the issue. Fianna Fáil members on Dublin City Council had tabled a motion calling on Dublin Corporation to withdraw its denial of liability in the Stardust cases. A similar Fianna Fáil motion was planned for the Dáil in relation to the State's defence. The Government was also concerned at plans for a major protest in Dublin that November by the Stardust families and their supporters. Thanks largely to media coverage of the Bradford fire disaster, there was now renewed public sympathy for the Stardust victims.

On September 25, 1985, Taoiseach Garret FitzGerald finally announced details of a Government scheme to compensate the Stardust victims. Those who suffered loss or injury in the fire were invited to have their claims for damages heard by a special tribunal, chaired by Mr Justice Barrington. Two expert assessors would also be appointed to hear the claims, now numbering close to three hundred. A deadline of January 31, 1986, was set for applying to the tribunal. Those who accepted *ex gratia* (meaning "as a favour") compensation had to agree to give up all claims in courts and not initiate further proceedings. However, anyone who was unhappy with an award would be able to reject it within a month and resume a court action. Another condition was that any settlement agreed with victims by the tribunal would have to remain confidential. The State would pay all legal expenses in claims brought before the tribunal. Significantly, those who accepted an award would also have their costs paid for past and ongoing legal proceedings up to November 15, 1985.

The tribunal was the brainchild of the Attorney General, John Rogers, who had to circumvent constitutional and legal difficulties before finalising the scheme with the Taoiseach and the Tánaiste, Dick Spring. One obstacle was the fact that legislation could not be enacted by the Oireachtas on matters which were the subject of litigation. The deal would have to be set up in such a way so as to allow the plaintiffs to pursue their court actions if they so wished. Accordingly, the compensation tribunal would not be allowed to determine the issue of liability. Before details of the new tribunal were announced, there were behind-the-scenes talks between the Attorney General and the Stardust Victims' Committee chairman. In fact, relations between John Rogers and John Keegan were said to be warm and cordial at all times.

The Attorney General told a press conference that the availability of up-to-date medical reports would be an important factor in dealing with the claims speedily. Mr Rogers urged the Stardust victims and families to "lie low" and consider the Government's offer very carefully. They did not have to rush into making a decision, he stressed. Asked why it had taken so long to establish the tribunal, Mr Rogers said it had not been possible for the State to intervene until it had an overview of the scale of the problem and had assessed the progress of the court cases.

Garret FitzGerald said the "many million of pounds" being set aside to compensate the Stardust victims would be paid from the Exchequer. A statement issued by the Government insisted that the establishment of the tribunal could not be construed as an admission of any legal liability. However, it added that "the agony suffered by the victims and their families should be brought to an end as soon as possible".

There was a guarded welcome for the compensation tribunal. Charles Haughey said that, at first sight, the tribunal seemed to be a satisfactory way of dealing with the situation. With its success dependent on the support of the legal profession, the initial reaction from the Incorporated Law Society was also positive. "It has gradually become clear that the sheer number of claimants, and the complex issues of liability which had arisen, were going to delay the final determination of the issues and the payment of compensation for several more years if the claims were all to be pursued through the courts," a statement from the Law Society read. "The responsibility for funding the compensation to the victims could well have ended up with the State ultimately, and its decision to accept the responsibility to meet the claims is welcome."

John Keegan said he expected that the majority of families and victims would opt to go before the tribunal, which he described as "a step in the right direction". For his own part, however, Keegan vowed to continue with his court action. "My family has survived until now and we'll survive another three years," he told *The Sunday Tribune*. "It's not just a question of money; it's just that someone will have to be held responsible for what happened. The law is always made [to] apply for people of a lower standard of life like us, so why shouldn't it apply to the rich and those in authority?"

John Keegan reiterated his reservations about the tribunal at a meeting of the Stardust Victims' Committee a few days later. He accused the Government of trying to dodge the core issue of liability by encouraging victims to have their claims processed through the special tribunal. Other factors relating to the workings of the tribunal would also need to be clarified by the Chief State Solicitor, particularly the potential exposure to costs from the defendants in existing High Court cases. Keegan told the packed meeting that the tribunal was an attempt by the Government to "divide and conquer" the victims and "side-step" the determination of liability. A motion was unanimously passed demanding that the Government pay for the costs of a selected Stardust family in taking a test case to the High Court to establish liability. The Committee also decided to proceed as planned with their November public rally in Dublin city centre and eventually take their case to the European Court of Human Rights in Strasbourg.

Over two hundred Stardust families and their supporters took part in the rally outside the GPO on O'Connell Street on November 2, 1985. The rally heard that the Stardust Victims' Committee was still not in a position to formally recommend the compensation tribunal, as the issue of costs remained unresolved. This was despite the fact that a conditional offer by the Butterlys to waive their costs had been made just days earlier. The conditions attached to the Butterlys' offer were: that the State would not seek a contribution from their companies towards the awards made by the tribunal; that the other parties sued either by the plaintiffs or the Butterly companies themselves would not seek to recover all or part of their costs from the Butterly companies; and that the plaintiffs would discontinue their actions against all Butterly-related parties.

Clearly, the issue of costs presented the biggest stumbling block to victims wishing to opt for the Government's compensation tribunal. The Butterlys had already incurred costs in the region of a million pounds as a result of the High Court actions taken against their companies. If victims discontinued proceedings by accepting a tribunal award, the Butterlys would have been automatically entitled to recover the amount they had spent from the people who brought the cases against them. Even if the victims agreed to drop their claims against all parties, the Butterlys' offer not to recover their costs was dependent, in turn, on the State and other defendants not seeking a contribution from them towards tribunal awards. Victims accepting a tribunal award faced the prospect of having to pay at least £11,000 each in costs to the various defendants in the abandoned Stardust court cases for their share in costs compensation to Butterly and other defendants. The Government's efforts to short-circuit the legal process in the Stardust compensation cases now looked certain to be snubbed by the majority of victims.

As the tribunal got underway at St David's School in Artane in the first week of November 1985, there was finally a breakthrough in the costs impasse. The Attorney General said he had advised the Government that the State would not be able in law to recoup the tribunal's awards from any other defendant in the Stardust cases, as any payment made would be *ex gratia*. His announcement cleared the way for the Butterlys to waive their costs. Dublin Corporation, too, had earlier agreed not to seek costs from any victim accepting a tribunal award. At a meeting of the Stardust Victims' Committee on November 6, 1985, John Keegan said the main problems with the Government's compensation tribunal had been ironed out. "The way is now clear for people to go to the tribunal and not be afraid that they will be given money in one hand and have it taken away for costs in another," he told the meeting.

Solicitor Liam Lysaght also felt that the way was clear for his clients to go to the tribunal. In a letter to John Keegan, Lysaght said he expected that the payments made by the tribunal would be as generous as any award made by the courts. However, under the scheme, social welfare benefits paid to victims since the fire would be deducted from the award made.

Victims would only have to prove that they suffered injury or

loss to qualify for an award, as the issue of liability for the fire
would not arise. This would simplify procedures and reduce the
likelihood of any victim losing a case, according to Lysaght. The
solicitor emphasised, however, that the tribunal would not establish
civil fault or apportion blame for the Stardust fire. "We are keenly
aware of the desire felt by all the victims and their relatives to have
civil liability established," he wrote. "Notwithstanding this, we feel
that the correct legal advice is to recommend the tribunal."

A small number of cases were heard at the special tribunal in
November 1985 before Justice Barrington and two assessors, Senior
Counsel Hugh O'Flaherty and Noel T. Smith, a solicitor specialising
in compensation claims. There was a flood of late applications to
the tribunal as the January 31, 1986 deadline approached. Details
of individual awards were leaked to the media. Despite the fact that
all settlements were supposed to be confidential, newspapers reported
that one seriously injured victim had been awarded over £100,000.
In the first few weeks of the tribunal other awards in the region of
twenty and thirty thousand pounds had also been made in cases not
classified as very serious.

In stark contrast to the trauma experienced in a typical court
case, the tribunal in Artane dealt with the Stardust claims in a humane
and compassionate manner. As Attorney General John Rogers put
it: "There were no courtroom dramatics. The hearings were in private
and the dignity of each claimant was therefore ensured." Some cases
were dealt with in the space of twenty minutes; others lasted no
longer than a day. There were 953 applications to the tribunal, of
which 195 were from persons not present in the Stardust on the
night of the fire. These were mainly from relatives of the deceased
or injured, who claimed to have suffered shock or mental trauma as
a result of the disaster. Of these, only sixty-eight were eventually
awarded compensation; sixty-three were refused; and sixty-four were
withdrawn.

Despite the fact that without John Keegan there might not have
been a compensation tribunal in the first place, he was among those
refused an award. He claimed that he had suffered nervous shock
and severe mental trauma as a result of the Stardust fire, which had
killed two of his daughters and seriously injured another. He had
suffered fits of alcoholism since the tragedy and had also been

convicted of assaulting the owner of the Stardust, Eamon Butterly. He challenged the tribunal's decision against him in the High Court but his claim was rejected. Even though John Keegan was now seriously ill with bowel cancer, he appealed the decision to the Supreme Court. On December 16, 1986, the Supreme Court turned down his appeal. The court heard that John Keegan's wife, Christine, had already received a tribunal award of fifty thousand pounds for nervous shock. Their daughter, Antoinette, had been awarded £66,200 for her injuries. This was in addition to payments of £5,000 for the loss of each of their two daughters. Justice Griffin said that, in his view, the awards were not indicative of a tribunal that had acted unfairly or irrationally. Mercifully, John Keegan would never be told of the Supreme Court's rejection of his appeal. Two days after the judgment, a solicitor called to the Keegans' home to break the news to the family. By then, the Stardust victims' champion had died, having lost a different battle.

By the time the tribunal ended on February 11, 1987 – almost six years after the Stardust tragedy – awards totalling £10.5 million had been paid out to 823 applicants. A further million was paid in legal costs by the State. There had been five awards ranging between £100,000 and £200,000. In the majority of cases, awards between £1,000 and £20,000 had been made. There were twenty awards of less than a thousand pounds. All the awards were accepted by the victims, who did not proceed with their court cases. The amount paid per dead child was just five thousand pounds but this was eventually increased by the Government to £7,500. After a five-year legal nightmare, the issue of financial compensation was finally closed.

* * * *

Hailed as a groundbreaking solution to the victims' dilemma at the time, the tribunal is today remembered with cynicism by many of the victims. The fact that awards were made with a confidentiality clause attached attracted criticism. It meant that the Stardust Victims' Committee was unable to monitor the success of the tribunal or assess individual damages awarded. Families, once united in a common cause, now often viewed each other with suspicion as rumours about the amounts paid out to certain victims did the rounds.

Christine Keegan firmly believes that the compensation tribunal ultimately proved divisive. "The Government put a gun to our heads, if you ask me," she says. "They knew we had no other choice but to accept the tribunal route due to the legal mess we were in. But it was never about money for us – it was about justice. Because we all went with the tribunal, no-one was ever held liable for the deaths of our children. I regret not taking my case through the courts and if I won a million pounds in the National Lottery I would still bring the case of the Stardust to the European courts."

William Mulvey is still a member of the Stardust Victims' Committee. His son, Emmet, received £32,000 for injuries he sustained in the fire; William himself was granted £12,000 for mental trauma. Mulvey remains one of the most outspoken critics of the compensation tribunal and has sought legal advice to see if the matter can be re-examined. "If I knew what still lay ahead of me back then, I never would have gone before the tribunal," he says. "People like my son had their youth stolen away from them and were never the same again. In my opinion, some of the money should have been put into a form of pension to provide security for the future. I believe we were badly advised and railroaded into going to the tribunal."

Solicitor Tony Hanahoe takes a different view. He attended every day of the tribunal and believes it was the most compassionate and speedy way of ending the victims' legal difficulties. "These were everyday, hardworking people who didn't have the finances to pursue such litigation," he says today. "Many of them were very young at the time and others weren't strong enough to go through the trauma of a protracted court case. People were asking at the time why the Government could not step in and do something to help the situation."

Hanahoe agrees that the Stardust victims faced considerable obstacles in pursuing their claims through the High Court, particularly given the number of defendants against whom liability would have had to be proven. He doesn't recall any of his clients being unhappy at the time with an award received from the compensation tribunal. "You have to remember that these were recessionary times in Ireland and the ten and a half million paid out by the tribunal was quite substantial," he says.

Hanahoe remembers actively encouraging his clients to wisely invest their compensation cheques. "I personally invested the money for some of them by opening investment accounts," he says. "Interest rates were very high at the time and investing the compensation cheques would have made some provision for the future. My clients' cheques were handed over at my office. I recall many of them turning up to collect the money, some accompanied by their advisers and consultants. I urged them to let me invest the money for them but some had already made alternative arrangements. I was worried that some of them would not be able to cope with the funds they had received."

There is certainly evidence to suggest that some victims were unable to manage their windfall. After they received their compensation awards, many spent it on holidays or extravagant shopping sprees. The compensation money gone, they settled down to lives dependent on disability payments or unemployment benefits. Some would never work again. A number of survivors turned to alcohol for refuge; others relied on drugs.

There's little doubt that the Government's compensation tribunal dealt adequately and fairly with the issue of financial compensation, in the short-term at least. Its ultimate legacy, however, was that the question of liability for the Stardust fire tragedy was never answered. In this context, fairly or unfairly, the tribunal is viewed by many as a State-backed whitewash and another nail in the coffin of truth.

Twelve

The Forgotten Victims

*"I feel like I'm a shadow of the Stardust. It has taken
my identity away. I'm always trying to break away from
it before it drags me into myself and I go mad."*

– Lisa Lawlor, who was orphaned as a result of the fire.

The Stardust fire left a trail of social devastation in its wake.
Long after the dead were laid to rest, many of the injured and
bereaved would struggle unsuccessfully to come to terms with an
event that had irrevocably changed their lives.

Some of the deceased had come from single parent homes.
Mothers had not only lost their beloved sons or daughters, but their
households' main breadwinners and sources of income. The issue of
financial hardship would only be partially addressed by the
compensation tribunal.

For the survivors and their families, guilt was the real enemy.
Stories of marriage break-ups abounded, as fathers and mothers
sought to blame each other for the deaths or injuries of their children.
There were suicides, too. One girl who had already been compensated
for her injuries had taken her own life, the High Court was told in
June 1986. There had been a further twenty-five attempted suicides
by people affected by the Stardust tragedy, it was claimed at the
same court hearing.

During the Stardust tribunal of inquiry, evidence as to the general
psychological after-effects of the fire on a number of survivors was
given by Professor J. McKenna. Professor McKenna had interviewed
twenty-four survivors, divided equally between the sexes. He found
a wide range of symptoms among them, including: mild anxiety;
general nervous tension; sleep disturbance; nightmares relating to
the fire; phobic reactions; conversion neurosis and hysterical

symptomology; mild and severe depressive reactions; disorientation; and increased alcohol intake. A common reaction to the fire shared by all the survivors, he said, was "personality decompensation". For some, this was a transient phenomenon from which they had made a satisfactory recovery; with others, it was of a relatively long-term nature. Those who lost immediate family members were more severely depressed, obsessional or tense than those who had lost close friends. However, those who had lost friends were more affected than those who had lost no friends or family in the fire.

The circumstances of the fire – particularly its rapid spread and the sudden extinguishment of all the lights – also had psychological consequences for the survivors, in Professor McKenna's view. At the height of the emergency, some only had thoughts of getting out of the building while others had tried to find their friends in the darkness. In the case of some survivors whose friends had died, their escape led to poorly concealed guilt reactions.

Professor McKenna believed that most of the survivors he interviewed would be able, from their own resources, to overcome their particular neurotic reaction to the fire. Some had already surmounted it, he found, and had integrated the event into their general life experience. There was, he warned, the possibility of a post-traumatic neurosis with some, particularly those with a vulnerable personality. He was satisfied, however, that in the majority of cases the fire would become an unhappy memory and would not lead to any radical changes in lifestyle. In the same way, he said, grief reactions to the deaths of close friends or family members should run their course. Where such grief reactions continued, they would, in Professor McKenna's opinion, be generally attributable to already existing personality weaknesses rather than the circumstances of the fire.

However, fourteen years after the tragedy, a report given to the World Congress of the Federation for Mental Health in Dublin found that seventeen per cent of grieving parents interviewed were still unable to come to terms with their loss. The report's findings were presented to the conference at Trinity College, Dublin, where delegates included doctors, psychiatrists, voluntary health workers and mental health experts from Ireland and abroad. Commenting on the study's findings, Dr James Mullaney said the Stardust disaster directly affected forty-five different families. Two years after the tragedy, forty per cent of the bereaved parents had no lessening of grief, he found. Mothers were particularly affected – 77.1 per cent, compared to 52.4 per cent of fathers. They were, in Dr Mullaney's view, "quite an ill population".

Dr Verena Keane, from St Ita's Hospital in Portrane, told the conference she had interviewed thirty-five parents and just over half of them had suffered psychiatric problems since the fire. Twenty eight per cent reported that their physical health had deteriorated, while seventeen per cent said they had no lessening of their feelings of loss since the fire at all.

Tom O'Meara was best placed to fully understand the impact of the tragedy on the local community. Although only in his early twenties at the time, O'Meara was appointed to oversee the administration of the Lord Mayor's Disaster Fund and would help shoulder the burden of the families' grief. O'Meara would un-wittingly become a social worker and confidant to hundreds of the bereaved and injured. Speaking on the current affairs programme "Today Tonight" in 1985, O'Meara said that one of the most frightening statistics to emerge was the fact that there were a number of separated or deserted wives among the forty-five bereaved families. "If you had handpicked all forty-five families, you couldn't really have handpicked forty-five families that could have been more affected . . ." he said. "In each case it was a major breadwinner in the family and it really couldn't have happened to people who were any worse off."

O'Meara also referred to the Northern Irish victims of the tragedy, including Robert Hillick and James Millar, who both perished in the fire. "They were in the Republic, working in generally low-paid jobs," he told the programme. "They were from poorer areas of the North, two from Twinbrook estate in Belfast, one from a very poor area in Derry. They were all from poor families living during the Troubles. It couldn't really have happened to [less fortunate] people in worse circumstances."

O'Meara said the tragedy had different effects on families but almost constantly present were feelings of guilt. "Most of the people involved were teenagers; very few were over the age of twenty. I think there was an awful feeling associated with letting these people go out, letting them leave the safety of the home and go to somewhere they would die. This guilt feeling was accompanied by an almost paranoia about their other children. You had cases where kids weren't allowed outside the door in case they were knocked down by a car. This may seem like a hysterical reaction but it was real for these people involved. Terrible nightmarish dreams went on with people who got out; who saw friends die behind them; who woke up in hospital the next morning and found that their girlfriend or boyfriend or whoever didn't make it. Their friends were in the City Morgue and they were alive. This brought on terrible feelings. We've had at least one wife deserted by her husband on account of this. We've had terrible guilt feelings that have involved parents visiting graveyards at two in the morning."

O'Meara went on to criticise the lack of psychological back-up services for the affected families. He claimed that the victims of the tragedy had been "abandoned" by the Government. "Politicians may argue that they said nothing; they made no promises. But I was there and I heard politicians on both sides say: 'We'll look after you.' People, in their emotional state, took that as meaning they would be looked after both financially and every other way that was required. The simple fact is that nobody, but nobody, has done anything about it. I think it's now time that we stopped using the excuse that there is no money. People must be seen as being more important, in particular the Stardust victims."

The former Minister for Health and Social Welfare, Dr Michael Woods, admits today that the psychological needs of those affected by the disaster were not sufficiently catered for by the Major Accident Plan in force at the time. While on record as saying the Plan went "like clockwork" on the night of the fire, Woods concedes that the lack of counselling for victims and the relatives exposed a weakness in the system. He stresses, however, that this shortcoming was addressed in subsequent reviews of the Plan, along with general improvements in the area of counselling and psychological services that occurred over the years.

The Irish Government's neglect of the psychological needs of the Stardust victims contrasts sharply with how other European countries have responded to recent major disasters. On October 30, 1998, a fire at a private disco party in Gothenburg, Sweden, killed

63 young people and injured 213. The Swedish Government took full responsibility for ensuring adequate support for the victims of the fire. "Help first, costs later," was the Swedish motto.

The official response to the Gothenburg tragedy has set an example for other countries. On January 1, 2001, a fire in a café in Volendam, Holland, killed fourteen people and injured 300. The Dutch authorities immediately allocated a sum of fifty million guilders (equivalent to eighteen million Irish punts) to provide the victims with adequate psychological and social care. This sum will be periodically reviewed to ensure it is sufficient to meet the victims' needs. This funding was provided by the Dutch Government in advance and irrespective of the outcome of litigation by the victims and families against the owner of the café and the municipality of Volendam. The Dutch Government also initiated a study to examine if it should take responsibility for damages not covered by insurance companies or liable parties, such as loss of earnings.

By comparison, Ireland's treatment of the Stardust victims was shamefully inadequate.

* * * *

Evidence of north Dublin's "ill population" can still be found to this day in most of the families affected by the Stardust disaster. Clearly, any improvements in State-funded mental health services came too late for them. Even with the passing of time, the Stardust's forgotten victims can still remember the most minute details of the fire, from the clothes their loved ones wore that night to the last words they heard their children speak. Every story is different, but equally tragic.

For over two weeks after the Stardust fire, an impossible charade was played out at Antoinette Keegan's bedside, as her family and friends struggled to prevent her from finding out that her two sisters, Mary and Martina, had died. The doctors and nurses warned her parents that she was still too weak to be told the truth. "Our parents told us to put on our happy faces," recalls Antoinette's younger sister, Lorraine. "We had to pretend that she looked fine and we'd all tell her how well she was coming along."

Visitors were warned to stick to the story that Mary and Martina were still alive. "There were sixty-five lads in the factory where I worked and every day two or three of them would come up to see me," says Antoinette. "I asked every one of them how Mary and Martina were doing and they all told me they were safe in the Mater Hospital. I started making plans to go and see the girls if I got out before they did."

Meanwhile, her heartbroken parents had buried her sisters in Balgriffin Cemetery. "I was screaming my heart out," remembers her mother, Christine. "I was in floods of tears every day. I had to change from my funeral clothes when I was going in to lie to Antoinette. One day she said: 'Ma, you can put your black clothes back on, I know they're dead.' I nearly fell through the floor."

A priest had seen Antoinette earlier that morning as he was making his rounds. When Antoinette told him her name, he innocently mentioned that her two sisters were deceased. Antoinette waited in disbelief for her parents to visit and when they arrived, she confronted them. "My mother broke down in tears, sobbing that she was sorry but that she wanted to keep me alive," recalls Antoinette.

The shock of hearing the truth spun Antoinette out of reality. "The night I got out of hospital I demanded that my father bring me up to Balgriffin Cemetery to see Mary and Martina's graves. Even though it was freezing cold and I was still very ill, I insisted that I was brought to see them. I lay down beside the graves and asked Mary and Martina to rise up out of the ground and come back to me. I wanted to stay up there in case they came back. In a way I knew they wouldn't but I wanted to stay, just in case."

For years, Antoinette harboured bitter feelings over being told "lies" about her two sisters. Today, the scars on her arms bear testimony to her many suicide attempts. "I tried everything to join my sisters," she admits. "On one occasion my dad had to chase me down the road after I had taken an overdose and force his fingers down my throat. I was in loads of different hospitals after taking overdoses. I've seen the inside of Beaumont Hospital I don't know how many times. Finally, I slit my wrists because I couldn't take it anymore."

Antoinette reckons she'd be dead today only for the birth of her son, Christopher, now aged nine. "He was all that stopped me from killing myself," she says. "I don't believe in God now – I pray to my dad and my two sisters."

The effects on the rest of the Keegan family were equally traumatic. Once a close-knit unit, the stresses and strains pulled each member in different directions. The first Christmas following the fire was a grim affair, as they sat around a table with two empty chairs. The family still dislikes Christmas to this day and wouldn't celebrate it at all, if it weren't for the youngsters in their lives.

Guilt weighed heavily on John Junior's shoulders. "I thank God that John wasn't allowed into the Stardust that night," says Christine. "There's no way he would have left without his sisters. I would have had four dead and injured in the fire. But it still eats him up terribly."

Lorraine remembers one night when John got so drunk that he couldn't get home. "He lay across the road outside the Swiss Cottage pub in Santry shouting that he hoped a car would run over him. Another time we visited the graves in Balgriffin and then went into Campion's for a drink. John again went outside and lay across that road, too. He couldn't accept what had happened to his sisters. To this day he can't talk about the Stardust. He visits their graves but he will not talk about that night."

Lorraine Keegan, just 13 years of age at the time of the tragedy, feels that her teenage years were stolen from her. Her father became obsessively protective about her and his other surviving children. She admits that she's now an overprotective mother herself. "I was denied a normal adolescence," she says. "When I was 19, I was engaged but I still had to be in by half eleven. The first time I smoked or drank in front of my father was at my wedding." Lorraine married Stardust victim Larry Stout, who was badly injured in the fire. They separated acrimoniously within a year.

Having already buried two of her daughters, Christine Keegan could not have known that the Stardust tragedy would later claim another member of her family. "At night John would break down in bed," she recalls. "He would open up and display his real emotions to me when we were alone. When he was with the family, he was trying to put on a strong face, but it would all come out at night in the years afterwards. His attitude was that the girls were gone and he couldn't ever get them back, but he was going to get justice for their deaths. He was determined to make Eamon Butterly pay. That's what kept him going. For years afterwards we would be sitting

together and I would glance up and catch him staring into space. I
would ask him if he was all right and he would repeat over and over
again: 'They died because of greed; it was all for greed.' John never
hated anyone in his life but he hated that Butterly man."

Christine watched helplessly as her husband was slowly
consumed by his hatred. When John became chairman of the Stardust
Victims' Committee, people started calling to the house all the time.
Everyone was asking his advice on making claims, even if they had
only lost a coat in the fire. "When we went out for an evening to try
and get away from it, all you'd hear out of John was the Stardust,"
says Christine. "When he realised that he would never get justice
for Mary and Martina, he became a demon."

A year before he died, John started complaining of terrible pains
in his back. He went to the doctor when he could no longer go to the
toilet. He was immediately referred for surgery and the doctors in
Jervis Street Hospital removed thirty yards of his intestine. It was
too late. He had advanced cancer of the bowel and doctors gave him
a few months to a year to live. Christine warned the hospital staff
not to say anything to John. "I told them he would throw himself out
a window if he found out he had cancer. He had seen his mother die
from it and he said he'd never let anybody close to him die like that
again."

Christine brought John on holiday to Spain to get over the
operation but during the second week there he fell seriously ill again.
A second operation carried out when they returned home revealed
that the cancer had spread to his kidneys. "When I got home, I told
the children that their daddy was going to die," says Christine.
"Antoinette ran out the door and jumped into her car and drove away.
Hours later we found her clinging to her sisters' headstone, begging
Mary and Martina to not let her father die."

Once a strong man who had been fighting fit in the British Army,
John's health rapidly declined. "I could see the flesh walking off
him," recalls Christine. "The second operation was in September
and he was given three months and that's all he got." Just before
Christmas, in December 1986, John Keegan died at home. In his
last hours he said he could see his daughters standing at the gates of
heaven. "He asked us to sing 'The Fields of Athenry'," remembers
Christine. "He looked at me and asked me not to scream in case the

kids got a fright. Then he closed his eyes and he was gone."

There was a massive turnout for the funeral of the man now regarded as the most vocal champion of the Stardust cause. He was given a police escort to Balgriffin Cemetery, where he was buried in the same plot as his beloved daughters. Christy Moore sang at the funeral. "I always asked what had I done to that man upstairs," says Christine. "I will carry three crosses for the rest of my life."

Concerned for her health, the rest of the family pleaded with Christine to drop out of the Stardust Victims' Committee. But, without hesitation, she stepped straight into her late husband's shoes. Christine developed serious psoriasis which the doctors attributed to the stress she was under. She is unable to cry for her lost family any more. "The Stardust took three members of my family and battered the rest, but my tear ducts are dry," she says. "I can cry no more."

* * * *

Jimmy Buckley is buried alongside many other victims of the Stardust fire, in St Fintan's Cemetery, Sutton. His mother, Elizabeth, was shattered by Jimmy's death. "I took it so badly that I couldn't find his grave when I went looking for it the next day," she recalls. Mrs Buckley was unable to settle back into her home in County Offaly after the loss of her son. "The family was in a mess. A few months later, my eldest son, Pat, told me he wanted to get married. I wanted him to cancel the wedding. I couldn't handle it at all. I couldn't understand how everyone was able to sing and dance and laugh while my heart was breaking. I couldn't see any sense in life at all."

Albert Buckley says the Stardust left a terrible legacy for the community of Donnycarney where he was brought up. "Everyone in the area was affected," he says today. "That's where many of the people had come from. Nobody was really right after it. The Stardust was a place where they all loved going to. It was their pride and joy; a place where they had a great time. They went out and bought their clothes and made an effort to get dressed up and look respectable. And that's where they died."

Albert is still angry about the death of his brother but not as much as he was twenty years ago. "It's something I'll never get over. But I'm married with kids and I have my own life now. I've picked up the pieces and moved on. However, I want to make sure my own children have a good life and that they never meet with a disaster like the one we went through. If the kids go out, I want to be able to close my eyes, rest my head and know they are safe."

Albert is adamant that there should never be another Stardust tragedy. "Nobody should have gone through what we went through," he states. "The only people who can ensure something like this never happens again are the people in Government. This year they bought six new fire engines but why didn't they buy them twelve years ago, or fourteen years, or twenty years ago? When I hear people saying that this could happen all over again it makes me feel that the Government are doing fuck all."

* * * *

Jimmy Fitzpatrick was described as a miracle of modern science by the doctors who treated him over the five months he spent in hospital. He suffered third-degree burns across his back, neck, face, most of his arms and both hands. Now married with two children, he lives in a beautiful home in the fashionable north Dublin suburb of Portmarnock. He is currently training to be a solicitor, a career route that was influenced by his various legal battles after the fire.

Jimmy is a lively person with a jovial nature and his face often breaks into a grin as he shares a joke. Those blue eyes that the nurse noticed when he finally regained consciousness in hospital still sparkle, but they cannot distract from the terrible damage his body suffered in the fire. The most visible damage is to his hands. The tendons in the joints were effectively burnt away and most of the fingers fused together. Through successive painful operations, the surgeons managed to construct new hands out of the welded stumps left by the blaze. Around the tops of each arm is a band of undamaged skin which was protected by his rolled-up shirtsleeves.

The doctors in the Mater Hospital were amazed that he lived. With horrendous burns covering a huge percentage of his body, Jimmy was declared the worst injured survivor. A ventilator sucked the poisonous soot from his lungs and other tubes ran from his arms and legs, replacing wasted fluids with fresh liquid every hour. He was sedated on a daily basis to quell the pain. His parents were quietly told that if he didn't respond to treatment, the surgeons would have to consider amputating his arms before gangrene set in.

"My mind was asking me how many days I had lost," recalls Jimmy. "I kept wondering how many days had I been there. For a while I remember thinking that I couldn't be that bad because I had walked into the place. I was sure that a couple of weeks in hospital and I'd be grand; that I'd be out in no time." As the days passed, his confidence faltered. "There were times when I got depressed but I knew it wouldn't get me anywhere. I clung onto this idea that when the bandages came off I would be good as new and that kept me going. Then I was told about my friends."

The first friend he heard about was David Morton. There was a news broadcast about him on the television. Usually the nurses would rush over to turn it off when anything about the Stardust came on but they weren't fast enough that time. Weeks later, a physiotherapist accidentally told him that his best friend, Liam Dunne, had died after four weeks in hospital. "When I saw my parents I told them I knew about Liam. They starting crying. As it turned out, they had gone to his funeral that very morning but didn't tell me because they didn't want to upset me. That was one of the lowest points of my life."

Jimmy would spend more than six weeks in the intensive care unit of the Mater Hospital before he was transferred to the National Burns Unit in Dr Steeven's Hospital. Over five months passed before he saw the outside world again. Jimmy stubbornly believed he would walk out of the hospital the same way he had walked in. "The day finally came when they said I could go home but I was still dependant on a wheelchair to get me around. I said to them: 'Do you remember all that shite about me walking out of here? Well fuck that, get me a wheelchair.'"

It was only when he got home that Jimmy learned the full extent of the Stardust tragedy. "They told me forty-eight had died. I just went blank. All I could think about was my friends. There was Liam Dunne and George O'Connor, Richard Bennett, David Morton, Martina Keegan and Michael Griffiths, who I went to school with." Jimmy is grateful for his surviving friends, who helped pull him through. "There were also the girls from work who my da called

'Jimmy's Angels'. They called up every day after work to keep me going."

Jimmy believes his family was treated very shabbily by the Irish Government in the weeks, months and years after the fire. "I went home incapacitated in a wheelchair. Nobody knocked on my mother's door to see how she was coping. Nobody called on the phone to ask how I was getting on. We were left on our own. Even the banks deserted us. My parents were paying a small fortune in taxi fares going to and from the hospital. They went to the bank, which they had been dealing with all their lives, and asked them for a small loan to see them through. Anybody else seeing our predicament would have given us a small bit of money to get us by. But they said no, they couldn't do that. When the Lord Mayor's Fund was divvied out, my share went straight into that bank. When the day finally came that I could walk, I got out of my wheelchair and stumbled over to the bank. I told them to take the money out, every penny, close the account and stick it up their arses. I never went back. There was a distinct lack of sympathy and that attitude came all the way down the line, from the Government through the social services to the banks. If they were that apathetic at the bottom, imagine how little they cared at the top."

Jimmy eventually accepted an award from the Government's compensation tribunal. "Unfortunately, I went down that road of compensation. In hindsight, I wish I had listened to my father. My dad was totally against taking the money but I was fed up by that time. I wanted to get this behind me and get on with my life. I hate the fact that they just got a carpet and swept everything under it. Not one person was asked if they needed counselling. That turned out to be a major factor in many people's lives. But I thank God that I had strong family support and friends and I made it."

Jimmy feels to this day that he is a living reminder of his friends who died. "A lot of people come up to me in the street and hug me, the Dunnes in particular. I see Liam's mother, Kay. We chat but we don't talk about Liam. There's nothing that needs to be said. I think of Liam whenever I go to a place where there is a ballad night because Liam loved traditional music. He knew all the old songs and he could sing them word for word. I hear David Bowie and I think of David Morton because he gave me my first David Bowie album and

I became a big fan. My sister went to his funeral and she told me his brother had laid out all his albums on each side of the coffin. Whenever I go to Northside Shopping Centre, where I used to work, I think of my friends. They were short friendships but great friendships. I don't doubt that if they had lived we would still have been friends to this day."

* * * *

Jimmy Fitzpatrick's best friend, Liam Dunne, from Coolock, died in the Mater Hospital twenty-five days after the Stardust fire. When his frantic parents, Kay and Jimmy, first rushed to their son's bedside, they knew he was dying. "He was barely with us but I could see his eyes were open a little bit," remembers his mother, Kay. "I said to him: 'Oh Liam, thank God, you're alive, you're alive.' And he looked straight up at me and said: 'Am I ma, am I really alive?' They were the last words he ever spoke to me."

When her husband, Jimmy, heard Liam utter those words he knew his son was dying. "Those words confirmed everything we were afraid of," he says. "I had built up some strength to prepare myself for the worst and with those words he destroyed any hope I had for him." Although their son was relatively unmarked and had suffered only superficial burns to his body, his lungs were failing him. Kay remembers the consultant saying: "I don't know how your son is still alive. He should have been dead a long time ago."

Kay and Jimmy watched their son's health deteriorating as the life support machine managed to keep him alive. "Liam was mumbling in bed, not really talking but making noises and you could hear the hurt in his body," remembers Jimmy. "You could hear the damage in his lungs. They took him off the life support a couple of times but he was too weak on his own." For almost four weeks Liam fought for his life. The trauma of those weeks is indelibly imprinted on the minds of Dunne family members to this day. "We know there are people out there who have suffered the same and worse," says Jimmy. "I don't want to sound like a whinger, but we had that inflicted on us for a whole month; day in and day out. It was sheer agony." Jimmy asked the doctors to spare Kay the grim details but they showed him an X-ray of Liam's lungs and only a tiny proportion was not black. "The doctor told me nobody had ever survived that much damage," says Jimmy.

On March 11, 1981, Liam Dunne became the forty-eighth victim of the Stardust fire. His shattered parents were at his beside as his life slipped away. "Even though we knew he was dying, it was still a shock when it finally happened," recalls Jimmy. "We were standing outside when all the doctors flew past us, nearly knocking the door off its hinges. It was a massive heart attack that finished him off. He had been fighting for so long but the body couldn't carry on. They were trying to resuscitate him but I looked at Kay and told her we didn't have to wait for them to come and tell us he was gone."

The Dunne family desperately tried to come to terms with Liam's death. "We felt that we were out on a limb after he died," says Jimmy. "Everyone else who lost someone in the fire seemed to be getting on with their grieving that month but we had been hanging on." Kay found solace in her local GP who became her "guardian angel". He urged her to talk about Liam. "He knelt down at my feet and said: 'I don't know if I can do anything for you but if I could take your tears away with me I would.'"

Jimmy maintains that his own strength got him through the trauma of his son's death, but he readily admits that his wife has helped him during the worst times. "It would take a lot to shock me but when I'm in the horrors I can rely on Kay to lead me out of it. Every year around the time of his death I get a little contrary. Every day of that month I can see myself sitting on the chair waiting to go to the hospital to see him. It's still a difficult month."

Visitors in the small but comfortable sitting room of the Dunnes' house in Coolock immediately notice the pictures of a cheeky 18-year-old Liam. His father holds on to the memory of his son. "You can have a thousand pictures that will fade but you will never forget your memories. Years pass but that person is still there, eighteen years of age and still young and vibrant. That is a great thing to be left with." Kay and Jimmy paid tribute to their son's gentle and laid-back spirit by etching his favourite phrase onto his headstone. "His attitude to everything was 'ah well'. He'd say 'ah well' about everything. And that's what we put on his gravestone."

* * * *

For eleven days after the fire, the O'Meara family from Coolock held a similar vigil over the blackened body of 24-year-old Brendan. They found him lying in a bed in Jervis Street Hospital, fighting for his life the day after the fire. "We only heard afterwards that Brendan had been seen outside the Stardust a number of times that night," recalls his brother John, who was only a year older than Brendan. "He was a strong lad, having just come out of the Army, and he was running in and out, dragging people outside. But he got caught up in the hall himself and he never managed to get out."

Firemen eventually found Brendan lying face down in the hallway of the ballroom. His back, arms and legs bore imprints of people's feet where he had been trampled after he fell to the ground. One side of his face was badly burnt. "The doctors showed me the burns on his legs and arms where his clothes had melted onto his skin," remembers John. "But he was alive and that was great. After running around all the hospitals it was just such a relief to find him alive."

Brendan was put on a ventilator to help him breathe and he was pumped full of drugs. "He was covered in tubes; there was so much machinery in there you could barely see him in the bed," recalls John. "But the doctors were quietly confident that he would be off the machines in a few days." John left the hospital one morning and returned home for something to eat. He was just in the door when a Garda knocked and asked him to step outside. "We had no father and, as the oldest boy in the house, I was the one who looked out for my younger brothers and sister," says John. "So I went outside to talk to the police. They told me that we had better get back to the hospital. I asked them why and he told me my brother had just died. I couldn't believe it. I just kept saying: 'No way, no way! We left him an hour ago and he looked great.'"

It was a particularly cruel shock for the family. Over the eleven long days they had watched optimistically as Brendan's condition appeared to improve. New skin had formed over the burns on his face and the swelling had left his body. This gave his family the impression that he was getting stronger. They were unaware that the doctors were concerned about the internal damage Brendan had sustained. Eventually he developed abscesses in his lungs from breathing in carbon monoxide. "He fought and fought and fought but his lungs were badly scorched," says John. "He held on for eleven days but his lungs just couldn't cope with what the carbon monoxide had done to him."

When his brother died, John lost his faith in God. "I never prayed as much in my life as I did over those eleven days," he says. "Every morning I would step into the small chapel in the hospital and pray. Then I prayed every evening before I went home. I prayed and prayed and then he died. It was such a shock that I just felt that God had deserted him. I mean, why did he keep him alive for so long and then let him die?"

The death hit the rest of the family equally hard. John's mother and sister had to be sedated by a doctor. "We talk about it today and I don't think the others remember that much about it," says John. "At the time I tried to stay strong because I was the oldest man in the house and I was trying to keep them together." Worse was to come for John when the police told him he would have to identify his brother's body in the morgue two days later. "I was asking them why did I have to do that. They knew who he was and I knew who he was. I didn't understand why I had to do this. The Garda told me I would have to give the body a name. He said: 'Look, there's loads of bodies without identities; we need to say this one is Brendan O'Meara.'"

John's experience in the morgue affects him to this day. "I was led into a room and I heard a voice asking me if that was him. That's the first time I ever remember feeling my legs going from under me. I don't think I ever felt so weak in my life. I went numb and I don't remember what I said to them. But fair play to the police. They brought me next door into Store Street Station and gave me a cup of tea. They explained that there were other poor families who had no body to grieve over. I felt better that we had identified Brendan but it was still the toughest thing I have ever had to do in my life."

John became a member of the original Stardust Relatives' Committee. "We met Charles Haughey in Coolock one night and he shook everyone by the hand and looked all concerned. We thought we might get some answers but then Garret FitzGerald came into power. When they came up with the compensation tribunal it struck me as a move to get us off their backs. In a blur we signed some papers and that was it. It was over. I had tried to stop my mother from signing because it sounded like they were just trying to wash their hands of us. But she was sick of it at that stage and she knew it was going to go on for years. We were told we would get £7,500 for the death. We also got a lump sum for trauma. My mother divided it all up and that was the end of that. It was over, except for our memories.

"I still miss him. We were friends as much as brothers. We used to play darts together in a pub in Coolock and we were really good. Every time I visit my sister, Brendan comes up in conversation. My nieces and nephews all know him as well as they know me. The kids talk about him as if he is still with us. We keep him alive by talking about him all the time. We'll keep him with us until the day we die. In the meantime, we wonder what he would look like. Would he be bald or grey? I'm just starting to go grey and I wonder if he would be too. My sister gave me a frame with a photograph of me and him stuck together and it is my treasured memory. We still have little bits and pieces belonging to Brendan. I have his suit up in my wardrobe. It's out of fashion now. I mean, it's twenty years old but I could never throw it out. I also have his ID card from when he was in the Army. The other stuff we have is worth nothing to anybody else but to us it's priceless."

* * * *

Just before the Stardust disaster, Gertie Barrett felt that, for the first time in her life, things were starting to go her way. For the previous eleven years Gertie had brought up her four children single-handedly after her marriage broke up. "At the time it was socially unacceptable to walk out of a marriage … But I wasn't stupid. I had my priorities. I was determined to keep my children in school."

Gertie's persistence paid off when her eldest son, 17-year-old Michael, got a job as an apprentice plumber. He was paid seventeen pounds a week which, together with the meagre children's allowance Gertie received from the Government, enabled his mother to breathe more easily for the first time in over a decade. Despite his youth, Michael now had his younger brothers and sisters – Carol (16), Mark (14), and David (10) – depending on him for their survival.

Michael was a hardworking young man who never got into

trouble. The only time a policeman ever knocked on the door of the Barrett household was on the morning of Monday, February 16, 1981, to inform his mother that Michael was dead. He had gone to the Stardust disco with his DJ friend, Colm Ó Briain, three nights before but had not come home. Michael would not usually stay at the disco for long. He would help Ó Briain with the equipment and then go home. The only time he stayed behind was on the night the Stardust went on fire. Michael was one of the last of the dead to be identified.

"How I ever lived through those days I'll never understand," says Gertie. "I think the fight was in me from rearing the kids on my own. I still cannot believe that we had come that close to finally getting somewhere when Michael was killed. I asked God: 'Do you realise what you have done?' Michael was the only man in our lives to mind us and look after us. At the time I resented the fact that he was so good. If he had been bad or out robbing cars, I might have understood why God took him, but I was left scrambling for a reason as to why he died. It was like having my own private hell in my own home; a place where we could all go mad. I didn't need to go to the mental hospital. I cannot to this day comprehend the eerie silence walking around that house. I couldn't accept he was dead. A psychologist later told me that when you don't see the remains, you'll always look for your child. I would open the door at 2 a.m. and walk the streets looking for Michael. The other poor children would ask me where I was going in the middle of the night. They would be in their night clothes, wandering the streets behind me. Sometimes the police would bring me home."

Gertie was forced to find a job only a week after Michael died. "Suddenly Michael's wages were gone and the child allowance was gone. The department that looks after the payments demanded that I brought my [children's allowance] book into them so they could take off the fifteen pounds I was receiving for Michael. I hounded them for three months to give me back my book and in the meantime I couldn't pay a bill. The morning Michael was buried, a man came to the door and said he was sorry but he was going to cut off the electricity."

At Michael's inquest one year later, Gertie learned the horrible details of his death. The State Pathologist, Dr John Harbison, said

Michael almost went to the grave without being identified. It was all too much for Gertie. "I had convinced myself for years that Michael was in one piece and then at the inquest I heard the gory truth. I heard how Michael had been cremated. I was shattered after the inquest. It took an awful lot out of me. I went to the doctor to get a tonic to keep me going. While I was there he did some tests and sent me away for ten days but he was back at my door the following morning. I was diagnosed with cervical cancer and I was brought in for an operation."

While Gertie was being treated for cancer, her family finally fell apart. "They all wanted Michael and he wasn't there. Oh God, I couldn't describe it. My son, David, became [very] disturbed in the years after. You could see the disturbance in his eyes. He was crying all the time and sleeping in his clothes. It just wasn't right. One morning he threw himself across my bed, crying: 'Please mammy, find someone to help me ...' When he was sixteen we went to the compensation tribunal and he was asked very hard questions about how he felt about his brother. I was told he just cracked. He opened the door one day and he never came back. There was a priest in the parish who found him and brought him down to the country."

David eventually left Ireland and moved to London. "He'd ring me in tears and hang up. I was afraid he would be washed up in the Thames." Her other son, Mark, also suffered from stress. "I would have sold my house to get Mark calm," says Gertie. "I don't know how he could ever breathe, as he was so tense." After years away from his family, David came home for his sister Carol's wedding in 1991. The event was the first time the family had been together for years. Since then, David has returned home for recent Christmases. "I only feel now, after twenty years, that a little bit of sanity has come back into our lives," Gertie confesses.

* * * *

Madeline Martin and Debbie Osbourne are cousins who both lived in Kilbarrack at the time of the Stardust fire. Both women were badly injured in the blaze and their circle of friends was wiped out. They lost two of their closest companions, Sandra Lawless and Paula Lewis. Another friend, George McDermott, lost his life along with his sister, Marcella, and brother, William.

Madeline was detained for three nights in St James's where she was treated for smoke inhalation. She didn't find out about the death toll until days later. "We hadn't a clue what had happened," she says today. "It never occurred to me that anybody had been killed. Even the badly burned people in the ward didn't look that bad. They looked dirty, filthy with smoke, but they didn't look in a serious condition."

Meanwhile, Debbie was in a serious condition in the National Burns Unit in Dr Steeven's Hospital. She almost completely lost the power of speech. When her mother finally got to see her, Debbie repeatedly asked for her two close friends, Paula Lewis and Sandra Lawless. The passing of time has not erased the memory of that terrible night. "If my eyes were cameras, I could replay it all for you in sharp focus," she says. "Not one memory has faded. In fact, my memory is too good. Sometimes it all comes flooding back. I cringe when I think of the heat; it came from nowhere in seconds. It felt like something physical, something alive. It crawled around you and it was evil. It was out to get you. It was out to kill you."

Debbie's last memory of her friends is seeing them in the middle of the bedlam of the burning disco. "There was smoke everywhere and we got separated in the panic. We were all holding hands but somebody broke through our grip. I was running into tables and chairs, blinded by the smoke. The metal was so hot that when you touched it, your skin would stick to it. Then I found Sandra, lying on the floor. I could see her so well. There was a big glow from the fire and I could see her face glowing in the heat. Sandra was a tough girl; she was strong. But I remember her holding on to me and saying: 'Deborah, I'm going to die, I'm going to die.' And I said: 'No, we're not, Sandra, we are not going to die.' I put my arms around her. I was just so happy I had found her that we just lay down together in the middle of all the noise and screaming. And I can still see her face; I can still see the way her hair was.

"I remember thinking at that moment that I was quite happy to lie there. I realised that I was prepared to die. At first I was frightened, thinking that I wouldn't see my mam again, and that sent me into a panic. I could never describe the effect of knowing you're never going to see your family again. Suddenly I was pushed through a door. To this day I don't know how. I only moved about a foot, or maybe the door just opened, but suddenly I was outside and cold air was waking me up."

The memory of losing her friends still upsets her. "I still see them," she says quietly. "They were my friends who I went to school with. We hung around and did everything together. I never had that experience of growing up with them. I went to school with other people but I missed Paula and Sandra every day. Twenty years later and I wish they were here with me now. There's no question we would still be together. The three of us went out one night and they never came home. I was afraid about coming home from hospital myself because they weren't there. Oh, God, the guilt I went through. I kept thinking: 'I got out and they didn't.'"

Debbie claims the Stardust robbed her of her youth. "We were very innocent. We only went to each other's houses in the evenings. We never drank and we didn't get up to anything. But the fire robbed me of all that. From that day on my whole outlook on life changed. At one stage I was afraid to go out in case I never came home. It was that simple."

Two decades have failed to cushion the pain for her. "Sometimes I don't know how I feel. Twenty years later and I'm still working it out. It's probably something I will bring to my deathbed. Just a couple of weeks ago I was going to London and I was sitting on my bed thinking to myself: 'What if I don't come back?' I have two young daughters now, Stacey [15] and Ann-Marie [10]. I was asking myself over and over what would happen to them. It's bloody awful, but I have to fight that fear every step of the way because that's no way to live your life."

* * * *

The parents of Debbie's friend, Sandra Lawless, battled to keep their large family together after their daughter's death. "For the first year we didn't cope very well at all," admits Bridget Lawless. "Paul's a brilliant husband but his friends took him out and my friends took me out. We had our own grief to deal with. He told me he could hear Sandra's voice when he was driving. She had asked him if she could go out that night and he told me that for years he could still hear her saying: 'Let me go out, dad.'"

The family were told Sandra was dead when she was identified in the City Morgue three days after the fire. They had feared the worst on learning of what had happened at the Stardust. "My husband went down there to see if he could find Sandra and I waited with a friend of mine who had a phone," says Bridget. "Paul came back the next morning and he still hadn't found her. I knew then she was one of those who died because she was the kind of girl who would have phoned or made some contact. I went straight down to the mortuary on Sunday morning and waited there until they showed us some rings and a strap off her watch. I knew then there was no hope."

The reverberations of Sandra's death ripped through the family. "The days and weeks were bleak," recalls Bridget. "It's something I'll never forget. It hit her other siblings very hard. I suppose we were all so wrapped up in our own grief that we never realised what was going on with each other. One of the hardest things for me to accept was that one of my children had died before me. My daughter, Annette, was always very ill from the day she was born and was sick all her life. There were a few times when we thought we lost her. She was the one we watched very carefully. I never suspected that one of the others would be taken from us behind our backs. Sandra's other sister, Valerie, lost her job in a toy maker's in Arbour Hill because she used to sit across from Sandra and she couldn't remain there looking at her empty seat."

Bridget felt that the family was left on their own in the wake of the tragedy. "I had a nun who used to come to me and she was like a counsellor. She helped get me through it. But apart from that we were never offered anything. The only help we got was from the Stardust Fund which paid for the funeral and the headstone. Sandra had helped me bring up the four younger children. The youngest girl, Fidelma, was particularly close to Sandra and it affected her very badly. She was afraid to cry in case she upset us, so she was keeping all her grief in. But we were lucky to have good friends and family who got us through."

The Lawless family still feels Sandra's loss. "We think about her all the time," says Bridget. "Sandra was our third girl and was only eighteen when she died. She was a lovely person and she was very giving. She would have been brilliant with children. We always wonder what sort of children she would have had. We have ten grandchildren, but there is still that massive gap."

Sandra's death hit her father particularly hard. "I went very heavy on the drink for a while," Paul Lawless admits. "For a few years the booze played a part in my life but I'm grand now and I wouldn't be that pushed if I didn't see a drink again. At the time, though, I was going out every night. I couldn't handle Sandra's death and I hit the bottle. But I was lucky that I had the family there for me. I think we have come out of the whole experience in one piece but there's no way I'll get over the Stardust disaster. Most of her mates were killed but the others who are scarred for life are the ones there to remind us of what happened."

Like so many others, the Lawless family were quietly confident that justice would prevail when the tribunal published its findings. They were bitterly disappointed when nobody was held accountable for the tragedy. Paul Lawless states: "Only for Charles Haughey we would never have got a penny ... I know he's been criticised in the past but in my opinion he did something at least."

Paul believes that Eamon Butterly got off on a technicality. "He was the owner and he should have been held responsible. I don't know about jailing him but he should have been heavily fined and had his licence taken away from him so that he could never open another place again. I still believe that he shouldn't have got away like that. I know he didn't go out to deliberately kill those people but he owned the place and he was responsible for getting them out alive."

* * * *

Sandra Lawless' closest friend, Paula Lewis, also died in the inferno. The death of the 19-year-old from Macroom Avenue in Coolock left a void in her family. As the eldest of six children, Paula had devoted her life to helping her parents bring up her five younger siblings. Money was scarce in the Lewis household. Mary Lewis would make a few extra pounds for the family by labouring over an industrial-sized sewing machine for twelve hours a day. Paula would always help her mother as soon as she returned home from her own job as a bookkeeper in a local printing firm.

"I have to say we had our squabbles but she was a great help to my mother," recalls her brother, John, who was 16 at the time. "I think Paula knew how to iron at the age of eight. But she was the leader; there was no doubt about that. When my mam went out to bingo, Paula was in charge. She was the eldest and she was the boss."

John first realised that something had happened to Paula when his father woke him from his bed in the middle of the night and told him to go look for his sister. "Myself and my brother arrived at Coolock Garda Station but things were crazy down there at that stage," he remembers. "They didn't have any information so we went straight to the City Morgue." The brothers found out that Paula was dead when a relative, who was in the Garda Fraud Squad, identified her body. "In my mind, that was a very generous thing to do," says John today. "It saved my father the ordeal. But it bothered my father for years after that he never saw his dead daughter. I think he wanted to see her with his own eyes one last time, but it was probably best that he didn't. As far as I know, Paula was pretty badly burnt."

Even though he was still a young teenager, John felt a strong sense of injustice at how the families were treated in the years after the disaster. "They should have levelled the Stardust instead of having another licensed premises there," he says. He took part in protests outside the Silver Swan and the Lantern Rooms when they re-opened in September 1981. "We shouldn't have had to picket that place to stop Butterly from getting another liquor licence," he feels. "But I went down there because, even though I was still a youngster, I was very aware that there had been no justice served and that someone should have been held responsible. I was convinced that somebody should pay."

A few years later, John attended some of the meetings of the Stardust Victims' Committee, but eventually stopped going because, he claims, they usually degenerated into shouting matches. "People were so upset, and I understand why, but I didn't think we were getting anywhere."

John is adamant that local communities paid a heavy price for being considered working-class areas. "If the families had had any money, the scenario would have been quiet different," he believes.

* * * *

Now aged 21, Lisa Lawlor is too young to remember the Stardust fire, but there is a unique bond that links the bright girl from Glasnevin with the tragedy. Of all the stories of loss and pain that stem from the disaster, Lisa's experience is particularly poignant. She hadn't even reached her second birthday when her parents, Francis and Maureen Lawlor, reluctantly decided to go to the Stardust that fateful night.

Lisa's father had left the Army and was settling down to begin a new life with his wife. They moved into a house in Finglas and doted on their first-born baby girl. The night of Friday, February 13, 1981, would be the first and last time that the young couple visited the Stardust complex. They had hired a babysitter for Lisa but were concerned about leaving her alone, as she had a bit of a temperature. However, a friend convinced the couple to go for a few drinks and leave baby Lisa with the childminder. They would never see her again. Lisa became the only orphan of the Stardust fire.

She was brought up by her father's parents, who she refers to as her mam and dad. Her aunts and uncles became her brothers and sisters, as the family wrapped their protective wings around the infant. When she began asking questions as she grew older, her grandparents told her the story of the fire and how her parents died. When she turned 16 questions began bubbling up to the surface. "I would always tell people: 'Oh, my parents got killed in the Stardust. My parents are dead and I'm an orphan.' But I didn't really know what I was saying," she admits today. Although her grandparents loved her as much as one of their own children and gave her everything, there was still something missing. "At the time it was almost good because I was getting bikes and dolls and prams but my grandparents couldn't really hug me. I suppose they couldn't show me affection because they didn't really know how."

With the questions came the tears. Lisa started crying and couldn't stop. Her concerned grandparents asked her what was wrong but she didn't know. Then she started saying: "I miss my mum and dad." Her grandmother knew the day of realisation had finally come. "Everybody goes through little bad patches when they are a kid but this was different," Lisa insists. "I kept saying to my nanna: 'Please don't die, please don't die.' I was petrified that I was gong to lose her too. I was always worried about what would happen to me if she died." She remembers those feelings as a constant in her life, with very little respite.

Her grandparents realised she needed professional help and Lisa embarked on two years of intensive counselling which, she feels, left her worse than she was at the beginning. "I nearly went mental. I was crying all the time and the counselling made it worse." However, Lisa stumbled on a breakthrough when she decided to highlight her story in *The Evening Herald*. "The newspaper ran a two-page story about me and this Finglas couple, Anna and Denis, saw it. They had been my parents' best friends and when they saw the article they started looking for me. Eventually they got in contact and Denis explained that he had been in the Army with my dad. We arranged to meet over the weekend but I couldn't wait. I loved any connection with my parents, so I went straight over to their house and met Denis on the doorstep. We both burst into tears. I was so happy and sad at the same time. The last time he had seen me was when I was two years old. But when I met him and Anna I realised this was what I needed. I loved their company. I don't know why I ever bothered with counselling."

However, the spectre of the tragedy was still stalking Lisa and she suffered a terrible setback in September 2000 when her beloved grandmother died. The shock brought all her insecurities flooding back. "She was buried on top of my dad and that was awful, seeing the two of them buried together. My granddad was great, even though he was watching his wife being buried next to his son. But I had confused feelings towards my aunts and uncles because they were kind of accepting that she was dead. She was old and they expected her to die, but for me it was devastating. She was the only one who could properly understand me without having to say anything. I'm better now and I can talk about it, but for months after her funeral I couldn't say a word."

Lisa was compensated £86,000 for the deaths of her parents. The money was put into a trust fund and when she turned 18 in 1998 she received an accumulated total of over £200,000. When the initial rush of happiness wore off, she realised the money came with its own price. "I skipped across the Ha'penny Bridge the day I got that cheque but two weeks later the feeling was gone," she says. "And now I'm left with the tag. I overhear people saying: 'There's the one who got the big claim.' But people don't know why I have that money. I've heard so many times that people are jealous because I have nice clothes or a nice apartment but they don't understand. I feel like I'm a shadow of the Stardust. It has taken my identity away. I'm always trying to break away from it before it drags me into myself and I go mad."

The compensation has done little to ease her anger towards Eamon Butterly. "There was a picture of me in the paper after I lost my parents and I had the face of an orphan. I don't believe he ever wondered about me, about how that little girl in the picture was getting on. We never got a 'sorry', not even a card over all the years. Nothing. He never made a gesture. I think it would have made such a difference if he had. All those years growing up on my own, I wonder sometimes if Butterly ever realised the damage he did. I really believe that he hasn't a clue about what happened to me. I missed out on so much. Everything. You really need that bond with your parents but I missed everything with them – birthdays, my Holy Communion, Christmases. Even the little things, like coming in and saying: 'Mam, I'm home.' The anger is there and it'll never go away."

Lisa has never met the man she holds responsible for her parents' deaths and she doesn't know what she would do if she ever did. "I don't know if I would fall to his feet and weep or if I would attack him," she confesses. "But I wouldn't kill him. I wouldn't want to see him dead because I wouldn't like to put his family through what we went through. All I want is for him to stand in front of me and apologise, to admit he was at fault."

Lisa feels she has a long way to go before she finally rids herself of the Stardust nightmare. She firmly believes she can put a gap between herself and the horrific memories by having her own family. "I want a baby," she reveals. "It's a want I've had since I was six. It's not natural to want a child at that age but it's been with me since then. I think that by having a baby I will finally be able to leave the Stardust behind me and get on with my own life."

Thirteen

Honouring the Dead

"This is the final act of reparation."

– Charles Haughey at the sod-turning ceremony
for the Stardust Park, Coolock, May 30, 1991.

In tandem with their painful battle for compensation, relatives of the Stardust victims campaigned tirelessly to ensure that their loved ones would never be forgotten. It would take more than a decade before successive governments would make good on a promise to provide a permanent memorial to the victims. The campaign to honour the Stardust dead is a story of political inaction, broken promises and profound disappointment. It is also a story of censorship.

Like so many others, Irish folk singer Christy Moore was deeply affected by the tragedy. Despite the countless number of gigs he had played at home and abroad since his career began in the 1960s, the singer remembers exactly where he was performing when he heard about the Stardust. At the time he was a member of the critically acclaimed band Moving Hearts, who were playing the first of two concerts in Thomastown, County Kilkenny, on the night of the fire. The band considered cancelling the second show on account of the news but decided to go ahead and donate the proceeds from the gig to the Stardust disaster fund. A minute's silence was observed during the emotional performance.

Christy Moore was renowned for performing socially conscious songs that covered topics ranging from Travellers' rights to the conflict in Northern Ireland. No stranger to controversy, Moore's emotive ballads about the hunger strikes of 1981 had been banished from the airwaves. One of his most popular songs, "Back Home In Derry", was banned after the authorities realised it was written by the late Bobby Sands, who died on hunger strike three months after the Stardust tragedy. The reaction on that occasion was no surprise to him; but little did the singer realise how much trouble he would be in over a song about a fire in Artane.

In the aftermath of the tragedy, Moore wanted to write a song in honour of the Stardust victims. The song's title came about after he heard a mother tell a television reporter that her daughters went out one night "but they never came home". Moore's acute sense of injustice was heightened by the fact that the families and victims had yet to receive any compensation for their loss and suffering. By this stage, the Butterlys had settled their malicious damages claim against Dublin Corporation. The irony of the situation was not lost on the singer. "I used Woody Guthrie's technique of describing events to create not only a picture of the event, but also the underlying inequalities and injustice and blatant discrimination that still exist in our society," Moore would write in his autobiography in 2000.

Reflecting on his inspiration for the song, Moore says today: "I just heard a mother utter that sentence and it struck a chord and convinced me that I needed to write about this. I wrote it because I try to write songs about things that affect me. I'm always seeking to express my anger or my sorrow or my sense of fun by the things I see around me. I certainly wanted to write about the Stardust because, I suppose, I felt there was a class thing involved as well."

After enjoying considerable success during the 1970s, both as a solo artist and with the influential traditional Irish group, Planxty, Moore hit the big time in 1984 with his "Ride On" album. His eagerly awaited follow-up, "Ordinary Man", was released during the summer of 1985. The Stardust song, "They Never Came Home", was the second last track on the album. The record was officially launched in O'Donoghue's pub on Merrion Row in Dublin on July 29. Journalist Gene Kerrigan, writing for *Magill* magazine at the time, noted: "There were good songs on the album, but the most deeply felt was 'They Never Came Home' – the Stardust song."

Just days after the launch, Clive Hudson of WEA, Moore's record label, received a letter from legal representatives of the Stardust owners. It claimed that "They Never Came Home" was in contempt of court. It contained, they contended, a comment on matters still before the courts. The album was already in the shops and had been receiving considerable airplay on the radio. WEA was forced to recall the album from record stores and contact radio stations, urging them not to broadcast the song in case the allegation of contempt was upheld in court.

Moore was stunned. It had never entered his mind that the song would be the subject of a legal challenge. "In my innocence, I didn't have the song vetted," he recalls. "We just went for it and I suppose that anybody who had heard the song prior to its release assumed that it was telling the truth."

Around twelve thousand copies of the "Ordinary Man" album had been produced and distributed. It was already number one in the album charts. "They Never Came Home" was also the B-side of Moore's latest single, "Delirium Tremens", which was number six in the Irish music charts. Despite every effort by WEA, both the album and single were still available in a number of Dublin outlets by the time the contempt case came before a special vacation sitting of the High Court on August 9, 1985. While Moore found the prospect of a court case stressful, he was more concerned about the effect it would have on the Stardust families. He feared they would think the song exploited their situation. He needn't have worried – many of the families turned up in court to express their solidarity with the singer.

"I was scared going into the High Court," Moore wrote in his autobiography. "It was a high-profile case and I was most concerned, both about the likely outcome and how the case itself would affect the bereaved families and the injured survivors. The court was thronged and there in the front seats were many, many families of the lost and injured who came out to support me. It was a very moving realisation for me."

The High Court action was based on complaints that the song would prejudice the outcome of litigation concerning over two hundred compensation claims resulting from the Stardust fire. The application by Eamon Butterly, Scott's Foods Ltd and Silver Swan Ltd was for an order of attachment for contempt against the author and singer of the song, Christy Moore; the song's producer, Donal Lunny; and WEA (Ireland) Ltd, distributors of the record.

Counsel for the Butterlys, Brian Dempsey, said it was his clients' view that some of the words of the song interfered with and prejudiced issues which were *sub judice* (in the course of trial) and in contention already before the courts. One lyric complained of went: "Just how the fire started, sure no-one can tell." This was inaccurate and misleading, Mr Dempsey argued, as Dublin Circuit Court had determined that the fire had been started maliciously in the case taken by the Butterlys' companies against Dublin Corporation. Mr Dempsey said it was also inaccurate to state, as the song did, that "hundreds of children are injured and maimed, and all just because the fire exits were chained".

An affidavit from Christy Moore was read to the court stating that the subject of the song was, in his opinion, a matter of public and social concern. He had been unaware that the subject matter and the words were capable of prejudicing the applicants' defence in other proceedings. If this was the case, it was deeply regretted. But counsel for the Butterlys claimed that the overall effect of the song was that, through the media and on radio, almost everyone in Dublin would come to know as a definite "fact" that the locking of the doors had caused the Stardust deaths.

Sean MacBride, Senior Counsel for Christy Moore, Donal Lunny and WEA, said his clients did not concede that there had been any contempt of court. He pointed out that the Stardust tragedy had been widely discussed and debated in the public arena for over four years, including on a number of television programmes. MacBride also described WEA's efforts to stop distribution of the record as soon as they learned of the contempt proceedings.

Mr Justice Frank Murphy found that the song was in contempt of court. He ruled that the lyrics of the song contained statements or comments calculated to prejudice a fair trial of matters already before the courts, in particular the statement about fire exits being chained. Justice Murphy said the question of punishment did not arise, as the statements complained of had been made unintentionally. He also took into account the fact that the parties involved had endeavoured, to the best of their ability, to limit the damage by stopping publication and halting distribution of the record.

The decision came as a bitter blow to Christy Moore and his record company. As a result of the verdict, the song could no longer be promoted, distributed or sold in shops in Ireland. "They Never Came Home", effectively, had been banned. "I was shocked," says

Moore of the verdict. "I didn't know to what extent the court case was going to run. I was very innocent of such things."

As a dejected Christy Moore and his manager, Mattie Fox, left the High Court, they were approached by a Stardust victim, Larry Stout, who wanted to say thanks to the singer. Stout, a painter/decorator whose hands were badly disfigured in the fire, felt the song had done the relatives and victims a great service by highlighting their case. Christine and John Keegan, who had also attended the court hearing, shook hands with the singer. "Thanks Christy, thanks," was all that Christine could say.

Although no punishment was imposed on Christy Moore or the record company by Justice Murphy, the implications of the ruling were punitive by their very nature. Thousands of singles and albums were recalled and destroyed by WEA and a new song had to be recorded in place of "They Never Came Home" for a reissued version of "Ordinary Man". Costs in the High Court case were also awarded against the singer. The whole episode cost Christy Moore, his manager and the record company in the region of £100,000.

Ironically, the new song was recorded close to where the Stardust had been, in Nicky Ryan's Artane studio. Up against a three-hour deadline, the song was literally recorded as it was being rewritten. The result was "Another Song Is Born", a powerful, emotion-packed ballad with an angry undercurrent. "I suppose in a way it's a much angrier song," says Moore. "Sometimes when you have to find a different way to say something, you find a more powerful way to say it."

The banning of "They Never Came Home" has not discouraged Christy Moore from writing controversial material. Since then, however, all songs are first vetted for potential legal problems before finding their way onto his albums. After the victims' compensation battle was over he continued to play the Stardust song live in concert, although it was suggested that he shouldn't sing the offending line. "It doesn't matter if that line is in or not," insists Moore, "because in a way it's not a particularly important line in the song. With or without that line, the song still tells the truth."

Christy Moore continued to support the Stardust victims over the next two decades. In 1986 he performed at the funeral of Stardust Committee chairman John Keegan. On a happier but equally emotional occasion in 1993, he sang "They Never Came Home" at the official opening of the Stardust Memorial Park in Bonnybrook, Coolock.

To this day Moore feels that in the case of the Stardust tragedy, justice wasn't served. "I think the whole thing was handled very cynically," he says.

* * * *

Coláiste Dhulaigh in Coolock is a secondary school located in the heart of the community where the Stardust tragedy hit hardest. Many of the victims were students at the school; others were former pupils and graduates. The two places are intrinsically linked by the events of that dreadful February night.

Phil McHugh was a year head at the school when the Stardust took the lives of fifteen students. Today he is the school's principal. He still remembers those who died as hardworking individuals who were determined to succeed, despite the uncertainties they would face in the economically bleak landscape of the outside world.

"Back then the first pre-employment courses were set up in response to the economic difficulties of the time," McHugh explains. "They were geared towards getting people into jobs and some students were doing very well from them. It would be inaccurate to describe the attitude of teachers and pupils as optimistic but we were certainly tackling a problem that existed. At the same time the horizon didn't look great for these kids and there was no prospect of immediate success in the days long before the Celtic Tiger. It was a case of doing your best and hoping that something would turn up."

McHugh taught English to Antoinette Keegan's younger sister, Martina. "She was doing a secretarial course after the Inter Cert," he recalls. "She was in a very good class and they were all very pleasant to work with. I also remember her sister, Mary, who had done very well in the Leaving Certificate. They had bright, long lives ahead of them. Mary was one of three girls from one Leaving Cert class the previous year who all perished. The other two were Mary Kenny and Paula Lewis. I remember them clearly. They haven't faded from memory."

McHugh remembers waking up on the Saturday morning and

hearing that the Fianna Fáil Ard Fheis had been called off. "I didn't know the Stardust well but we quickly realised what had happened. Myself and a few teachers went around the pubs on the Sunday to try and find out who had been involved. It took a number of days before we found out the scale of the tragedy. We knew something big had happened but it took some time before the terrible details began to emerge. We were totally shocked. It was so difficult to comprehend. Being involved in a school, we were conscious that we should be doing something to help but I remember thinking: 'Well God, what do I do?' I remember a feeling of helplessness."

Empty desks in many classrooms were a daily reminder of the impact of the disaster on the school. Senior students came up with a plan to develop a memorial garden within the grounds of the school. With the co-operation of school staff and management, work on the garden got underway.

The memorial was officially unveiled by the Lord Mayor of Dublin, Councillor Dan Browne, on February 17, 1983, just over two years after the Stardust fire. "We have wished for some time to do something special to reach out to our people and tell them that we will never forget the pain in their hearts," a statement from Coláiste Dhulaigh read. "The memorial garden is our way of saying this. May it be a lasting memorial to our young people who have died so tragically."

A second memorial to the Stardust victims was unveiled in 1987 at the newly opened Beaumont Hospital. Located at the main entrance to the hospital, the memorial was made possible through a £30,000 donation from the Lord Mayor's Disaster Fund, which had been set up in the week following the fire. The impressive monument is inscribed with the names of the forty-eight young people who died in the fire.

While both the Coláiste Dhulaigh and Beaumont Hospital memorials were deeply appreciated by the Stardust families, a campaign got underway to lobby for the development of a memorial park in honour of the victims. While such a proposal was on the Stardust Victims' Committee agenda for many years, it was overshadowed by their fight for compensation. Proposals for a memorial on the site of the Stardust had been abandoned due to objections from a number of families. It was decided that a park would serve the dual purpose of honouring the dead and providing badly needed local amenities, such as football pitches.

The campaign for the park was spearheaded by Christine Keegan, chairperson of the Stardust Victims' Committee since the death of her husband, John. A site had been acquired by the Committee from Dublin Corporation on Glin Road in Coolock for the purpose of developing a park. Architects Kevin and John McCarthy had designed the memorial garden, with a water fountain and eternal flame as its centrepiece. The plan also incorporated a youth centre and sports facilities. All that was missing was the money: the park plan would cost an estimated £1.5 million.

* * * *

During the 1989 general election campaign, Christine Keegan was visited by a familiar face, Taoiseach Charles Haughey, who was canvassing in the area. Haughey had been one of the first politicians to visit the scene of the tragedy on that dreadful St Valentine's Day in 1981. He had held back tears as he pledged a full inquiry into the disaster. In the mid-1980s, as leader of the Opposition, Haughey had raised the question of compensation for the Stardust victims in the Dáil, repeatedly pursuing the Minister for Justice, Michael Noonan, on the matter. To some, Charles Haughey was the undisputed champion of the Stardust families. Others, such as John Keegan, viewed Haughey with deep suspicion, as he believed there had been a State-assisted cover-up of the cause of the disaster: no evidence has ever been adduced to support this theory.

Numerous attempts had been made over the years by the media and Stardust victims to link Haughey with the Butterly family. They had certainly moved in the same business circles. *The Irish Times* discovered a connection between the Taoiseach's former accountancy firm, Haughey Boland and Company, and Mensaform Ltd, of which Patrick Butterly was one of the original directors and shareholders. One of Haughey Boland's directors, the late Des Traynor, was also a major shareholder in Mensaform.

Haughey had severed his connection with his accountancy firm in 1966 when he became Minister for Finance. Traynor became a director of Mensaform in 1968, a year after it was first registered as a company. Traynor would later go on to handle Haughey's personal financial affairs. His less than transparent dealings on behalf of his boss would lead to years of public scrutiny of Haughey's extravagant lifestyle by the McCracken and Moriarty Tribunals.

There were personal links with the Butterlys, too. Haughey's long-time friend, solicitor Pat O'Connor, was a brother-in-law of Patrick Butterly. O'Connor himself was a controversial figure, having been famously accused – but later acquitted – of voting twice in the 1982 general election for Haughey. O'Connor was Haughey's election agent at the time of the "two votes" scandal. Although there is no suggestion that O'Connor had any part in decisions relating to the Stardust tragedy, the mere connection, however tenuous, between Haughey and the Butterly family was enough to cause suspicion within the ranks of the disgruntled victims.

In his memoirs, Patrick Butterly gives the impression that he profoundly disliked Haughey. While admitting to being a staunch Fianna Fáil supporter, Butterly sniped that it was a great party "until that fella Haughey got a hold of it". Butterly admitted that Haughey's former accountancy firm carried out work for his companies, so it is reasonable to assume that the two men knew each other personally. It appears, however, that relations between Butterly and Haughey soured in the immediate aftermath of the fire. Butterly also appears to have been close to the former Taoiseach, Jack Lynch, who was ousted from power by Haughey in 1979. Butterly clearly resented Haughey for establishing the Stardust tribunal of inquiry so quickly. He was particularly bitter that he had to cough up almost a million pounds for legal costs after the tribunal ended, while the victims had theirs paid by the State.

Dr Michael Woods, who was a member of Government at the time of the disaster, is dismissive of talk about links between Haughey and the Butterlys. "He had dealt with a lot of business people, so I couldn't answer for him on that," he says. "As I would have seen it, he dealt with a lot of people in north county Dublin in business and would have known them in that way but I don't know what type of relationship he had with any of them. In relation to the Stardust, I believe his motives were absolutely sincere. I honestly believe that he was totally shocked and traumatised and it affected him really deeply. He couldn't come near the morgue. He'd visit the families in their homes or in the hospitals but he just couldn't bring himself to go there."

The various conspiracy theories surrounding Haughey's role in the Stardust were at odds with his unstinting support for the relatives when they were seeking compensation. He had also objected to the renewal of a number of licence applications by the Butterlys for the Silver Swan bar. Yet, despite his public record on the Stardust, Haughey would continue to be under suspicion. Christine Keegan recalls her late husband remonstrating loudly with Haughey in their living room. "John asked Charlie directly if there was any truth in the rumours about his connection with the Butterlys. Charlie emphatically assured him that there was no truth whatsoever in these allegations."

Just two days before the general election of June 1989, Haughey was back in the Keegans' livingroom. He nodded enthusiastically as Christine showed him the architects' drawings of the Stardust park plan. Although advising that the cost of the project be reduced, Haughey made a pre-election promise to provide funding for the park. It was a promise that would come back to haunt him. "He seemed genuinely impressed by what we had done and, although he wanted a price cut, he gave a definite undertaking to provide funding," insists Christine Keegan.

Haughey found himself back in power after the June 1989 election, albeit in coalition with his archenemies, the Progressive Democrats. By April 1990 there was still no official movement on the park proposal. Fine Gael TD, Michael Joe Cosgrave, tabled a Dáil question to the Taoiseach asking him to account for the delay. In a written reply to Deputy Cosgrave, Haughey stated that since there was already a memorial for the Stardust victims in Beaumont Hospital, no money for the park project would be forthcoming.

The news came as a crushing blow to the Stardust Victims' Committee. "It is the Government's responsibility to provide this park," Christine Keegan told *The Northside People* newspaper. "I lost two daughters in that fire and all I have to show for it is a burnt ring and necklace. You don't have to be well educated to fight the Government on this one. We are demanding National Lottery funding for our park and I don't care what I say or do – we'll get that money."

By the time of the tenth anniversary of the Stardust disaster, there was still no sign of funding for the park. Haughey's refusal to honour his pre-election promise was described as "a national disgrace" by William Mulvey, a member of the Stardust Victims' Committee. "We were lied to and Haughey has betrayed our trust," he said. The Committee vowed to take the park campaign to the streets. The then editor of *The Northside People*, Joe Lowry, wrote to prominent politicians and community figures urging them to publicly express their support for the memorial park. Pledges of support for the park proposal were published over the following weeks by the paper, including one from the Taoiseach's son, Councillor Sean Haughey.

On February 14, 1991, Charles Haughey received a Valentine's Day card from the Stardust Victims' Committee. As the card was delivered by hand to his palatial new offices at Government Buildings – built at a cost of seventeen million pounds to the taxpayer – members of the Committee picketed outside, cold but defiant. "We're not leaving until we get a meeting with Haughey," Christine Keegan told reporters. "I don't feel too good today – I never do on February 14 – so I hope we won't be waiting too long." A secretary from the Taoiseach's office approached the Committee and told them that Haughey was too busy to meet them. The protest continued and twenty minutes later the same secretary returned and informed the Committee that the Taoiseach would meet them at 1 p.m. Christine Keegan burst into tears of relief.

During the meeting, Haughey reiterated his support for the park but stressed the need for the project to be scaled down. The plan had already been reduced in cost from £1.5 million to £400,000 by Dublin Corporation. The park would now be located on Greencastle Road. Again, Haughey promised to consider allocating Government funding for the project. Later that week in the Dáil, Haughey was urged to give a definite commitment on the Stardust park. He responded that, having met with the Stardust relatives, he had indicated his support for a suitable memorial but on a greatly reduced scale. Haughey described the original proposals put forward for the park as "extravagant". In hindsight, this was a bit rich coming from a man who spent thousands of pounds on Charvet shirts and entertaining his mistress in exclusive restaurants or on board his yacht.

The Stardust Victims' Committee made it clear that they wanted the first sod turned on the memorial park before the local elections in June 1991. They were determined that the park would not be used as a political football or vote-catching exercise by any party. Just one month before polling day, Haughey came up trumps. The Taoiseach told relatives that the revised plan for the twenty-six-acre park was now ready and finance was finally available.

Not for the first time in his controversial career, Haughey had gone from villain to hero. He was even invited to turn the first sod of the park at a special open-air Mass on the site of the park on May 30, 1991. Speaking at the ceremony, Haughey said: "The Stardust was a terrible tragedy which shattered the local community here and will never be forgotten. You can be assured that the memory of the Stardust tragedy will always be in the minds of those in our society who have responsibility for the fire service and other safety measures. They must work to prevent such a tragedy occurring again." Haughey added that the park would be "the final act of reparation".

* * * *

As work on the park got underway, members of the Stardust Victims' Committee celebrated one of their few victories in the ten years that followed the fire. Their celebrations were to be short-lived, however, as a row over funding for the park erupted between the Government and Dublin Corporation. In October 1992, work on the park was suspended as funds for the project dried up. The memorial, as it stood unfinished, took on the form of a local eyesore. Dublin Corporation laid the blame squarely with the Government. Its spokesperson, Noel Carroll, explained that the Corporation was committed to spending a total of £130,000 from its own resources on the park. He said there were to be three annual instalments of £100,000 each from the National Lottery. However, just one instalment had been received and the Department of the Environment informed the Corporation that the rest of the money would not be forthcoming. "This must be the greatest three-card trick of all time," quipped Carroll.

The Department of the Environment hit back, accusing Dublin Corporation of "holding the State to ransom on this sensitive project".

The official reason given for the discontinuance of funding was because of "the mid-year correction of public finances". A spokesperson for the Department of the Environment said: "Much of the work involved is being done or could be done by the Corporation's own parks department. A very substantial body like Dublin Corporation, which is in a reasonably healthy state, should have no real difficulty in providing the necessary funding out of a current spending budget of well over £200 million."

But Noel Carroll was not letting Dublin Corporation take any of the blame for the cash crisis. "We were told that the funds would be available to complete the park but the Department of the Environment has now done a complete U-turn and has effectively let both us and the local people down," he said.

The Stardust relatives were devastated but refused to accept defeat. "We've been promised that the park will be completed and we intend to see that promise fulfilled," Christine Keegan told *The Northside People*. Charles Haughey, who had since resigned in disgrace to be replaced as Taoiseach by Albert Reynolds, was said to be surprised and disappointed at the suspension of funding by the Government. Senator Sean Haughey issued a statement condemning the hold up. "Given that there is now doubt as to whether the project will be completed, it would have been better if it never got underway at all," he said. "The families have every right to feel upset at what has happened. Work undertaken to date at the site is now deteriorating and it would seem that public monies have, in fact, been wasted."

Yet again, members of the Stardust Victims' Committee found themselves picketing outside Government Buildings. In the face of mounting political pressure, the Government suddenly found money for the project and a sum of £100,000 was immediately sanctioned. This followed a meeting between members of the Stardust Victims' Committee and the Minister for the Environment, Michael Smith. Within days of the meeting, work had recommenced on the park. "I'm only too aware that the upcoming election had a lot to do with speeding everything up," stated Christine Keegan. "But that doesn't matter to us. The fight is over and we've got what we want. I couldn't have gone on like this for too much longer. Hopefully the next time I'll have to deal with a politician will be at the official opening of the park."

The Stardust Memorial Park dream was finally realised on September 18, 1993. As the sun shone down on Coolock, the park was officially opened by the Lord Mayor of Dublin, Tomas MacGiolla. The park included an all-weather floodlit football pitch and a modern playground for local youngsters. Its centrepiece was a bronze statue depicting a young couple dancing, surrounded by 48 jets of water flowing into the illuminated fountain. The sculptor, Robin Bewick, had been chosen through a competition and the Stardust families were delighted with his finished work. The project was a credit to Dublin Corporation's parks department staff and the FÁS Community Youth Training Project members who had assisted with the work. The eventual cost of the park ran to almost £500,000.

Hundreds of friends and relatives of the Stardust victims attended the opening of the park. The Archbishop of Dublin, Dr Desmond Connell, was chief celebrant at a special Mass held earlier in Bonnybrook to honour the occasion. There were emotional scenes as members of the Stardust Victims' Committee were reunited with their old friend and long-time supporter, Christy Moore. The singer was too overwhelmed by the occasion to speak. Instead, he sang his banned Stardust song, "They Never Came Home", as eyes everywhere glistened with tears. Christine Keegan thanked everyone involved for making her late husband's dream come true.

Later in the year, Republic of Ireland soccer star Niall Quinn officially opened the all-weather football pitch at the Stardust Memorial Park. Christine says she will never forget his kindness. "He spent so much time talking to local children and signing autographs – he was exceptionally decent to us and I will always remember him fondly for it."

* * * *

As the twentieth anniversary of the tragedy approached, the Stardust Victims' Committee announced plans for a very special night. The AUL complex in Clonshaugh was booked for a "healing event" and invitations were sent to the families of those who had died in the fire. As the evening would cost in the region of £4,500, the committee wrote to ninety-three TDs requesting a financial donation towards their costs. The response was pathetic, according to Christine

Keegan. "After we sent the letters out to politicians I expected to wake up and find the hallway full of envelopes with offers to help us," she said. "I think we received fifteen responses at most, including one from Taoiseach Bertie Ahern, with a measly offer of a hundred pounds – he even wanted a receipt." The Committee described the poor response from politicians as "a direct insult" to the memories of those who died.

The Stardust relatives were forced to highlight their grievances through the media. "Stingy", "tight-fisted" and "miserly" TDs were lambasted by members of the Committee on television and in newspapers. *The Northside People* launched an appeal on behalf of the healing event's organisers, which received an overwhelming response from the public. The cash crisis was averted when a local businessman, Pat McNamara of Elite Kamino International Transport, donated two thousand pounds towards the night. Christine Keegan said she was touched by the response to the appeal from the local community but remained bitter that politicians, yet again, had let the Stardust families down.

The majority of families contacted by the Committee attended the healing event, which went ahead as planned on the twentieth anniversary of the Stardust fire on February 14, 2001. With trembling hands and quavering voice, Antoinette Keegan picked up a bouquet of flowers and called out the name of each victim. Bravely, she struggled through the roll call of the dead, which seemed like it would never end. The strain almost proved too much when she reached the names of her own sisters, Martina and Mary. Rounds of applause greeted each name: Mary Kennedy, Kathleen Muldoon, Robert Kelly, Julie McDonnell...

Despite the tragic undertones of the event, the atmosphere on the surface was one of quiet celebration of life carrying on. "It's good to look around and see so many people getting on with their lives," said Gertie Barrett, who lost her son, Michael, in the Stardust fire. "The last time I saw some of these people they were fainting in Garda stations and hospitals, clinging to the hope that their child was not the corpse covered with a blanket that the ambulance men were bringing in."

Today, the campaign to honour the Stardust dead continues. The Committee is lobbying the Government to designate February 14 an annual day of mourning, with a special commemorative Mass in honour of the victims. "We want the State to officially organise this Mass so we can bring together the forty-eight families who lost children every St Valentine's Day," explains Christine Keegan. "There have been special Masses for the soldiers who have died in the Lebanon, yet there is no official State or church recognition of the Stardust tragedy."

One family's recent attempt to honour their Stardust dead emerged in the media in August 2001. Their deceased loved one is one of the five unidentified male victims of the Stardust disaster. Because the five individuals could not be positively identified at the time of their funerals in February 1981, their graves in St Fintan's Cemetery, Sutton, north Dublin, are simply marked by numbers.

At the time of writing, there was rising speculation that the five bodies could be exhumed for DNA testing. The DNA issue arose when the family of one victim requested permission from Fingal County Council to erect a headstone above where they believe their loved one lies. Representations were also made on the family's behalf to the office of the Taoiseach, Bertie Ahern. The coroner's office, which was contacted about the headstone request by the Taoiseach, brought up the question of advances in DNA technology.

Although Fingal County Council approved in principle of the erection of the headstone, it warned that the grave could not be used as a family plot in the absence of positive identification. The Council, too, raised the possibility of DNA testing to help resolve the matter. If families could ascertain which of the five deceased was a relation, then each body might be re-interred under headstones bearing the victim's name.

Exhuming the five bodies would also require the permission of each of the other four families involved. A licence would then need to be issued by Fingal County Council. This latest development in the story of honouring the Stardust dead first broke on Dublin radio station 98FM. More details were later uncovered by *The Sunday Times* and this book's authors. Any proposal to exhume the bodies would require the permission of all five families. At the time of writing, at least one family said they would be opposed to such a move.

Fourteen

Could it Happen Again?

*"Could the Stardust happen again? The answer is yes.
It could happen any morning."*

– Michael Fitzsimons, chairman,
Chief Fire Officers' Association, July 2001.

T he Stardust fire caught Dublin off guard. The city authorities
and the emergency services were left reeling in the aftermath
of the tragedy. As the smoke settled over Artane on the morning of
February 14, 1981, a disturbing picture of blatant mismanagement,
shameful neglect and sheer ignorance emerged from the ashes.

Despite concerns expressed by increasingly nervous city
managers and Government-appointed working groups regarding low
morale and poor efficiency in the fire service during the 1970s, little
had been done to stop the rot. Tragically, those in authority paid no
attention to the ominous warning signs.

Just two years before the Stardust disaster, An Foras Forbartha
(the development authority) had questioned regulations governing
fire safety precautions for public places of entertainment. It would
later be claimed by the Chief Fire Officers' Association that the
Stardust tragedy could have been avoided if fire safety guidelines
recommended in 1979 by An Foras Forbatha had been implemented
by the Government. The report contained specific guidelines aimed
at preventing the rapid spread of fire in public resort buildings. It
recommended that such buildings would have to satisfy rigid "flame
and ignitability" criteria.

Even before the Stardust tragedy, a former chairman of the Chief
Fire Officers' Association, Brian McMahon, warned of the fire
hazards posed by discos. He said that escape routes were inadequate
in many venues. In addition, furnishings and decorations were often

combustible and could lead to a rapid spread of flame. After the Stardust fire, McMahon solemnly described the disaster as "predictable".

Other warning bells had been ringing throughout the preceding decade. On August 2, 1973, a fire swept through the Summerland Entertainment Centre in Douglas, in the Isle of Man. It was believed to have been started maliciously by two youths. There were hundreds of Irish holidaymakers among the two thousand people inside the massive complex when the fire broke out. A total of forty-nine people died in the blaze, one more than the Stardust death toll eight years later. Over eighty people were injured, many of them critically. The rapid spread of the flames was blamed on materials used to cover the interior of the building. Witnesses claimed in newspapers that emergency exits were locked. Back home in Ireland, the Chief Fire Officers' Association prophetically warned: "This country is open to a Manx-type tragedy."

In August 1980, less than seven months before the Stardust disaster, an electrical fault in the Central Hotel in Bundoran, County Donegal, resulted in a fire that killed ten people. John Boden, the manager of the nearby Palace Hotel, blamed low water pressure for contributing to the deaths. He told a newspaper that it had taken firemen over an hour to connect their hoses to a local swimming pool where an alternative water supply had to be sourced.

On Wednesday, November 5, 1980, just three months before the Stardust tragedy, a fire was discovered by two brothers attending a wedding reception in the Clare Manor Hotel. Located on the Malahide Road, the hotel was less than two miles from the Stardust complex. The fire started in the kitchen and the hotel was vacated immediately. There were no deaths or injuries. On the same night, over one hundred guests fled the Springfield Hotel in Leixlip, County Kildare, after grease fell onto a gas cooker and ignited. The fire was extinguished quickly by the Fire Brigade and there were no casualties.

However, the stage was now set for the worst fire disaster in the history of the State. The Stardust tragedy would be directly responsible for a radical overhaul of the emergency services in Ireland.

* * * *

The report of the tribunal of inquiry into the Stardust fire made unsettling reading for the authorities when it was published almost twenty years ago. It outlined, in detail, a sweeping range of changes which would be vital if another disaster on the scale of the Stardust was to be prevented. The report has become the yardstick by which all developments in the fire services in Ireland are measured. Although many of its recommendations have been implemented over the last two decades, veteran fire experts today claim that significant shortcomings in the system still remain which give rise to the potential for another Stardust-type tragedy.

The tribunal of inquiry was satisfied that the Stardust fire highlighted the inability of an outdated Dublin Fire Brigade service to deal with a disaster of such magnitude. Not one aspect of the service escaped criticism. In essence, the report called for a complete overhaul of the Fire Brigade, along with updated regulations on fire prevention. The tribunal report commended the firemen who had fought the Stardust fire for their bravery, but it was unrestrained in its criticisms of the fire services in general.

Nor could the bravery of individual firemen conceal the fact that Dublin Fire Brigade was crippled by disorganisation and internal strife. The lack of a proper command structure at the scene of the Stardust fire resulted in some firemen having to act on their own initiative in the battle to save lives. The firemen were seriously hampered by their lack of knowledge of the immediate area. They were unaware, for example, of the existence of a static water tank; this lack of information led to an interruption in the water supply at a crucial stage in the rescue operation. Nor did they know where the local fire hydrants were located, which caused further serious delays in fighting the blaze.

As established by the tribunal, even when the firemen eventually connected the hoses to the hydrants, the water pressure was, for a time, inadequate. No cutting equipment such as oxy-acetylene or compressed air-cutters – standard equipment carried today – was available. A lighting rig had to be supplied by Dublin Airport authorities because the equipment available to the fire brigade was not adequate. There was an insufficient number of breathing apparatuses to go around; some firemen had to take huge gulps of air before they ran into the burning building.

As the scale of the emergency became apparent, the Major Accident Plan was implemented. However, some serious deficiencies emerged in the operation of the plan on the night. The tribunal said it was not acceptable that some of the bodies who were furnished with the Plan should have differing versions of it. It found that the Garda Síochána should have ensured that all officers manning the Central Control room in Dublin Castle had an adequate working knowledge of the Plan.

According to the tribunal, the lack of proper training, from senior management down to the firemen, contributed significantly to the shortcomings in the rescue operation at the Stardust. The report highlighted the fact that firemen and officers had not received any instruction beyond their initial eleven-week recruitment training. There were occasional ad hoc courses available that instructed on the use of breathing apparatus equipment, but these were attended on a voluntary basis only. The tribunal concluded that, in the absence of ongoing compulsory training, there was a dependence on actual experience gained from fire-fighting operations. The fact that most of the firemen who attended the Stardust had never experienced an inferno on such a scale exposed the harsh reality that this method of training was completely inadequate.

At the time of the Stardust tragedy, the entire structure of Dublin Fire Brigade was riddled with failings. The communications systems that were in place to alert a unit of the brigade to an emergency were dangerously out-of-date. Although the initial alarm call from the Stardust disco was received at 1.43 a.m., the first unit did not arrive until 1.51 a.m. This seemed "unduly lengthy" to the tribunal, considering that the first fire crew on the scene had travelled a distance of just 2.5 miles (4 km) from Kilbarrack in light traffic conditions.

The tribunal report described an inspection of the central control room of Dublin Fire Brigade headquarters in Tara Street in 1981, shortly after the tragedy occurred. "The shabby and makeshift appearance of the room made it difficult to believe that it was the nerve centre of all the fire-fighting operations for the capital city and the largest concentration of population in Ireland," it stated. "Such surroundings can only have a demoralising effect on the personnel who are required to operate the control room. The fact that (these conditions) have been tolerated for so long reflects a most disturbing absence of concern on the part of senior management of Dublin Corporation."

It was not only the frontline units of Dublin Fire Brigade that were suffering from a distinct lack of organisation and resources in the years before the Stardust fire. The Fire Prevention Department, which dealt with all applications referred to the Fire Brigade under the Planning Acts and bye-laws, was seriously understaffed. There were only eight officers available in the early 1970s to carry out annual inspections of every dance hall, registered club and gaming establishment in the city. By 1980, this number had halved. The acting head of the department said at the time that there should have been at least twelve inspectors working full-time. To put the situation in perspective, when Patrick Butterly sought planning permission to convert his factory in Artane into an entertainment venue in 1976, his was just one of a total of 1,127 applications referred to the overworked Fire Prevention Department that year.

The tribunal established that the backlog of referrals to the Fire Prevention Department had dire consequences. The fire requirements of the department were not communicated to the planning section of Dublin Corporation until after a decision to grant permission to Butterly for the conversion of the factory had already been made. This meant that the Stardust was allowed to open without any inspection whatsoever by a member of the Fire Prevention Department of Dublin Fire Brigade.

The responsibility for fire prevention and fire-fighting in the State rested with the local authorities under section 2 of the Fire Brigades Act, 1940. If a complaint was made in writing to the Minister for the Environment alleging that a local authority had failed to comply with the Act, the Government had the power to order an inquiry and direct the authority to take steps to remedy the matter. The Stardust tribunal established that a general complaint had been made by the Chief Fire Officers' Association to the effect that no local authority in the State had fulfilled its duties, as laid down by the Act, by 1981.

* * * *

Today, more than twenty-one years after the Stardust tragedy, fire safety in Ireland is undergoing a period of change. In recent years there has been a flurry of activity by local authorities and the Government as more money and resources are ploughed into the country's cash-starved fire services; antiquated legislation and fire regulations have also been updated considerably.

At the Chief Fire Officers' Association annual conference in May 2001, the Minister for the Environment, Noel Dempsey, said it was time to commission a wide-ranging strategic review of the fire service. He stressed the importance of the impending findings of the "Review of Fire Services and Fire Safety in Ireland". The review was undertaken by independent consultants Farrell, Grant and Sparks Ltd, and was still awaited by the Minister at the time of writing. "The importance of the review cannot be over-emphasised, as it will shape the future of the fire service for many years to come," Minister Dempsey said.

The review took place against a backdrop of increased investment in the fire service. The capital allocation for the programme in 2001 was fifteen million pounds, the highest on record and an increase of seven million pounds on the previous year's provision. In the same year, Minister Dempsey revealed that local authorities had been invited to submit tenders for the purchase of forty new fire engines at a total cost of eight million pounds. This would bring the total number of new fire engines he had approved in the last four years to just over a hundred.

Since the Stardust tragedy, the Department of the Environment has spent over £110 million on capital investment in the fire service. Four hundred fire engines have been purchased and 115 new or reconstructed fire station projects have been completed. In order to keep abreast of technological developments, the fire authorities, in conjunction with the Department of the Environment and Local Government, are developing a new computer-based call-out mobilisation and communications system (CAMP), which will eventually cover the entire country. Dublin is one of three regional control centres that will benefit from this system by 2002. The others are Limerick (Munster region) and Castlebar (West region).

There have also been sweeping legislative changes in the area of fire prevention. In April 2001 Minister Dempsey admitted that

existing licensing arrangements governing indoor events like rock
concerts did not cater for issues such as safety and crowd
management. Accordingly, he announced the publication of the
Licensing of Indoor Events Bill. When enacted, the legislation will
ensure that public safety and crowd management will be taken into
account when an event goes through a new licensing process. One
of the provisions of the new Bill is the right of a fire inspector to
impose conditions on the granting of a licence. It empowers the fire
authorities to inspect indoor events while they are being organised
or in progress. Crucially, it enables a fire officer to serve a notice
cancelling an event if they have reason to believe that the organisers
have contravened any of the conditions.

The Licensing of Indoor Events Bill, 2001, clarifies the powers
of fire authorities to prosecute for summary offences. It will put,
beyond doubt, the onus of duty on owners of a premises to make
adequate provision for fire safety. In effect, the new Bill is the latest
measure brought in to close off loopholes and anomalies discovered
in the Fire Services Act, 1981. Introduced in the immediate aftermath
of the Stardust disaster, this Act replaced the seriously outdated Fire
Brigade Act, 1940. Essentially, the 1981 Act assigned responsibility
for fire safety on a premises to its owners and occupiers. Regulations
introduced under this Act in 1985 made the locking of exits and the
blocking of escape routes from places of assembly a specific offence
punishable by a fine of up to ten thousand pounds or six months of
imprisonment.

Although the Act strengthened the powers of the authorities, it
was still legally weak. The Chief Fire Officers' Association found
that legal challenges to the Act meant it was an almost impossible
task to punish anyone who transgressed it, except in cases of very
serious offences. Michael Fitzsimons, the chairman of the
Association, warned in 1999 that the ability of the fire authorities to
prosecute for overcrowding of premises and the locking of doors
was almost impossible. "Fire safety notices are now all but
unenforceable," he said. "Unfortunately, that Act is now all carrot
and very little stick."

Another key recommendation of the Stardust tribunal of inquiry
resulted in the introduction of the Building Control Act, 1990. The
lack of appropriate regulations governing the construction of new

buildings and changes in existing properties had been severely criticised by the tribunal at the time. Under new laws, a Fire Safety Certificate is now required for all new buildings (except housing), extensions, material alterations and changes of use.

Responsibility for compliance now rests firmly with the owner, builder and designer of the building. However, enforcement of the regulations is primarily the duty of the local authorities and it was in this area that a significant flaw in the Act was uncovered. While the introduction of the Fire Safety Certificate was certainly a step in the right direction, it was not backed by the staffing numbers required to enforce it. In 1999, 1,037 planning applications were referred to the Fire Prevention Department in Dublin Fire Brigade. The department was in a position to process only 222 applications that year. Dublin Corporation admitted in March 2001 that the operation of the Fire Safety Certificate process imposed an extra workload on its fire prevention staff, "sometimes to the detriment of other work".

Further improvements in fire education were consolidated in 1988 with the establishment of the National Safety Council. The body is primarily charged at national level with publicity campaigns about fire safety. The council addressed one concern expressed by the Stardust tribunal twenty years ago: that the impact of the disaster would "fade with time". The Council promotes public awareness in relation to fire safety by continuing to disseminate a programme of information at school level and through the media. The Council is comprised of the Fire Prevention Council, the Road Safety Council and the Water Safety Council. Fire authorities get involved with the National Safety Council in public information campaigns. One ongoing prominent message relates to the installation of smoke detecting systems in private houses. Over half of the annual budget of the Council comes from the insurance industry.

Although one major recommendation of the tribunal – the establishment of a national fire-fighting training centre – was never acted upon, Dublin Corporation's training centre, located in the north city suburb of Marino, has gone some way towards improving the situation. The centre provides a dedicated base for the extensive and detailed training of new recruits. Other improvements in levels of training are due, in part, to the efforts of the Fire Services Council (FSC). Since it was established in 1983, the Council has held over two hundred training courses at local level for over four thousand fire service personnel. This highly focused programme supplements the training carried out by individual fire authorities and helps ensure that recruits are kept fully up-to-date with new technological developments in the area of fire service equipment.

The National Safety Council today strives to ensure that all firemen have the necessary skills to deal with the changing and evolving circumstances in which they operate. At fire-fighter level, every man is now provided with breathing apparatus and given regular, routine refresher training. At educational level, too, the fire service has been totally turned around. All ranks now have the opportunity to pursue courses leading to university degrees through a Dublin Corporation scheme.

The flaws exposed in the Major Accident Plan by the Stardust fire have since been significantly addressed by the formulation of the Major Emergency Plan for the Dublin Metropolitan Area. It involves the co-operation of the Garda Síochána, the Eastern Regional Health Authority, Dublin Corporation, the Irish Marine Emergency Services and the local authorities of South Dublin, Fingal, Dun Laoghaire-Rathdown, Meath, Kildare and Wicklow. Under section 26 of the Fire Services Act, 1981, all local authorities in the country are required to have Major Accident Plans.

Regrettably, by the time of the twentieth anniversary of the Stardust fire in February 2001, ten local authorities had still failed to approve fire and emergency procedures as part of their plan. Three local authorities – Limerick Corporation, Athlone UDC and Dundalk UDC – had not drawn up any plans at all; seven other local authorities – including Dublin Corporation – had yet to approve their plans, although they had been drafted. At the time of writing in July 2001, the Department of the Environment was unable to confirm whether it had received the Corporation's Major Accident Plan. Dublin Corporation also failed to clarify to the authors the position in relation to the Plan.

* * * *

Despite significant improvements in the fire service over the last twenty years, it is clear today that much work remains to be done.

As recently as May 1999, Dublin Corporation was served with notice of strike action by firemen who were determined to improve their rates of pay and conditions. A senior Fire Brigade officer told *The Irish Mirror* newspaper that the planned industrial action was not just about money and warned that the city was on the brink of another Stardust disaster. "People will think we are being selfish by going on strike for money," said the unnamed officer. "But this is about safety and how we can look after this city. Dublin is a tinder box just waiting to go up."

The industrial unrest offered a behind-the-scenes glance at a shabby fire service teetering on the brink of falling apart. Reports in national newspapers described how Ireland's fire brigades were the worst equipped in Europe. It was revealed how the cash-strapped service was forced to purchase fifteen-year-old fire engines discarded by the British fire service, which were originally destined for the scrap heap or Third World countries. According to *The Irish Mirror*, one of Dublin Corporation's most recent purchases was a 1984 Dennis fire engine from Britain. The authorities had originally planned to donate it to Nigeria when it was decided that it was too dilapidated for use in the United Kingdom. In fact, firemen complained that it took over two minutes to start some of the engines. Other vehicles still in use in Dublin had been in service at the Stardust fire eighteen years earlier. Despite their age, they were still on the road, some with over 750,000 miles on the clock.

In 2001 one-third of Dublin Corporation's fifty-eight frontline vehicles were more than fifteen years old, even though international experts agree that fire engines should not be used for more than twelve years. At the time of the industrial dispute, the chairman of the Chief Fire Officers' Association, Michael Fitzsimons, said the fire service was seriously over-stretched and under-resourced. He confirmed that much of the equipment available to the Fire Brigade was outdated.

Fitzsimons has a favourite phrase that he uses to describe the state of Ireland's fire service today: "It's working but it's creaking." According to the man who represents members in 37 fire authorities across the country, the fire service is struggling to deal with simple day-to-day demands. Something that keeps him awake at night, he admits, is that there be may be a challenge out there that the Fire

Brigade is not up to meeting. "You never know if you can face down a challenge until you are up against it," he says.

Although the fifteen million pounds spent on the capital funding of fire services across the country in 2001 sounds like a lot of money, it pales in comparison to what the Chief Fire Officers' Association estimates is the least amount that needs to be spent. "Capital funding in the order of £28 million is required to maintain the fire service at an acceptable level of operation," the Association stated in a recent report. "This figure does not take inflation into account or any new developments." The Association's ballpark figure of £28 million simply covers vehicles, stations and large equipment. "When you are talking in terms of fire service expenditure in this country, it works out as ten times less than what our neighbours in Europe are spending," reveals Fitzsimons. "In terms of years, we are so far behind that it is difficult to imagine the European services at the stage that we are at now."

Fitzsimons explains that many European fire brigades were developed after years of wartime experience which this country avoided through its neutrality. "We have had so few big fires in our recent past that the Stardust has become something of an urban legend," he says. "But what people have to be aware of is that the money you spend on your fire service should not be based solely on the size of fires, or how many they attend every year, but the availability of the emergency response; in other words, how quickly a unit can get out there to deal with an emergency. In cities, we have to be rolling out the doors with all the necessary equipment within sixty seconds of getting a call."

Fitzsimons concedes that training for firemen has improved, but almost exclusively in Dublin and other urban centres. "It has come on in leaps and bounds over the last twenty years," he admits. "For a start, Dublin Fire Brigade have their very own training centre in Marino and it is a fantastic facility for them and the other counties that use it. That centre is at the core of the efficiency of Dublin Fire Brigade as it is today. However, the situation is not so rosy when you look at the rural counties. There are some training centres around the country but generally the firemen have to be sent away to be trained. The Fire Safety Council, which is responsible for the training of officers and fire fighters, is grossly under-funded and under-resourced when it comes to manpower and premises from which to operate. Their annual budget is only about £250,000, which is the equivalent of buying one fire engine.

"One of the recommendations of the Stardust tribunal was that we should have a national training college with an inspectorate whose responsibility would be to ensure that fire services across the country meet at least a minimum standard. We don't have the training college and we don't have the inspectorate. This is a subject which was raised by the Stardust report but not taken on board."

According to veteran fire officers like Fitzsimons, no amount of investment in the fire services will make up for the dangerous ignorance of fire safety displayed by the public. The potential for another Stardust is only too evident in the packed pubs and clubs across the country on any night of the weekend. In the immediate aftermath of the Stardust tragedy, there was a heightened awareness of the importance of fire safety among the public at large. Patrons checked the fire exits in their local pubs; owners ensured that exits were clear and there was an adequate number of fire extinguishers available. However, the impact of the Stardust fire continues to fade with each passing year, Fitzsimons believes.

"We have no safety factor out there," he declares. "The most relevant question today is: 'Could the Stardust happen again?' The answer is 'yes'. In the present climate, and this is not a fire service issue – this is a social issue – it could happen any morning. We've had two major tragedies in Europe in the last couple of years. There was the Gothenburg disco fire in Sweden, in one of the best-regulated societies in the world, and they lost more people than we lost in the Stardust. The same thing happened recently in Holland. There's no reason why it couldn't happen here again.

"There are a lot more young people out there now, certainly more than there was in the 1980s. They are drinking and entertaining themselves while putting their lives into the hands of young, inexperienced staff who are trying to cope with this massive influx of money, business and work. Meanwhile, nobody is thinking about the safety of those young people on these premises."

Fitzsimons relates a story that proved to him how little has been learned since the Stardust by today's generation. "I was involved in an organisation called the 'No Name Club' which is run to encourage young people to go out and enjoy themselves without consuming alcohol. They asked me to go in and speak to this group of young teenagers. I was chatting away, talking about the Stardust, and I was met with these blank expressions. So I asked them if they had heard about the tragedy and, out of twenty-five, only two or three put their hands up. It frightened me because I've lived with the Stardust all my life and so have most of the people I know inside and outside the fire service. But these young people, who were the same age as those who died back then, had never heard of the fire or its consequences.

"When you realise there are so many teenagers out there who never even heard the word 'Stardust', you know we have gone wrong somewhere. We have not sold the message of fire safety in the places where these young people congregate. From time to time, we get the message across in primary schools because we get the attention from the younger kids. But we find it very difficult to interact with the teenagers because they don't have the same interest or attention. Because they are more work, we tend to ignore them."

Fitzsimons is highly critical of venue owners who routinely allow overcrowding in their bars and clubs. "The management of these places, where something like the Stardust is likely to happen again, do not have a proper sense of responsibility for the safety of the people on their premises," he claims. According to Fitzsimons, the attitude of the managers and staff of Irish bars and nightclubs, generally, leaves a lot to be desired.

"It must be kept in mind that, on the night of the Stardust, over-crowding wasn't even an issue," he says. "If it had been filled to capacity, never mind overcrowded, the death toll would have been unbelievable. Now when you go out around Dublin and step into any bar or disco, every place is jammed to the doors. You stand in any of these places on any night of the week and consider what would happen if a fire broke out, for whatever reason. It wouldn't necessarily have to be a big fire or involve a huge volume of flames and smoke, but I wonder how many people would die in the panic to get out. How many would be crushed, never mind killed by the flames?

"Overcrowding of premises is a massive issue today. I could go up to any club at one in the morning and ask them how many people are in there and they can just tell me the figure which is permitted by their licence – and there is no way to prove otherwise. There should be something in the legislation which requires owners to have a controlled mechanism that allows him to know how many people are on the premises and, more importantly, will allow us to know if the law has been broken."

Ireland has one of the highest rates of fire accidents in the world. Official statistics show that, on average, there are fifty-eight fire-related deaths every year in this country. Almost eight fires occur for every thousand people. Only the United States has a marginally higher rate in official fire statistics for western countries. However, America spends nearly three times as much per person on prevention than the Irish Government. In the United Kingdom, which has a lower rate of fire incidence, the Government spends twice as much as Ireland.

According to Dublin Corporation, Dublin Fire Brigade attended 46,256 fires in 2000 compared to a figure of 49,690 for the entire country in 1980.

Epilogue – January 2006

This book was originally published on September 25, 2001, in the shadow of the 9/11 atrocities in America. The significance of the previous fortnight's events was not lost on those attending the book launch. In her speech Christine Keegan, Chairperson of the Stardust Victims' Committee, expressed her condolences to the thousands of families affected by the terrorist attacks. Like the other Stardust families, she could acutely relate to the sense of pain, loss and anger being experienced in the United States by the thousands of victims' loved ones.

It was against this backdrop that our book on the Stardust was launched. There had been renewed media interest in Ireland's worst ever fire disaster that year, with February 2001 marking the 20th anniversary of the tragedy. Earlier in the year, RTÉ's flagship current affairs programme, *Prime Time*, had carried a special report on the Stardust. The report not only revisited the pain of the victims; it highlighted the scandalous circumstances of the aftermath of the disaster. It was difficult not to feel a profound sense of anger and shame as the programme exposed a dark side to modern Ireland.

A few days later, at a St Valentine's night healing event in Clonshaugh organised for the Stardust families, talk inevitably turned to the *Prime Time* programme. Most families agreed that, in twenty years of media analysis of the Stardust disaster, the *Prime Time* programme had come the closest yet to getting to the truth, something that had eluded the victims for two decades. This lingering wish to analyse the tragedy in even greater detail was the genesis for our book.

It is something of a media tradition to feature the Stardust tragedy once a year, usually around St Valentine's Day. For the remainder of the year, the Stardust is forgotten, a disaster consigned to history. Until the publication of this book, the Stardust families had only scrapbooks full of press cuttings to commemorate their losses and injuries. We felt that a book on Ireland's worst fire tragedy would be a fitting tribute to the victims and their families. We also wanted to get closer to the truth.

As a result of Ireland's antiquated laws on defamation and libel, it can often be difficult to lay the facts bare, even when the truth appears to be on your side. The Stardust is a highly emotive subject and it was, at times, difficult to take an objective overview. We did, however, attempt to be fair to everyone involved, particularly Eamon Butterly, who is subject to much criticism in these pages. We wrote to Mr Butterly on two occasions inviting him to be interviewed; he did not respond. After failing to hear from him, we approached him as he left his Malahide home one afternoon. When asked if he had received our letters, he replied: "I'm not giving any interviews." He refused to accept another copy of our letter.

This book could have provided Eamon Butterly with the perfect opportunity to finally face down his critics or, if he wished, to express regret for the loss of so many young lives on his premises. Eamon Butterly continues to be demonised by the Stardust victims and families. Some, like Stardust orphan Lisa Lawlor, simply want him to say sorry. Eamon Butterly's failure to co-operate with this book – for whatever reason – was a missed opportunity on his part.

Patrick Butterly went to his grave in January 2000 not having made his peace with the Stardust victims. When we were conducting interviews for this book, a recurring grievance expressed by the families was that Patrick Butterly never publicly expressed remorse or regret for the tragedy. His posthumously published private memoirs, "From Radishes to Riches", mentions the Stardust disaster in just a few paragraphs and refers to it, mostly, in terms of what he lost financially. Patrick Butterly's memoirs were once described by a Sunday newspaper as "a two fingers snub from beyond the grave to the Stardust victims".

How should the Butterlys' role in the Stardust disaster be summed up? It's fair to say that they didn't set out to kill anyone and no doubt suffered their own personal anguish after the fire. On reflection, however, they should never have been allowed to open the Stardust in the first place.

The Butterlys were able to use sub-standard materials when

converting the former jam factory into Ireland's largest entertainment complex and there was no supervision, by either professional architects or engineers, of the conversion work carried out. Patrick Butterly had already, by his own admission, breached fire safety regulations in his first disco, the Two Ages, at the back of his former Silver Swan pub on George's Quay. How could a man with such a poor safety track record ever be allowed to open an entertainment venue for the public? When Butterly's application for the Stardust came before them the earlier episode at the Two Ages should have been a warning to Dublin Corporation's planning department.

Despite the fact that the Stardust was in breach of numerous building bye-laws and fire safety regulations, the Butterlys were able to carry on unchecked and unsanctioned. The only Corporation inspections carried out were by Martin Donohoe, whose brief was to simply check the electrical installations at the Stardust – not fire standards. It is to Donohoe's credit that he raised the issue of locked fire exits and overcrowding with his superiors in Dublin Corporation. The Corporation's response was to simply write to the owners of the Stardust and threaten to object to the renewal of their licence. At the very least, Dublin Corporation should have insisted on shutting down the Stardust pending a full safety inspection.

Disturbingly, there was not one fire safety inspection carried out on the premises from when it first opened in the spring of 1978. More worrying still was Eamon Butterly's recklessly dangerous practice of keeping fire exits locked until at least midnight on disco nights. There's little doubt that the exits caused security concerns for management at the Stardust. The simple solution would have been to station a doorman at each exit during discos to deter gatecrashers. But this would have meant spending money on extra staff; something Patrick Butterly, in particular, wasn't inclined to do easily.

Eamon Butterly's behaviour in the immediate aftermath of the fire was most astonishing, particularly his comments to the media about re-opening the Stardust, which were insensitive in the extreme. Eamon Butterly was also less than co-operative with the Garda investigation and much of his evidence was treated with caution by the tribunal of inquiry into the fire. The D.P.P.'s decision not to prosecute anyone for negligence in relation to the Stardust tragedy was, perhaps, the most bitter blow of all to the families.

In our view, the real scandal of the Stardust story is the fact that the Butterlys were able to remain in the licensed trade and re-open their Silver Swan pub and Lantern Rooms on the site of the tragedy. It beggars belief that a man held responsible for ordering fire exits to be chained could ever be allowed to manage a public venue in any shape or form again. It's little wonder that the majority of the Stardust families now view our legal system with cynicism and suspicion.

This is the same legal system that ruled, in 1983, that the Stardust fire was started maliciously, paving the way for the Butterly companies to sue Dublin Corporation – and, by extension, the Irish taxpayer – for malicious damages. A year earlier, the tribunal of inquiry into the Stardust disaster had been unable to conclusively determine the cause of the fire. It found that it was "probably" started maliciously, a view not shared by Gardaí. It's important to bear in mind that no new evidence had come to light about the cause of the fire when Dublin Circuit Court later decided that it was started maliciously.

More than 25 years after the fire, Gardaí are no closer to finding the supposed arsonist or arsonists involved in the Stardust disaster. The only real line of enquiry was followed in 1988 when a member of the notorious criminal gang, the McKenzies, claimed in a newspaper interview that some of his men had started the Stardust fire. According to the report, the gang had only intended to divert attention while they robbed the nightclub's tills. Despite being hailed at the time by Gardaí as their first breakthrough in seven years, nothing ever came of the lead. Most likely it was just bravado on the part of an anonymous criminal.

Justice Keane admitted in 1982 that the cause of the fire would "probably never be known". His conclusion of "probable" arson has always rested uneasily with the families. Not only did it exonerate the owners of the Stardust of any real blame for the tragedy, it indirectly cast suspicion on every person who was in the disco that night, from the deceased and injured, to the staff on duty.

Following the authors' own investigation into the cause of the Stardust tragedy, it is our contention that the fire was accidental. The contents of a confidential Garda report, in our opinion, seem to point to an accidental origin. This report raises many questions. A number of patrons gave statements about experiencing excessive heat in the west alcove area of the Stardust just weeks before the fire. Why was this information not included in the tribunal's final report? Why was the west alcove area of the Stardust closed on the night of the fire when it was usually open to the public? This is one question that only Eamon Butterly can answer.

One patron, who was sitting beside the sectioned-off west alcove area, recalled feeling cold on the night of the fire. This was despite the fact that the heating system had been on since 9 a.m. the previous day. According to the tribunal report, she remembered the heating coming on at about 1.30 a.m. and she started to feel warm all of a sudden.

What of the sightings of sparks flying across the ceiling of the Stardust during a concert shortly before the tragedy? What about the fact that staff had complained of a burning rubber smell on a number of occasions? Is there an adequate explanation for the sightings of dust or smoke that apparently disappeared when the heating system in the Stardust was switched off? Significantly, the Garda report also revealed that Butterly had to replace a motor in the heating system just weeks before the fire. There is no mention of this in the tribunal report.

It is reasonable to speculate that there was a problem with either the heating system or lighting that directly affected the room temperature in the west alcove area. Could this explain why it was closed off to the public on the night of February 13, 1981?

It is also possible that the fire had originated in the roof space and not on the seats in the west alcove, as eyewitnesses have claimed. A doorman spoke about feeling intense heat above him as he aimed the fire extinguisher at the small flames on the seats. One theory put forward to explain this sensation was that the heat from the flames was simply reflecting down from the ceiling. However, the fire would appear to have been quite small at this stage, scarcely advanced enough to cause the doorman to feel such a strong burning sensation.

Doorman Patrick Murphy, in evidence to the tribunal, described the suspended ceiling collapsing and a large volume of black smoke suddenly pouring into the ballroom. This would also seem to suggest that the fire was already well advanced in the roof space and staff were actually only fighting a smaller, secondary fire in the west alcove.

What about the taxi driver who noticed flames shooting through the roof of the Stardust shortly after 1.30 a.m. that morning? On his arrival, he could still hear music playing inside. This is at variance with the evidence of a doorman who was tackling the fire in the west alcove area. He told the tribunal that the music had stopped before the ceiling collapsed. This would indicate that, although the fire may have appeared to be just confined to the chairs in the west alcove, it was actually raging above the roof space.

There were also serious shortcomings in the forensic investigation by the Gardaí and Department of Justice. In some instances, samples of material which could have proved "crucial" – according to the tribunal – were not taken and important tests were not carried out. This implies that the forensic evidence was incomplete. If so, how could an accidental fire be deemed less probable? Two forensic experts who gave evidence before the tribunal did not rule out the possibility of an electrical fault.

All these questions raise the possibility that an error of judgment occurred in determining the cause of the Stardust fire, both at the tribunal of inquiry and during the Butterlys' case for malicious damages in Dublin Circuit Court.

Since the publication of this book in 2001, the Stardust Victims' Committee has attempted to expand on the theories we put forward regarding the cause of the fire. According to information obtained by the relatives, a number of potentially flammable substances – including cleaning products and boxes of toilet rolls – were allegedly stored in the roof space over the nightclub. They also claim that important evidence relating to electrical problems at the Stardust, dating as far back as July 1980, was not given to the tribunal.

While contact between the relatives' legal advisors and senior Government officials is ongoing, their key objective – a new inquiry into the fire – has so far eluded them. A spokesperson for the

Department of Justice, Equality and Law Reform seemed to pour cold water on their campaign in May 2003 when he told a newspaper: "All I have heard so far are theories, not evidence. Theories are one thing, hard evidence is another."

In a letter to Christine Keegan, dated July 25, 2003, the Taoiseach, Bertie Ahern, wrote:

> 'I note the criticisms which you make of the findings of the Stardust Tribunal. However, I should point out that the Tribunal sat in public session for many days and heard an immense amount of evidence upon which its conclusions were based. After so many years it would be extremely difficult to re-open the findings of the Tribunal in the absence of fresh evidence which would stand up legally. However, you will be aware that a bill to set up simpler forms of inquiry has been published. I note that you are in discussions with the Department of Justice, Equality and Law Reform and you might perhaps raise with the Department the possibility of the new procedure being used for a further inquiry into the Stardust tragedy if further evidence becomes available.'

The official response to the Stardust disaster was always a curious mix of compassion and neglect. The tribunal of inquiry into the fire, while speedily sanctioned by the then Government of the day, had limited terms of reference and precluded Justice Keane from conducting a thorough probe of the fire services. This sparked claims from the victims that the Government, led by Charles Haughey, was orchestrating a cover-up of the circumstances surrounding the disaster. It's a rumour that has continued to dog Haughey to this day, particularly in light of his former accountancy company's business dealings with Patrick Butterly.

The authors wrote to Charles Haughey, inviting him to be interviewed for this book, but he never responded. Again, this was a missed opportunity by a central figure in the Stardust story to set the record straight. In the authors' view, the links between Charles Haughey and the Butterlys were tenuous to begin with. There's little doubt that Haughey was personally devastated by the Stardust disaster and that his concern for the victims was heartfelt and sincere. It's also important to remember that Haughey spent most of the 1980s on the Opposition benches; he was hardly in a prime position to influence Government decisions, let alone a cover-up, relating to the Stardust. As Opposition leader, Haughey played a key role in eventually securing compensation for the victims by putting pressure on the Fine Gael/Labour Government to establish a special tribunal. Haughey has since been exposed as a liar and a cheat in his financial dealings and personal life. But nothing – other than speculation and innuendo – has ever emerged to suggest any wrongdoing on his part in relation to the Stardust disaster or its aftermath.

Although the Butterlys received financial recompense for the fire in 1983, it took the injured and bereaved almost five years to receive theirs. After their claims were tangled up in a legal labyrinth for years, the Government finally stepped in and set up the compensation tribunal. It addressed the issue of financial compensation, but families who accepted awards were precluded from pursuing further litigation against the parties they blamed for the tragedy. This continues to be a source of regret for many victims today.

After the compensation issue was dealt with, the Stardust survivors were abandoned by the authorities and left to cope on their own. The suicide attempts, marriage break-ups, and incidences of alcohol and drug abuse attributed to the Stardust fire could possibly have been avoided if the State had provided ongoing counselling to the victims. In this regard, successive governments have been guilty of shameful neglect.

A Stardust memorial park in Coolock was begrudgingly provided by the authorities after years of broken promises and disappointments. It is agreed by many victims, however, that the most fitting tribute of all to the Stardust dead would be a modern, effective fire service. The Stardust tragedy was undoubtedly a catalyst for change, but the pace of that change has been frustratingly slow.

Much depends on the outcome of the 'Fire Services Change Programme' which was published in February 2005. Speaking at its launch, the Minister for the Environment, Heritage and Local Government, Dick Roche TD, said it would "create a better awareness of fire and how to guard against it."

The aim of this programme is to bring about a significant improvement in the safety of property and people. It involves projects in four closely linked priority areas identified in the 2001 Farrell Grant Sparks review of the fire services and is based on what is happening internationally and best practice.

These include the development of community fire safety programmes to shift the current focus from responding to fires to involving the community at large in the task of preventing fires; the development of a risk based approach to the determination of fire and emergency response cover; the introduction of a competency based approach to recruitment, retention and career progression in the fire service; and the enhancement of health, safety and welfare programmes within the fire service.

A high level 'Implementation Group' has been tasked with determining priorities, while four steering groups will offer expert technical advice and guidance on each of the projects. When completed, the programme will be issued to local councils for implementation as stated fire policy. However, this is an ongoing process and in late 2005 did not have a completion date attached to it.

Meanwhile, the Licensing of Indoor Events Act, 2003 introduced a new licensing system for indoor pop concerts and other entertainment events. It strengthened the powers of enforcement of fire authorities under the Fire Services Act, 1981, to ensure that public safety and crowd management will be taken into account when an event is going through the new licensing process.

But despite these developments, the fact that Ireland has so far avoided another Stardust can be put down to sheer luck rather than a result of direct action by those in power. To ignore the warnings once was tragic; ignoring them twice would be criminal and unforgivable. The authorities cannot afford to sit on the findings of this book for another 25 years, as they did with many of the Stardust tribunal's recommendations.

On a personal note, we would like to pay tribute to the late Albert Buckley, who is a central character in this book. The Donnycarney man – who lost his brother, Jimmy, in the fire and was a crucial eyewitness to the events that unfolded that dreadful night – was an invaluable source to us throughout the writing of this book. His support for this project was unstinting from the outset and we hope we did his story justice in our retelling of the Stardust disaster. His untimely death deeply affected those who had the privilege of knowing him.

We were also glad to hear that the Christy Moore song from which we took the title of this book, 'They Never Came Home', has now made a welcome return after almost 20 years in exile. In an earlier chapter we recounted the controversy that followed the release of the song in 1985. Contempt of court proceedings were brought against the folk singer and the album on which the song featured was withdrawn from record shops. 'They Never Came Home' eventually had an official re-release in 2004 when it was included on 'Christy Moore – The Box Set (1964–2004)'.

* * * *

Today, the Stardust relatives and victims continue to fight for justice, although their campaign of late has been less public and more legally driven. We wish them well in their endeavours.

This was not an easy book to write and will not have been easy to read, particularly for those directly affected by the tragedy. Likewise, the RTÉ commissioned drama, which is directly based on this book, will have been difficult – impossible, even – to watch for many of the Stardust survivors and relatives. This is understandable. But if the Stardust story manages to instil a greater sense of fire awareness in club and pub owners – and the public at large – then the deaths of forty-eight young people will not have been entirely in vain.

Appendix

Notable Club and Cinema Fires of the past Thirty-Five Years[1]

November 1, 1970: 146 die in disco in Saint-Laurent-du-Pont, France
September 1, 1972: 37 die in cabaret in Montreal, Canada
June 25, 1973: 29 die in nightclub in New Orleans, U.S.A.
June 30, 1974: 24 die in disco in New York, U.S.A.
November 3, 1974: 88 die in nightclub in Seoul, Korea
October 24, 1976: 25 die in nightclub in New York, U.S.A.
May 28, 1977: 161 die in nightclub in Southgate, Kentucky
June 9, 1977: 42 die in Abidjan, Ivory Coast
October 10, 1978: 25 die in disco in Caracas, Venezuela
August 14, 1980: 59 children die in cinema in Baghdad, Iraq
August 16, 1980: 37 die in two private clubs in London, U.K.
February 14, 1981: 48 die in Stardust nightclub in Dublin, Ireland
February 1, 1983: 64 die in cinema, Turin, Italy
December 17, 1983: 82 die in disco, Madrid, Spain
April 21, 1985: 44 die in cinema in Tabaco, Philippines
January 14, 1990: 43 die in disco in Zaragoza, Spain
March 25, 1990: 87 die in arson attack on New York club, U.S.A.
November 27, 1994: 234 die in disco in Liaoning, China
December 8, 1994: 325 die in cinema, Karamay, China
February 15, 1995: 67 die in karaoke bar in Taiwan
April 25, 1995: 51 die in karaoke bar in Xianjiang
March 18, 1996: 153 die in disco in Manila, Philippines
April 16, 1997: 13 die in arson attack on disco in Amarante, Portugal
June 13, 1997: 57 die in New Delhi cinema, India
October 30, 1998: 63 die in disco in Gothenburg, Sweden
January 1, 2001: 14 die in pub fire in Volendam, Holland
September 1, 2001: 44 die in club fire in Tokyo
December 1, 2002: 50 people die in bar and club in Caracas, Venezuela
February 20, 2003: 100 die in nightclub fire in Rhode Island, U.S.A.
December 30, 2004: 175 die in disco fire, Buenos Aires, Argentina

---

[1] *The Irish Times*, October 31, 1998, and the authors.